BRUTE SCIENCE

"This is as important a book in applied ethics as one can hope to find. It mounts an impressive scientific and moral case against the current practice of animal experimentation, demanding that we either provide an adequate defense of that practice or radically change it."

James P. Sterba (Philosophy), University of Notre Dame

"Brute Science provides a careful, historical and interdisciplinary analysis of scientific experimentation using non-human animals. Everyone seriously interested in biomedical experimentation – those who use animals and those who use the results of experimentation – should read this book."

Marc Bekoff (Biology), University of Colorado

"One need not accept all of the authors' arguments and conclusions to benefit from their clear and perspective analysis of the scientific and philosophical issues involved ...Their policy recommendations deserve serious consideration from both scientists and animal rights advocates."

John Parascandola, medical historian

Are humans morally justified in conducting sometimes painful experiments on animals in their search for a cure for cancer, heart disease, and AIDS? Apologists for animal experimentation claim for practice is morally justified, because humans are more valuable than animals, and scientifically justified, because the data derived from these experiments profoundly benefits humans. *Brute Science* investigates this standard defense of animal experimentation.

Hugh LaFollette and Niall Shanks show, on methodological and empirical grounds, that defenders of animal experimentation seriously exaggerate its benefits. The authors' analysis reveals that, although these experiments may be a rich source of hypotheses about human biomedical phenomena, they can never prove or establish anything about these phenomena. Consequently, we need to reassess, scientifically and morally, our use of animals in biomedical experimentation.

Brute Science is a ground-breaking analysis that should be read by philosophers, public policy analysts, animal rights activists, medical students, and anyone involved in research using animals.

Hugh LaFollette is Professor of Philosophy at East Tennessee State University; he is the author of *Personal Relationships: Love, Identity, and Morality* (1995) and editor of *Ethics in Practice: An Anthology* (1996). Niall Shanks is Associate Professor of Philosophy and Adjunct Professor of Biological Sciences at East Tennessee State University.

PHILOSOPHICAL ISSUES IN SCIENCE
edited by W. H. Newton-Smith

Also available in paperback

BRUTE SCIENCE

Dilemmas of Animal Experimentation

Hugh LaFollette and Niall Shanks

London and New York

First published 1996
by Routledge
11 New Fetter Lane, London EC4P 4EE

Simultaneously published in the USA and Canada
by Routledge
29 West 35th Street, New York, NY 10001

Typeset in Baskerville by
Ponting–Green Publishing Services, Chesham, Buckinghamshire
Printed and bound in Great Britain by
Mackays of Chatham PLC, Chatham, Kent

British Library Cataloguing in Publication Data
A catalogue record for this book is available from
the British Library

Library of Congress Cataloging in Publication Data
LaFollette, Hugh, 1948–
Brute science: dilemmas of animal experimentation / Hugh
LaFollette and Niall Shanks.
p. cm. – (Philosophical issues in science)
ISBN 0–415–13113–8. – ISBN 0–415–13114–6 pbk.)
1. Animal experimentation–Social aspects. 2. Animal
experimentation–Moral and ethical aspects. I. Shanks, Niall,
1959– . II. Title. III. Series.
HV4915.L34 1996
179'.4–dc20 96–18248
CIP

CONTENTS

PREFACE

> Vivisection is a very old procedure. It has been practiced since the beginning of scientific medicine, in ancient Greece and Rome. Through the seventeenth and eighteenth centuries it even acquired a certain degree of popularity. Doubt about vivisection, however, whether of a medical or moral kind, has been virtually coeval with the existence of the practice. But this doubt did not develop into a major public controversy until the second half of the nineteenth century. By then, experimentation on living animals had become a quintessential part of physiology as an institutionalized profession (Rupke 1990: 1–2).

The American Medical Association (AMA) estimates that biomedical researchers in the US use between 17–22 million animals each year (1992: 15); others estimate the number is higher. Although we can finally judge the scientific and moral legitimacy of the practice only if we determine more precisely the number of animals used in research, on all available estimates, the numbers are sufficiently high to demand that we evaluate the practice.

Most debates about the practice of animal experimentation are moral debates. Although parties to these debates disagree about the moral appropriateness of animal research, they often agree that the research is scientifically legitimate. Of course, some opponents of animal experimentation challenge the scientific validity of certain types of research. However, many of these objections, although perhaps suggestive, are inadequately developed and scientifically uninformed.

Nevertheless, there are scientific questions about the validity of animal experimentation that both sides of this debate should consider seriously. A careful scientific and methodological assessment of the practice reveals that claims about the enormous benefits of animal research – claims made in both public policy statements designed for public consumption and in scientific texts – are exaggerated. More generally, we have reason to question whether the legitimacy of straightforwardly extrapolating the results of animal experimentation to humans.

Doubts about the grand claims made for animal experimentation emerge from a careful examination of evolutionary biology. Evolutionary theory is no mere adjunct to contemporary biology; rather, it is at its center. It is intricately connected to genetics, population biology, systematics, and ecology; evolutionary biology is the theoretical glue that holds these disparate fields together. Especially important to the current inquiry, evolutionary theory helps us understand the biological significance of speciation. Modern physiology and biomedicine assume we can legitimately extrapolate laboratory findings from one species to another. That is why a proper understanding of the nature of species and species differences will be central to a scientific evaluation of these practices.

In the popular debate about animal experimentation, these deeper scientific questions are seldom discussed, and when they are discussed they are discussed in ways that often distort rather than clarify the issues. Neither the critics nor the defenders of these practices have adequately explored the implications of evolutionary theory. We wish to remedy this deficiency. We will carefully analyze the scientific, methodological, and epistemological merits of the practice of animal experimentation. There are, contrary to some apologists, legitimate criticisms of the practice of animal experimentation. And, contrary to some critics, there are scientifically legitimate reasons for conducting research using animals. A proper understanding of the scientific issues will illuminate the ethical and public policy debates about animal experimentation. By some estimates the National Institute of Health currently allocates about 40 percent of its resources for animal research, 30 percent for human studies, and 30 percent for alternative research methodologies. Whether this is the best allocation of scarce research resources depends partly on the scientific and moral legitimacy of biomedical experimentation using animals.

THE STRUCTURE OF THE ARGUMENT

In Part I we set out the background information essential for a proper scientific evaluation of biomedical experimentation. We present prima facie cases for and against animal experimentation. These reveal the typical argumentative strategies employed by each side of this debate. Although both cases are plausible, neither plumb the deeper epistemological and methodological questions we think are so important. Both sides rely heavily on examples to defend their respective cases. Although this is an understandable strategy, it is not especially productive. Among other things, it overlooks the centrality of animal experimentation to the current biomedical paradigm, and how that central role affects our interpretation of these examples.

We first explore the roots of this paradigm in the work of the nineteenth-century French physiologist, Claude Bernard. Then we set out the contours of the current paradigm. We specifically explore the role of the *Intact Systems Argument*, the use of scaling principles, and the paradigm's commitment to biological reductionism. We end this section by introducing contemporary evolutionary theory. We focus on those elements of the theory especially relevant to a critical assessment of the current biomedical paradigm.

In Part II we explain how a proper understanding of the theory of evolution, in tandem with laboratory findings, undermines the claim that, since animal models are strongly analogous to the human conditions they model, we can straightforwardly extrapolate findings in laboratory ar.imals to humans. We then explore other defenses of animal experimentation, including the claim that animal models, although not strongly analogous, are still useful. We show how the study of complex systems theory exposes weaknesses in the standard defenses of the practice. Then we discuss researchers' attempts to evade and avoid the consequences of causal disanalogy. Finally, we discuss basic research. Throughout the book, and in this section particularly, we quote extensively from evolutionary biologists and biomedical researchers. Although these citations may seem excessive, they provide the necessary background for evaluating animal experimentation.

Although the arguments in this book will expose the weakness of animal experiments whose results are to be directly extrapolated or applied to humans, the relevance of these arguments to other uses of animals is unclear. Animal experimentation is not all of a piece. There are different scientific uses of animals, and these must be evaluated differently. Some specialized uses of animals will not be touched by the methodological arguments raised in this section (though perhaps some moral arguments developed in Part III will be relevant to their assessment). Some of these are: (a) using animals as hosts for viruses (e.g., the early use of rhesus monkeys to preserve strains of polio virus), (b) using animals as "bio-reactors" to produce biologically active compounds, or (c) epidemiologists' and pathologists' experiments on wild animals to uncover the natural hosts of human viruses, for example the Ebola virus.

For still other uses of animals our arguments may have some application, although not as direct as for applied research. For instance, our methodological arguments do not have direct bearing on the use of animals in education. Perhaps what is more important, these methodological arguments have less direct bearing on *basic research*, be it anatomical, physiological, toxicological, virological, and so on.

In Part III we build on the analysis from the previous chapters to evaluate animal experimentation morally. We first set the moral debate in historical context, showing how the moral understanding of non-human animals has evolved over time – especially after the advent of evolutionary theory. We argue that, although some arguments that humans have strong moral obligations to animals are plausible, any widely accepted evaluation of experimentation must be based on weaker moral assumptions. The assumption that non-human animals have some moral worth is sufficiently weak to be acceptable to most people, while also being sufficiently powerful to generate potent questions about the morality of the practice.

We first discuss speciesism, and, more generally, deontological defenses of animal experimentation. Then we consider the utilitarian defense of the practice, which claims the practice is justified because of its enormous benefits to human health. We conclude that the practice of using animals in medical research is morally questionable, partly because we cannot straightforwardly apply findings in animals to humans. However, as we noted earlier, the evaluation of basic research, will, by its nature, be somewhat different.

We end the book with some public policy recommendations about the continued use of non-human animals in biomedical experiments.

ACKNOWLEDGMENTS

Earlier versions of several chapters have previously appeared in print, albeit usually in very different form. Parts of Chapters 6 and 13 appeared in "The Origin of Speciesism," in *Philosophy*, 1996, 41–61. Parts of Chapters 10 and 14 appeared in "Utilizing Animals," in *Journal of Applied Philosophy*, 1995, 13–25. Parts of Chapters 7, 8, 9, 10, and 12, appeared in "Two Models of Models in Biomedical Research," in *Philosophical Quarterly*, 1995, 141–60. Part of Chapter 3 appeared in "Animal Experimentation: The Legacy of Claude Bernard," in *International Studies in the Philosophy of Science*, 1994, 195–210. Part of Chapter 9 appeared in "Chaos Theory: Analogical Reasoning in Biomedical Research," in *Idealistic Studies*, 1994, 241–54. Parts of Chapters 4–8 appeared as "The Intact Systems Argument: Problems with the Standard Defense of Animal Experimentation," in *Southern Journal of Philosophy*, 1993, 323–33. Finally, parts of Chapters 1, 3, 4, 5, 6, 7, and 8, appeared in "Animal Models in Biomedical Research: Some Epistemological Worries," *Public Affairs Quarterly*, 1993, 113–30.

We would like to think William Newton-Smith, series editor, for his encouragement and support in this project. We would also like to thank the Research Development Committee at East Tennessee State University, who gave us travel funds to do the extensive library work necessary to complete this project.

Many people gave us feedback on early expressions of the ideas contained in this book. These include, but most assuredly is not limited to, John Bailar III, Andrew Brennan, Stephen R.L. Clark, Dale Cooke, Anthony DeLucia, George Gale, George Graham, John Hardwig, Jeff Gold, David James, Andrew Petto, Mark Parascandola, Lee Pike, James Rachels, Tom Regan, Andrew Rowan, David Sharp, Peter Singer, and Lynn Willis. We are especially grateful to Larry Carbone, Stephen Kaufman, John Parascandola, and Rebecca Pyles, for their thoughtful comments on a draft of the entire manuscript. We would also like to thank Eva LaFollette for helpful philosophical and stylistic comments on successive versions of the manuscript.

Part I

UNDERSTANDING
THE DEBATE

1

A FIRST LOOK
The prima-facie cases

Why investigate the scientific and moral value of animal experimentation? We know that it increases our knowledge of the animal species under study. Don't we also know that it has promoted human health and well-being? Isn't the very act of questioning the scientific, epistemological, and moral status of animal research either misplaced, silly, or simply misanthropic?

Certainly there is a prima-facie case to be made for animal experimentation. Any adequate assessment of the scientific, epistemological, and moral appropriateness of animal experimentation cannot ignore this case. Although branding researchers and their public policy advocates as barefaced liars may be rhetorically effective, it is intellectually indefensible. Doubtless advocates on all sides of this debate have exaggerated their respective cases. However, this does not license the inference that researchers (or their opponents, for that matter) have nothing important to say, or that all or most of their claims are false.

Indeed, the public debate over animal experimentation has been unproductive largely because both sides have been reluctant to seriously consider their opponent's claims and to critically examine their own presuppositions. Were both sides to scrutinize the arguments, they would discover that the "opposition," even if mistaken, is neither crazy nor wholly off the mark. So we begin by setting out the prima-facie cases for and against biomedical research using animals, snapshots of the cases made by opposing sides in this debate. These prima-facie cases are not irrefutable. They do, however, offer evidence that suggests that there is a case to be considered – much as a preliminary hearing in a court of law does not establish guilt or innocence, but rather determines whether there is a case to be heard.

3

THE PRIMA-FACIE CASE IN FAVOR OF ANIMAL EXPERIMENTATION

What, precisely, is the case for animal experimentation? We begin by summarizing the arguments of the research community and their policy advocates. Then we shall briefly outline the principal philosophical defense of the practice. Finally, we will discuss some arguments offered by individual researchers and biologists.

Sigma Xi

Sigma Xi, the scientific research society, defends the use of non-human animals in biomedical research by citing what they take to be the enormous benefits of that research:

> Results from work with animals have led to understanding mechanisms of bodily function in humans, with substantial and tangible applications to medicine and surgery (e.g., antibiotics, imaging technologies, coronary bypass surgery, anti-cancer therapies), public health (e.g., nutrition, agriculture, immunization, toxicology and product safety) . . . As the Surgeon General has stated, research with animals has made possible most of the advances in medicine that we today take for granted. An end to animal research would mean an end to our best hope for finding treatments that still elude us (1992: 74).

In their view animal experimentation is not a scientific technique that has outlived its usefulness. Biomedical inquiry would be seriously hampered were scientists unable to continue their reliance on animal experimentation:

> Research with animals has been remarkably successful in generating both basic and applied knowledge. Without such research, many of us would not have survived diseases that were once common. Without further research with animals, there will be no vaccine for AIDS and dramatically fewer advances for treating and preventing heart disease, cancer, and other serious health problems (1992: 74).

Doubtless, the development of alternatives to animal research (e.g., computer simulations, cell and tissue cultures) may reduce the numbers of animals used for certain purposes:

4

However, these developments will not entirely replace the use of animals. Indeed, the number of animals used in research may actually increase, for several reasons: First, virtually all of these alternative methods are now adjuncts to the use of animal subjects in research, not replacements for such subjects. Second, because of complex interactions between organ systems, some physiological processes cannot be studied in isolation, but require entire animals. Third, new lines of animal research (e.g., transgenic animals) will be needed to reap the benefits of recent progress in fields such as molecular biology and genetics. Finally, results of computer simulations may raise research questions that can be addressed only by the use of animal subjects (1992: 75).

This Sigma Xi statement encapsulates the central features of the argument for animal experimentation, namely that (a) no matter how useful non-animal research methodologies are, they are mere adjuncts to animal research; (b) most significant research must be performed on whole, intact, animal systems; (c) research using whole animals has been the primary engine of biomedical advance.

The American Medical Association

The AMA White Paper, *Use of Animals in Biomedical Research,* echoes the Sigma Xi Statement's triumvirate of claims in support of research using animals. Such research, the authors claim, "is essential to improving the health and well-being of the American people, and the AMA actively opposes any legislation, regulation, or social action that inappropriately limits such research."

Why are they so concerned to maintain animal research? Because, they say,

virtually every advance in medical science in the 20th century, from antibiotics and vaccines to antidepressant drugs and organ transplants, has been achieved either directly or indirectly through the use of animals in laboratory experiments. The result of these experiments has been the elimination or control of many infectious diseases – smallpox, poliomyelitis, measles – and the development of numerous life-saving techniques – blood transfusions, burn therapy, open-heart and brain surgery. This has meant a longer, healthier, better

5

life with much less pain and suffering. For many, it has meant life itself (1992: 11).

The White Paper not only argues for the value of animal experimentation, it responds to some claims of critics. For instance, some animal activists claim that increased longevity and well-being are due to public health measures. However, the White Paper avers that these activists are mistaken.

[F]or most infectious diseases, improved public health and nutrition have played only a minor role. This is clear when one considers the marked reduction in the incidence of infectious diseases such as whooping cough, rubella, measles and poliomyelitis. Despite advances in public health and nutrition, eradication or control of these and most other infectious diseases was not achieved until the development of vaccines and drugs through research using animals (1992: 11–12).

In short, according to the AMA, the bulk of the improvement of longevity and well-being in the twentieth century is a consequence, directly or indirectly, of biomedical research using animals. Animal experiments are the core of current biomedical research.

Carl Cohen

In 1986, the *New England Journal of Medicine* published an article by philosopher Carl Cohen defending the use of animals in bio-medical research (Cohen 1986). Cohen builds on the claims of researchers about the enormous benefits of animal experimenta-tion to mount a utilitarian argument in favor of research:

When balancing the pleasures and pains resulting from the use of animals in research, we must not fail to place on the scales the terrible pains that would have resulted, would be suffered now, and would long continue had animals not been used. Every disease eliminated, every vaccine developed, every method of pain relief devised, every surgical procedure invented, every prosthetic device implanted – indeed, virtu-ally every modern therapy is due, in part or in whole, to experimentation using animals (1986: 868).

For Cohen, the moral to be drawn is clear. Had opponents of

6

animal experimentation been heeded, "Untold numbers of human beings – real persons, although not now identifiable – would suffer grievously as a consequence of this well-meaning but shortsighted tenderness" (Ibid.).

Like the scientific defenders of the practice, Cohen is pessimistic about the possibility of replacing animal-based research with non-animal research methodologies:

> No other methods now on the horizon – or perhaps ever to be available – can fully replace the testing of a drug, a procedure, or a vaccine, in live organisms. The flood of new medical possibilities being opened by the successes of re-combinant DNA technology will turn to a trickle if testing on live animals is forbidden (1986: 868).

In fact, Cohen thinks it would be a mistake to maintain, let alone reduce, the current level of animal experimentation: "Should we not at least reduce the use of animals in biomedical research? No, we should increase it, to avoid when feasible the use of humans as experimental subjects" (Ibid.).

Cohen's argument is considered by many scientists to be the definitive moral defense of animal research. The cogency of that defense, however, rests entirely on claims about the profound benefits of animal experimentation for humans' health. To this extent the moral defense of the practice rests upon scientific claims about its enormous benefits.

The perspective of bench scientists

The prima-facie case for animal research, however, does not rest solely on public policy statements or the writings of philosophers. Most theoretically sophisticated scientists assert that animal research has played a pivotal role in human biomedical research. For example:

> There is no question that most medical progress – perhaps all, in fact – has been attained through knowledge derived initially from experiments in various animal species. There is practically no way of replacing animals in these investigations and so-called "alternative methods" are in reality merely complementary. Tissue cultures, cell, microorganisms, en-zymes, membranes, mathematical models – all are useful for

7

preliminary screening tests and for testing hypotheses, but the complexity of a living organism is such that *in vivo* studies are essential before any test can responsibly be made in man (Garattini and van Bekkum 1990: vii).

However, it is not merely that animals have been useful historically. Rather, knowing how to continue research without using them is difficult if not impossible:

Historically, models of human diseases reproduced in animals have long been a requisite for discovering new therapies. It is in fact difficult to imagine how to set up *in vitro* techniques for diseases which are expressed under the influence of complex systems such as blood circulation, nervous system regulation, neuroendocrine secretion, immune defenses (Garattini 1990: 1).

Doubtless clinical investigation has prompted some great medical advances. However, according to Sir Peter Medawar, were it not for animal experimentation we could not have made most of these advances (e.g., vaccination against smallpox). Thus, animal experimentation is "unconditionally necessary":

It is better that laboratory animals should be used than that tests should be made directly upon human beings. So far as insulin is concerned, it was only by experimentation on dogs that it came to be learnt that removal of something manufactured by the pancreas caused diabetes ... In the continuing debate between experimentalists and champions of the rights of animals, the discovery of insulin remains a shining example of the benefactions experimental animals have conferred upon man (1991a: 113).

A vast majority of researchers agree: they think experiments on non-human animals play a vital role in biomedicine. If two objects are relevantly similar, we naturally assume that the results of experiments on one will, under appropriate conditions, be legitimately extrapolated to the other. Since, researchers argue, we know humans and non-human animals are similar, then results of tests on animals can be applied to humans. Moreover, we know humans and non-human animals are similar in many significant respects. Schmidt-Nielsen identifies four common features of all organisms:

(1) It was realized early in the last century that all animals and

plants are made up of cells ... (2) In this century it has become clear that the energy metabolism of animals, the use of fuel, the metabolic enzymes and pathways, etc. universally are based on the same general principles. (3) More recently, revolutionary progress has been made with the revelation of striking similarities in the transmission of genetic information at the molecular level. (4) Another area in which general biological similarity has been established is concerned with cell membranes, membrane potentials, action potentials, and the very active field of membrane transport processes. These areas ... are all examples of striking, unifying principles of biological similarity of the greatest importance (1975: 287).

The claim that there are pervasive biological similarities between non-human animals and human beings is often linked to the further claim that many biomedical phenomena can be studied only in intact animal systems. Studies on isolated (non-intact) animal systems (like cell and tissue cultures) may uncover some simple, isolable biological facts. However, since such systems lack the organizational complexity which exemplifies intact systems, then these isolated systems cannot accurately model most significant biomedical phenomena. When discussing carcinogenicity and risk assessment, Chouroulinkov states this explicitly:

Thus, the epigenetic systems and control mechanisms in a complex organism cannot be entirely elucidated using cellular models in culture, which have only to do with cellular biology. The *in vivo* reference is absolutely indispensable for investigation of these mechanisms and for assessment of cancer risks. There remains the decision concerning choice of species – human or rodent. Personally I recommend the rodent (1990: 208).

Of course animal researchers are not silly: they recognize biomedical similarities between organisms are not biomedical identities. That is, researchers realize there is no panacea species – no species that, while sufficiently different from humans in morally relevant respects to permit experimentation on them, is nonetheless sufficiently similar in relevant biomedical respects so that we can learn important biomedical information about humans by experimenting on this non-human species. Nonetheless, researchers do think that, under the appropriate conditions, we can legitimately extrapolate findings in laboratory animals to humans.

9

A brief summary

In short, the prima-facie case for animal experimentation asserts that:

- most medical advances in the twentieth century have resulted, directly or indirectly, from biomedical research using animals;
- halting such research would have serious consequences for human health and well-being;
- there are currently no alternatives to animal experimentation. Cell and tissue cultures, and computer simulations are at best adjuncts to animal experimentation;
- animal experimentation is scientifically justified because of the pervasive biological similarities between humans and non-human animals.

THE PRIMA-FACIE CASE AGAINST ANIMAL EXPERIMENTATION

Exaggerated contributions of medicine

Medicine has benefited humans. Nevertheless, opponents argue that its role in extending human life and in controlling human disease is much less than medical scientists have led us to believe. Consider, for example, the AMA's claim that the dramatic increase in lifespan is directly attributable to medical interventions based on animal research. Many medical historians disagree. Death rates attributable to tuberculosis, pneumonia, influenza, scarlet fever, measles, whooping cough, diphtheria and typhoid fever had dropped dramatically before the advent of vaccinations and chemo-therapeutic treatments for these diseases. For instance, approximately 90 percent of the total decline in mortality rates from the most common childhood killers – scarlet fever, whooping cough, measles and diphtheria – occurred before the advent of the treatments and vaccinations for these diseases (McKeown 1976: chapter 5).

Other historians deny that interventionistic medicine has single-handedly led to the elimination of smallpox, often cited as a triumph of interventionist medicine:

The history of smallpox of the later years of the nineteenth century does not support the contention that vaccination was fully or finally responsible for the eventual disappearance of

10

the disease in Britain. It was in those years, in fact, that there was developed the system for control of the disease that became the basis for the successful modern campaign for its eradication (Hardey 1983: 126).

More generally, many of these critics claim that much, if not most, of the decrease in mortality is traceable not to medical intervention but to preventive measures, especially improvements in diet and sanitation. As *Lancet* explains it in discussing risk assessment: "public health legislation and related measures have probably done more than all the advances of scientific medicine to promote the well-being of the community in Britain and in most other countries" (1978: 356–7). As McKinlay and McKinlay state it:

> In general medical measures (both chemotherapeutic and prophylactic) appear to have contributed little to the overall decline in mortality in the United States since 1900 – having in many instances been introduced several decades after a marked decline has already set in and having no detectable influence in most instances . . . More specifically, with reference to these five conditions (influenza, pneumonia, diphtheria, whooping cough and poliomyelitis) for which the decline in mortality appears substantially after the point of intervention – and on the unlikely assumption that all this decline is due to intervention – it is estimated that at most 3.5 per cent of the total decline in mortality since 1900 could be ascribed to medical measures introduced for the diseases mentioned here (1977: 425).

The limitations of interventionistic medicine are manifest in its inability to control some diseases like cancer. Forni *et al.*, note that

> [T]he overall incidence of tumors is rising but gains in survival time of cancer patients and reductions of cancer death rates are marginal. Of those diagnosed with cancer, only half will be alive in five years time. Surgery, radiotherapy and chemotherapy are improving continuously, but there seems little to support the hope of major breakthroughs (1990: 128).

These limitations of curative medicine are not really surprising. After all, cancer and most serious human diseases are caused, in no small measure, by environmental factors.

11

Rates of heart disease ... have changed much faster over recent decades than can be explained by genetic changes, implicating dietary and environmental causes. And the fact that no single cancer affects every population at the same rate suggests that factors external to the human body cause 70% to 90% of all cancers ... Only a few of these environmental factors are known – cigarette smoke for lung cancer, or sunlight for skin cancer – and epidemiology seems to provide the best shot at identifying the others (Taubes 1995: 165).

For diseases caused by environmental conditions, it is more prudent to eliminate the conditions which cause the disease than to try to cure the disease once it has occurred. That is why some prominent epidemiologists and physicians, like the former director of the US's "War on Cancer," advocate policies that emphasize prevention:

Research opportunities in other areas of cancer prevention may well merit sharp increases in support, even if this requires that current treatment-related research must be substantially curtailed. Certainly, the background of past disappointments must be dealt with in an objective, straightforward and comprehensive manner before we go much further in pursuit of a cure that always seems just out of reach (Bailar and Smith 1986: 731).

Exaggerated role of animal research in medical advances

Many opponents of experimentation argue that not only is modern medicine not the sole cause for the decline in mortality, many medical advances that did contribute to human health were not the result of animal experimentation. Defenders of research have claimed that since there is a strong correlation between the practice of animal experimentation and medical advancement, the former caused the later.

Opponents of research reject this inference. After all, we have independent reasons to expect these phenomena to be correlated. Since the law (at least in the US) prescribes that all new drugs, prosthetic devices, and surgical techniques be tried on animals before they are used in humans, we will subsequently find that all (recent) medical advances are correlated with prior experimentation on animals. Consequently, the correlation between animal experimentation and medical discovery is the result of legal necessity, not evidence that animal experimentation led to medical advances.

Moreover, several prominent physicians have offered historical evidence that animal experimentation has not been *as* responsible for biomedical discovery as advocates suggest. They claim that clinical discoveries played a more substantial role than animal researchers have led us to believe. As Paul Beeson explains in the *American Journal of Medicine*:

> Progress in the understanding and management of human disease must begin, and end, with studies of man . . . Hepatitis, although an almost "pure" example of progress by the study of man, is by no means unusual; in fact, it is more nearly the rule. To cite other examples: appendicitis, rheumatic fever, typhoid fever, ulcerative colitis and hyperthyroidism (1979: 368).

Apparently, the diseases and conditions cited by Beeson are not unique. "Similarly, key discoveries in immunology, anesthesia, and the treatment of depression were based on human clinical research and investigation" (MRMC 1990: 3).

Additionally, according to the former director of the Sloan Kettering Cancer Institute, the discoveries of insulin and of the mechanisms necessary for heart transplants were primarily the result of clinical investigation. In his Presidential Address before the American Society for Clinical Investigation, Robert Good challenged the claim that animal experimentation has been single-handedly responsible for medical advances:

> Recently a leading basic physiologist (cited) . . . a number of examples . . . in which basic contributions had paved the way for heart and organ transplantation. Included were such major advances as development of the science of circulatory physiology, control of infection, development of anesthesiology, pharmacological support of cardiovascular function, technological progress permitting secure diagnosis, control of the immune rejection, and others.
>
> From my somewhat prejudicial position, I seemed to hear a dramatic recitation of example after example in which investigation (of human patients) had led the way, asked the

13

critical questions, established the incisive view . . . Certainly
the control of infection is in great measure attributable to
leadership of clinical investigators . . .

The discovery and application of anesthesiology, to me,
also derives from interpretation of several natural experiments and conduct of critical clinical investigations. The
professional physiologists have contributed much to the understanding and control of the circulation, but was not the
discovery of the circulation of the blood primarily an interpretation of a clinical experiment of nature? I think so . . .
(1968: 1466).

Of course we should note that these physicians are not critics of
animal research. Nevertheless, if these investigators are correct,
then animal experiments have not played as central a role as the
public has been led to believe. Substantial credit must go to the
clinical sciences.

Places where animal experiments have misled us

A more serious criticism is that animal experimentation has sometimes resulted in measurable harm to humans. Opponents argue
that the case of thalidomide, a "miracle" drug introduced in
Britain in 1957, is instructive. Although at the time researchers did
not test prospective drugs for teratogenic effects (birth defects),
the drug did successfully negotiate the then current battery of
animal tests. Researchers discovered that animals could tolerate
massive doses of the drug without any ill-effects; they inferred the
drug was safe for humans. Unfortunately they were mistaken: more
than 8,000 children were born crippled or deformed.

As noted above, no animal tests had been done on pregnant
animals. This leads defenders of research to argue that the
thalidomide disaster in no way shows that animal research is flawed
(Willis and Hulsey 1994: 213). As it turns out, that fact is of little
solace to experimenters since what researchers would have learned
from such tests had they been conducted before the appearance of
human epidemiological data is not at all obvious. After all, the drug
has since been shown not to produce detrimental effects in several
strains of pregnant rats, mice, and other mammals:

In approximately 10 strains of rats, 15 strains of mice, eleven
breeds of rabbits, two breeds of dogs, three strains of ham-

sters, eight species of primates and in other varied species as cats, armadillos, guinea pigs, swine, and ferrets in which thalidomide has been tested teratogenic effects have been induced only occasionally (Schardein 1976: 5).

Hindsight is 20–20. Although animals have since been found which produce teratogenic effects when exposed to thalidomide, these animals may not have been the experimental test subjects.

Opponents of animal research point out that the thalidomide case is not unique. For example, when Lilly introduced Opren (called Oraflex in the US) as a potential treatment for arthritis. It passed all animal tests, yet there were more than 3,500 documented cases of severe reaction and sixty-one deaths in Britain alone (*British Journal of Medicine* 1982: 459–60). More recently, FIAU, a drug to treat hepatitis B, passed all animal trials, yet had disastrous results in humans: it killed five of the fifteen human subjects who were given the drug in clinical trials. Even after the disaster, officials determined that increased or altered animal tests would not have avoided the problem.

A retrospective evaluation of the material available in 1993 still supports [the original decision] . . . There was nothing in the preclinical toxicity studies that was suggestive of the tragic episode that transpired in the PPPC clinical trial. Furthermore, unfortunately, there is nothing to indicate that other laboratory animal studies would have been more appropriate or capable of better prediction of the fatal outcome (IOM 1995: 250).

Toxicologists openly acknowledge that different species often react differently to xenobiotics. Many researchers contend, however, that these differences disappear when doses are adjusted for differences in size, weight, and metabolism. We cannot make these adjustments until we know how humans respond to the xenobiotic – and that would undermine the predictive value of animal tests. Furthermore, it appears this assumption is false since, even when we do have data from both humans and non-humans, there is no straightforward way to correlate it. As Klaassen and Eaton note of cancer-causing agents: "All known chemical carcinogens in man, with the possible exception of arsenic, are carcinogenic in some species but not in all laboratory animals" (1993: 31).

Finally, some opponents of research question a basic assumption of toxicology. Toxicologists assume they can administer large doses of test substances to laboratory animals (who have short lifespans) and then extrapolate findings to humans. However, this testing procedure is flawed. For example, large doses of insulin produce deformities in the offspring of laboratory animals (Friedman 1969: 499). However, we have no reason to think insulin is teratogenic to humans when administrated in standardly prescribed doses.

Moral concerns

Some philosophers, like Carl Cohen, support animal research; others morally oppose it. Peter Singer is probably the best known moral critic of our treatment of animals, including the use of animals in research laboratories. He writes:

> If a being suffers, there can be no moral justification for refusing to take that suffering into consideration. No matter what the nature of the being, the principle of equality requires that its suffering be counted equally with the like suffering . . . of any other being (1990: 8).

Singer sees speciesism – a bias in favor of members of one's own species – as morally odious, on a par with such evils as sexism and racism. He comments:

> The experimenter, then, shows a bias in favor of his own species whenever he carries out an experiment on a non-human for a purpose that he would not think justified him in using a human being at an equal or lower level of sentience, awareness . . . No one familiar with the kind of results yielded by most experiments on animals can have the slightest doubt that if this bias were eliminated the number of experiments performed would be a minute fraction of the number performed today (1989: 80).

These moral concerns go beyond the scientific concerns mentioned earlier. That is, some people, like Singer, claim that even if research is highly valuable we should not do it – at least not unless we are willing to do the same research on some humans. That is, most people consider non-consensual human experimentation morally odious; Singer and some critics of animal experimentation also see the practice of vivisection as morally odious for the same reason. Others may not go quite as far. They may claim that research can be morally justified if the benefits are sufficiently substantial. What most critics would contend is that animal research cannot simply be evaluated on scientific grounds; it must be evaluated morally as well.

A brief review of the prima-facie case against animal experimentation

The prima-facie case against animal experimentation, as stated, is far from a knock-down refutation of the claims made by researchers. Rather, it is based on a series of examples intended to *deflate* researchers' claims:

- the contribution of interventionist medicine to the observable decline in mortality has been exaggerated;
- the contribution of animal research to interventionistic medicine has been exaggerated;
- the results of animal experimentation have occasionally been highly misleading;
- despite its scientific fecundity, the practice of animal experimentation is morally odious.

In short, even if animal research has played some role in prolonging life and improving health, its role has been less than defenders of research have claimed.

WHY AN ASSESSMENT OF THE SCIENTIFIC MERITS OF EXPERIMENTATION IS IMPORTANT

During the past twenty years, philosophers and others have written a great deal about the moral acceptability of using animals in research. Their arguments have doubtless raised people's moral sensitivities and prompted adoption of laws and policies that eliminated the most blatant cruelty to laboratory animals. Nonetheless, animals continue to be used extensively in research, both in the United States, the United Kingdom, and elsewhere in the world. Apparently the public does not find the moral arguments sufficiently persuasive, they think that the benefits to humans outweigh the suffering of animals, or they just don't care about moral issues.

Each of these responses reflects the public's firm belief that medical research pays enormous dividends for human health. Seeing why is not difficult: the research community has effectively

17

presented their prima-facie case for animal experimentation. As we stated earlier, ignoring this case would be silly, and dismissing all animal experiments as scientific fraud – as some critics (Reusch 1978) are wont to do – would be rash. Humans have benefited from some forms of animal research, and doubtless some beneficial medical research will cease if we abandon the use of animals. However, as we also argued, there is much room for disagreement about the extent of benefits (and loss of benefits, were the practice to cease). There are grounds for skepticism about the grand claims made for such experimentation.

In summary, although fanatical advocates and opponents of animal research think the opposition does not have even a prima-facie case, we think both sides offer arguments worthy of consideration. Yet often each side dismisses the other as misinformed, silly, or even malevolent. We hope the arguments in this book make each side less willing to reject opposing arguments out of hand. Only then are we likely to come closer to understanding the scientific merits of animal experimentation; only then are we likely to find a solution which most people will find reasonable. For, although both prima-facie cases are plausible; neither case, as it stands, is convincing. We must delve deeper to determine the scientific and methodological merits of animal experimentation. Only after we have done so will we be able to morally evaluate the practice.

2

THE PROBLEMS OF RELEVANCE

It is also a good rule not to put too much confidence in observational results until they are confirmed by theory. Sir Arthur Eddington (quoted in Riordan 1987: 136).

Each prima-facie case is plausible, but which is the most defensible? That question is not easy to answer. Our attempt to answer it will take us over rugged argumentative terrain. Before we venture further into this treacherous landscape we should briefly discuss human experimentation, for some people might wonder why experiments on non-human animals are carried out when we are trying to gain information about human disease. Why not just experiment on humans?

THE RELEVANCE OF HUMAN RESEARCH

The researchers' first answer comes quickly to the fore: doing so would be immoral. We should not perform randomized, *controlled* toxicological and teratological experiments on human beings, at least not experiments like those we standardly conduct on non-human animals. Such experiments would violate the interests (or rights) of the human subjects; they would be grossly immoral.

Researchers not only have moral qualms about scientific experiments on humans; they have methodological qualms as well. They think clinical and epidemiological studies on humans are scientifically second-rate. In well-designed scientific experiments, researchers strictly control all relevant variables. Then they introduce some stimulus and record the results. Without those controls, the experimenter cannot know exactly what caused the results.

19

However, by using strict controls, experimenters can gain crucial causal information. As Patton puts it, "It was the introduction of deliberate intervention into the study of natural phenomenon, as opposed to observation, which so inspired the investigators of the 17th century onward" (1993: 26).

Observational studies of humans, however, cannot be properly controlled. Humans live different lifestyles and in different environments. Thus, they are insufficiently homogeneous to be suitable experimental subjects. These *confounding factors* undermine our ability to draw sound causal conclusions from human epidemiological surveys. Confounding factors are variables (known or unknown) that make if difficult for epidemiologists to isolate the effects of the specific variable being studied. For example, Taubes argued that since many people who drink also smoke, researchers have difficulty determining the link between alcohol consumption and cancer (1995: 167). Similarly, researchers in the famous Framingham study identified a significant correlation between coffee drinking and coronary heart disease. However, most of this correlation disappeared once researchers corrected for the fact that many coffee drinkers also smoke. If the confounding factors are known, it is often possible to correct for them. However, if they are unknown, they will undermine the reliability of the causal conclusions we draw from epidemiological surveys.

The value of epidemiological surveys may also be subverted by biases in experimental design. For instance, the methods used to select the control population may introduce irrelevant factors, thereby confounding the results. For example, in a 1988 study of the influence of electromagnetic fields (EMF) on cancer rates, researchers selected the control population by randomly dialing phone numbers. This method likely produced a control population that underrepresented the poor. As Taubes notes, "Poor people, it seems, are less likely to be home during the day to answer the phone, less likely to want to take part in a study, or less likely to have an answering machine and call the researchers back" (1995: 167). Taubes continues:

> Indeed, the North Carolina researchers reported that their data showed that the risk of leukemia and brain cancer rises not just with exposure to EMF but also with higher levels of breast-feeding, maternal smoking, and traffic density, all of which are markers for poverty. This suggests . . . that the

study group was poorer than the controls, and that some poverty-associated factor other than EMF could have resulted in the apparent increase in cancer risk (1995: 167).

Studies are also biased if researchers do not know the extent to which subjects were exposed to the suspect causal factor. In randomized controlled animal studies, researchers can precisely control relevant variables, and then predict the likely results of human exposure to the substance. However, researchers cannot know the extent of "natural" exposure from the environment. Therefore, identifying a population of human subjects who have been similarly exposed is difficult. Often such studies are skewed by *recall bias*. As Taubes notes:

> Equally uncertain are those risk factors recorded only in human memory, such as consumption of coffee or dietary fat . . . underweight individuals tend to overreport fat intake on questionnaires or in interviews and obese subjects tend to underreport it (1995: 167).

Together these confounding factors and problems of experimental bias make the "use of human subjects difficult or impossible" (AMA 1992: 6).

These methodological worries about human research have led researchers to rely instead on animal subjects. Since the experiments on laboratory animals can be properly controlled, then the results will be scientifically valid; since the subjects are non-humans, the experiments are morally unobjectionable. As Craig puts it:

> Because of the many limitations and restrictions on the possibility of obtaining meaningful data from man himself, experimental surrogates of human functions or diseases have played a central role in the development of biomedical knowledge. In carcinogenesis, concepts of causes, mechanisms and fundamental nature of the disease process are derived primarily from the study of other species, primarily rodents (1992: 107).

Thus, animal experiments can yield scientifically respectable data without doing anything immoral. At least that is the governing assumption of most biomedical researchers.

THE RELEVANCE OF ANIMAL STUDIES TO HUMANS

Although it is misleading simply to assume, without argumentation, that findings on laboratory animals are extrapolable to humans, many defenders of animal experimentation appear to do just that. When they do defend the practice, they typically do so by citing examples of experimental success. Consider, for example, the now classic article "Ben Franklin and Open Heart Surgery" (Comroe and Dripps 1974). This article presumably shows just how pervasive and how important animal experimentation has been in the development of new medical treatments. What evidence do the authors offer in support of this claim? Basically they simply state, on grounds of authority, that animal experimentation was crucial for a variety of biomedical discoveries. What evidence they do provide is simply historical: the mere presence of some animal experiments before a particular biomedical discovery is interpreted as showing that those experiments were the cause of that discovery. However, more care must be taken before we claim that the former caused the latter. Although examples may establish a correlation, there is a large gulf between correlation and cause.

This is especially so for animal experimentation. For, as we argued in the prima-facie case against experimentation, since the law (at least in the US) requires experimentation before marketing of all new drugs or the introduction of new surgical procedures, then we know in advance that there will *always* be a correlation between animal experiments and scientific discoveries. Yet that does not show that the animal experiments were the source of biomedical discovery. We cannot, simply by observing a correlation, know what role, if any, animal experimentation played. We must know that the findings in animals are causally *relevant* to biomedical conditions in humans.

There are, however, two different though related questions of relevance. The first is an *ontological* problem of relevance: are humans and non-human animals sufficiently similar so that we can extrapolate results of experiments on one to the other? We cannot simply assume they are. After all, we not only observe differences between the species, we also know that the species have different evolutionary histories. This would lead us to expect some ontological differences, differences that might undermine extrapolation from one to the other.

There is also an epistemological problem of relevance: even if non-human animals and humans were sufficiently similar onto-logically, unless we *knew* they were ontologically similar – and that requires evidence of the similarity – then inferences from the former to the latter would be suspect. That is, we need some way to test the ontological claim that humans and non-human animals are relevantly similar. How, specifically, can we determine the legitimacy of such extrapolations? It appears there is only one way: we must compare the results of our findings in laboratory animals with the results of tests in humans. That is, to prove that animal models of human biomedical conditions are legitimate, we must rely on some form of human research, research that is, according to animal researchers, scientifically second-rate.

Researchers' doubts about human research methodologies thus come back to haunt them. They are faced with a dilemma: they can determine the relevance of animal research for humans only by testing these results in humans. Since in many contexts doing non-consensual, fully controlled, randomized experiments on humans would be immoral, then they must rely on epidemiological and consensual clinical studies. However, if these human methodo-logies are of questionable scientific value, as advocates of animal research claim, then we cannot obtain good, scientific data proving the relevance of animal experiments to humans. If we cannot establish the relevance of animal experiments, then we are left with a wealth of high quality data on, say, genetically homogeneous rodent populations, and considerable empirical uncertainty about this data's relevance to humans. On the other hand, if epidemio-logical and clinical experiments on humans *do* yield sound scient-ific data, then this undercuts one reason for experimenting on animals rather than humans.

Of course many researchers are well aware of the problem of relevance. In a discussion of animal models of hypertension, Ganten *et al.* note:

> Inbred hypertensive strains provide a homogeneous popu-lation of hypertensive animals. The onset of high blood pressure occurs early, and complications occur at a predict-able age if the environment is controlled. This is not the case with human primary hypertension; where age of onset varies widely and other factors are uncontrolled; its course, there-fore, is much less predictable with respect to severity and complications. Thus, the homogeneity of inbred hypertensive

rats is advantageous for scientific investigations, but caution must be exercised in extrapolating research results to humans because of the etiological heterogeneity of human hypertension (1990: 91).

Wiebers *et al.* likewise acknowledge this problem in their discussion of stroke research:

> Molinari eloquently summarized the rationale for using animal stroke models in stroke research, pointing out several advantages including the uniformity of the models, the quantitative gradation of the ischemic insult in certain models, and, in general, the quantifiable pathologic outcomes. However, he too points out several therapies for acute stroke which have proven effective in reducing lesion size in animal models while being clinically ineffective in humans. To explain this lack of correlation between animal studies and the human condition, he points to the lack of clinical pathological correlation in humans and concludes that "unless we use analytic methods in the clinical tests in humans similar to those used in the animal models originally suggesting the efficacious treatment, we are destined to repeat the now familiar and recurrent sequence" (1990: 1).

Molinari thus recognizes the problem of relevance, but places all the blame on the sloppy methodology of human clinical studies. However, even if he is right about the source of the problem, he fails to recognize that the inadequacy of human studies undermines the reliability of animal studies.

Other researchers recognize this problem and therefore urge that we try to ensure that the animal models are similar to the human condition they are supposed to model. Thus Wiebers *et al.* continue:

> Molinari suggested we modify measurement of human outcomes to conform to animal research so that we can reproduce the results of animal research in humans. We suggest the converse, namely that there is a great need to design experimental projects and therapeutic interventions in such a way that they have relevance and practical application to the human condition (1990: 2).

Although some researchers, like Wiebers *et al.*, recognize the full scope of the relevance problem, Molinari's attitude appears to be the norm. Many researchers do not interpret the failure to correlate the findings in non-human animals and humans as suggesting *disanalogies* between model and subject modeled. Instead, they contend that human and animal data would correlate, if only we could do properly controlled experiments of humans. However, as Wiebers *et al.* point out:

> We assert that the discrepancies between animal research observations and those in humans will not disappear by developing ways of improving clinical research. Although clinical research may well have much room for improvement, the discrepancies are rooted primarily in the challenging task of modeling human disease and assessing relevant measures of therapeutic efficacy in mammals (1990: 2).

In short, the assumption that carefully controlled experiments on humans would yield data consistent with animal data may be illusory. After all, the results of animal studies may also be skewed by confounding factors. There are many differences between laboratory animals and the humans they supposedly model. These differences may be causally relevant in the following respects: (a) differences in anatomy and physiology; (b) differences in the etiology of disease (most diseases and conditions in laboratory animals are artificially induced); and (c) different sources and extent of stress (laboratory animals are confined in artificial conditions). Consequently, *controlled* animal experiments undoubtedly yield information about non-human animals that are suffering from an (often) artificially induced condition and are raised in a highly artificial environment. However, whether this data is relevant to *anything* outside the laboratory is speculative, and cannot be assumed a priori.

RELEVANCE AND DRUG TESTING

In making a prima-facie case against animal research, we suggested that we could not always safely extrapolate findings in non-human animals to humans. There we gave a few examples of documented differences between animal and human reactions to drugs. Here are a few more: morphine sedates humans but stimulates cats (Brodie 1962: 375); penicillin has adverse effects on guinea pigs and hamsters by wiping out their intestinal flora, leading to disease and death (Koppanyi and Avery 1966: 250–70); and the industrial chemical benzene causes leukemia in humans but not in mice (Sax 1981: 385); nitrophenol produces cataracts in humans, ducks, and chickens, but not other animals (Zbinden 1963: 75–97); fenclozic acid produced no effects on more than thirteen species, but immediately caused liver toxicity in human subjects. Even the most common drug given to humans does not have uniform effects in non-human animals. According to Davis, aspirin causes birth defects in rats and mice, poisons cats (who metabolize it very slowly), but does not affect horses (because of their rapid metabolism, a given dose/mass has much less effect than in other animals) (1979: 1014–15). Thus, there are many cases of false positives and false negatives: some drugs are safe for animals but toxic for humans; others are detrimental to animals yet are valuable for humans. These cases raise, in concrete form, the problem of relevance.

Consider the thalidomide disaster again. The AMA claims this tragedy shows we need more – not fewer – animal tests when evaluating new drugs for safety. Let us ask the following question: would broad spectrum, multi-strain/multi-species tests serve as devices to protect the public from the marketing of harmful substances?

In dealing with this question, we note that no one disputes that thalidomide is a potent human teratogen. This is a brute ontological fact, uncovered through human clinical and epidemiological investigations. According to the AMA, thalidomide would have never been marketed had scientists conducted an appropriate battery of tests on many species. Eventually a species (or strain) would be found that indicated teratogenic risk.

This response, though, won't do. Even if more extensive testing solved one problem, it would have created another in its stead. Had we adopted a conservative approach and withheld thalidomide because it led to detrimental effects in some species, the decision would have been beneficial to humans here but detrimental elsewhere. Adopting such a conservative attitude would lead us to withhold many beneficial drugs. Had more rigorous testing been standard practice, aspirin and penicillin might not have been marketed. Both would have failed animal trials.

To avoid *this* problem – to ensure we do not withhold potentially valuable drugs –we could insist that results in a single animal test will not force us to suppress a drug. That is the procedure advocated by Patton. He claims that although penicillin harms several species of rodent, researchers would not have withheld the drug from the market: "Nobody would have abandoned a substance with such outstanding antibacterial properties, even if the impure extract was found to be harmful to a further species" (1993: 167). This response successfully evades the current problem (withholding valuable drugs) – but at the cost of reintroducing the original problem. For if we follow Patton's procedure we may release a drug that has devastating results in humans. For instance, we could easily envision researchers reasoning that since thalidomide had positive benefits for humans (it is still used for some purposes), and it produces teratogenic effects in a relatively small number of animal species (and then only if given in large doses), we should have released the drug, despite its detrimental effects in those species.

The problem is this: once we recognize that different species react to drugs in different ways, how can we know, before testing the substance on humans, which animal tests to believe? Which animal tests indicate human risk, and which ones are irrelevant? Animal trials precede human trials, but if we do not know whether the animal trial is relevant to the problem in humans it will lose even minimal predictive value. If we knew which species *would* adequately predict a drug's efficacy and safety for humans, then, of course, we would not need to conduct tests on different strains and species. The continued use of broad spectrum multi-strain/multi-species testing vividly shows that researchers do not know which results in laboratory animals can be legitimately extrapolated to humans. After we know a drug's effects in humans, we can often find some animal that reproduces those effects. For instance, after the thalidomide disaster researchers discovered that some rabbits were good models of the effects of thalidomide in humans. However, this does not show that we can use toxicological and teratological tests on animals to *predict* what will happen in humans.

The failures of predictive tests can be stated more generally. Consider the record of animal tests in determining the safety and efficacy of drugs. The Food and Drug Administration requires extensive animal tests before clinical trials in humans. These tests are designed to increase the likelihood that new drugs will be efficacious and safe. It appears these tests fail to do what they purport to do; certainly they are far from perfect. Less than one out of four potential drugs that successfully negotiate initial animal tests are ever approved by the Food and Drug Administration. This figure is a bit misleading: there are other reasons why drugs are never marketed. Still, if we give the most generous interpretation of the data, of those drugs that successfully completed animal trials and began clinical trials, 47 percent are discontinued because the drugs are later deemed unsafe or inefficacious in humans (FDA 1988). (The others are discontinued because of economic considerations, including, presumably, the "economic" consideration that drugs that do not work will not sell.)

What does this suggest? Minimally this: of those drugs that are safe and efficacious in animals, the animal trials are no better than 50 percent accurate in determining a drug's safety and efficacy. Defenders of the practice will reply that we are considering only those drugs that pass animal tests. For all we know the tests are still immensely valuable since they screen out many drugs that would be harmful to humans.

True, but misleading. For all we know there may be few false negatives. But the reverse is also true: for all we know there may be many. Perhaps these tests eliminated drugs which, although not great advances, would be safe and efficacious in humans. Perhaps, too, we scrapped a cure for lung cancer or a way to control hypertension. Since drugs that fail animal trials are typically not tested on humans, we do not and could not know. We are still faced with the problem that undergirds this entire chapter: how can we demonstrate the relevance of tests in animals to humans?

THE RELEVANCE OF EXAMPLES: THE RHETORICAL HYDRA

The previous discussion, coupled with the prima-facie cases, should now make it abundantly clear that the bare appeal to examples to resolve the debate is unlikely to be productive. Despite their differences, we can now see that there are important methodological similarities between the disputants in this debate. Both prima-facie cases are largely a patchwork of presumably relevant examples, woven together by claims of authority. Both sides think they have provided a sufficiently compelling list of examples (of successes or failures) which presumably support their respective positions; both sides think their cases are sufficiently backed by the power of authority. So, if we wish to evaluate their respective cases – and thus the practice of animal experimentation itself – we must scrutinize their use of examples.

Although each side's case relies on examples, the function of examples differs. Understanding this difference helps explain why researchers think their examples are convincing and why they think their position is relatively immune to their opponents' counter-examples. It likewise helps explain why opponents of the practice are generally unpersuaded by examples adduced by advocates.

Proponents cite cases that purportedly show that animal research has enormous utility; opponents cite cases that purportedly show that animal research has misled us or has failed to contribute to human health and well-being. For each example cited by proponents, opponents respond with a counter-example. For every "problem" identified by opponents, proponents offer another success story. If one example is shown to be inadequate, another is found to make the same point in a different guise. In this debate, examples come and go like the heads of the mythical Hydra.

It is not difficult to see why both parties rely so heavily on examples. The presentation of their respective cases is designed to garner public support. Both sides plausibly assume that the public is scientifically ignorant and unlikely to understand more sophisticated arguments. Therefore, both sides resort to a judiciously selected collage of examples because they think the public will more likely understand, and perhaps be swayed by, them.

Although the "examples game," when played well, is rhetorically effective, it is not as simple an argumentative strategy as it appears, and as both sides assume it to be. Single examples, or even a carefully selected cluster of examples, cannot, in and of themselves, show that the practice is either bankrupt or sound. Opponents of research are prone to interpret single failures of experimentation as showing that the entire practice is scientifically bankrupt. However, this is a mistake that reveals their ignorance of scientific methodology. *Most* experiments fail to support the hypotheses they are designed to test. Experimental failure is the norm in good science, not the exception. No one should be surprised to find that some animal experiments failed; rather, we would be shocked and suspicious if they all succeeded. To evaluate the practice of animal experimentation, we must not just tally failures. We must assess their significance. Are the failures what any knowledgeable scientist would expect for these types of experiments? Or do they reveal some deeper problem with the entire practice? Perhaps it is the latter; perhaps it is the former. Either way it is egregious to assume that the failures demonstrate that the practice is flawed.

Failures are evidence of a flawed practice only if we have some theoretical reason to think those failures reflect a methodological defect that undermines the legitimacy of the practice. A theory gives us the appropriate conceptual framework from which we can interpret the experimental failures. Without that theory, singular failures are just that: singular. They do not show that the practice is scientifically illegitimate.

It is likewise misguided to assume that an isolated experiment, or even a cluster of seemingly successful experiments, establishes that the practice of animal research is successful. We must have some theoretical framework from within which we interpret the experimental results as successful. Normally that will be provided by the governing scientific paradigm.

THE ROLE OF PARADIGMS

It is not merely that examples are explicable only in the light of some theory. Also theory is explained by – indeed, important aspects of science are characterized by – the citing of examples. The relationship between theory and examples is best illuminated using the Kuhnian notion of *scientific paradigms* (Kuhn 1970). According to Kuhn, a scientific paradigm is a scientific practice that is bound together by certain laws, theories, applications, and instrumentation. These "provide models from which spring particular coherent traditions of scientific research" (Ibid.: 10). These paradigms are (a) sufficiently novel to attract the interest of scientists away from other kinds of scientific activity, yet are (b) sufficiently open-ended that they leave problems for the "ordinary" scientists to resolve. Kuhn calls scientific activity that aims to solve the scientific problems under the aegis of a particular paradigm, "normal science."

All normal science is governed by some paradigm or other: the paradigm is a set of recurrent and quasi-standard examples of the theory's conceptual, observational, and instrumental applications. It is the conceptual framework by which scientists perceive, study, and evaluate problems of interest. That is, the paradigms characterize particular forms of scientific activity for practitioners working under its influence. The scientific community uses these illustrations, in textbooks, lectures, and laboratory exercises, to teach aspiring scientists their trade (Ibid.: 43). According to Kuhn, examples play a special role within normal science.

I mean to suggest that some accepted examples of actual scientific practice – examples which include law, theory, application, and instrumentation together – provide models from which spring particular coherent traditions of scientific research ... The study of paradigms ... is what mainly prepares the student for membership in the particular scientific community with which he will later practice. Because he there joins men who learned the bases of their field from the same concrete models, his subsequent practice will seldom evoke overt disagreement over fundamentals ... That commitment and the apparent consensus it produces are prerequisites for normal science, i.e., for the genesis and continuation of a particular research tradition (1970: 10–11).

Thus, the examples constitutive of a scientific paradigm are not merely proof of the paradigm's success; rather, they characterize a way of scientific life. Put differently, for the normal scientist examples are not so much evidence for the success of the practice as they are articles of faith – statements about what constitutes the best current scientific practice. So, when normal scientists cite examples of the successes of animal experimentation, although they may see themselves as defending the practice, they really are just articulating that practice. For instance, when Medawar cites the discovery of insulin as a "shining example" of the triumph of animal experimentation (1991a: 13), he is merely give an example which articulates the paradigm.

To the outsider, this appears to beg the question. In a sense it does. However, in the sense that it does, it is the very same sense in which the modern physicist would appear to beg the question when explaining to neophytes how current physics is practiced. The normal scientist cites examples to train aspiring practitioners into the scientific order; such a scientist is not accustomed to defending the practice from external criticism. For most scientists, the mere existence of the practice is justification enough. That helps explain why, once a paradigm is established, scientists engaging in normal science simply rely unquestioningly on the paradigm's concepts and practices. As Kuhn notes:

Closely examined, whether historically or in the contemporary laboratory, that enterprise seems to force nature into the preformed and relatively inflexible box that the paradigm supplies. No part of the aim of normal science is to call forth new sorts of phenomena; indeed those that will not fit the box are often not seen at all. Nor do scientists normally aim to invent new theories, and they are often intolerant of those invented by others. Instead, normal-scientific research is directed to the articulation of those phenomena and theories that the paradigm already supplies (1970: 24).

Animal experimentation is clearly the central element in the current biomedical paradigm. Thus, the Kuhnian account of paradigms correctly describes the situation of most contemporary biomedical researchers. It helps explain how the typical researcher engages in the examples game. Researchers think their own examples carry much weight – after all they define the practice – while examples offered by their opponents are mere gadflies on the body of science. From the vantage point of the bench scientist, objections by "outsiders" are an annoyance with which they must cope, not criticisms they need take seriously. As Patton puts it, "Judgements of this sort [about the quality and validity of their work] can only be judged by other scientists" (1993: 196). Since the critics are not trained scientists, they do not see the force of the proferred examples.

To this extent normal science is immune to what appear to be counter-examples to their practice. Seeming counter-examples, like those mentioned earlier in the chapter, are not interpreted as evidence against the practice but rather as problems to be solved, using the best current scientific techniques. Since the current technique is animal experimentation, then the failure of animal experimentation is seen as a reason for still more experimentation, not as a reason to abandon the practice.

That is not to say paradigms cannot change. They can. As Kuhn notes, stable scientific regimes can be beset by empirical and theoretical woes. At first these problems are merely treated as anomalies. However, if the paradigm continues to be unable to solve a problem, that problem may seem more sinister. If there is a network of seemingly intractable problems, then a sense of crisis may emerge within the scientific community.

Although the biomedical sciences are not in a state of crisis, those sciences have developed some internal tensions in the latter part of the twentieth century. Especially ominous is a methodological schism, a schism that has decided relevance for the current debate. Twentieth century biological theory, deeply infused with the theory of evolution, has moved away from the mechanistic physiological paradigm established by Claude Bernard, discussed in the following chapter. Contemporary, evolutionary biologists have begun to distance themselves, theoretically, from mechanistic physiology. The causes and consequences of this methodological schism will loom large in what follows. The paradigm of evolutionary biology casts a very interesting light on the mechanistic physiologists' favorite examples, as well as those of the opponents of animal research. The significance of examples will shift with changing theoretical contexts. Thus, the debate over the scientific worth of animal experimentation will be inextricably intertwined with this methodological schism. The existence of competing paradigms in the biomedical sciences provides new theoretical contexts against which the significance of cited examples can be assessed.

THE RELEVANCE OF METHODOLOGY

We are now a long way from the territory where both sides merely trade examples. We are wading into relatively uncharted theoretical waters. So we should. Science is not just a random amassing of discrete facts. Rather it is a way of giving a general theoretical account that unifies, explains, and predicts facts. That is why the problems of relevance must be addressed before either side of the debate can profitably play the examples game. In isolation from the relevant theory, examples settle very little. Their significance generally comes to light only against a background of theory that unifies them and explains their import.

For instance, before Darwin, examples of anatomical homologies were seen as evidence of a grand cosmic designer. After Darwin, scientists had a new theoretical vocabulary that allowed them (and us) to interpret these homologies differently, to see them as evidence of descent from a common ancestor with evolved modification. Examples make sense in the light of theory. Of course, once we have a satisfactory theory, examples can play a satisfactory role: they help illuminate the theory and isolate potential anomalies which must be explained.

One central thesis of this book is that examples of the successes and failures of animal research are best explained using the tools of our current best biological theory: the theory of evolution. If we try to understand the examples in isolation from theory, we could not understand their import. Likewise, if current practice continues to be guided by an outdated theory, then the practice will be scientifically questionable. Another central thesis of this book is that current biomedical practice continues to be unduly influenced by a nineteenth century scientific paradigm: a paradigm established by the great physiologist Claude Bernard. This is a paradigm that has been substantially rejected by many contemporary biologists for its failure to accord with the consequences of biological evolution.

Before we can fully explore this schism, we must first explain the governing paradigm in the biomedical sciences. Nevertheless, the current paradigm cannot be understood in isolation from its history. Just as Sir Isaac Newton established the paradigm that governed the practice of physics for 200 years, so Claude Bernard, the great nineteenth century physiologist, established the paradigm that initiated, and continues to govern, the practice of biomedical research. In the following chapter we explore that Bernardian paradigm.

3

CLAUDE BERNARD
The founder of the paradigm

Claude Bernard is the father of modern biomedicine. The AMA
claims he set down the principles of experimental medicine, and
bench scientists who wish to provide a scientific justification of
animal experimentation often cite Bernard as their intellectual
progenitor. Nobel Prize winner Sir Peter Medawar shows his deep
admiration for Bernard when he says: "The wisest judgements on
scientific method ever made by a working scientist were indeed
those of a great biologist, Claude Bernard" (1987: 73). More than
a century after his death, his basic methodological assumptions
permeate the theory and practice of biomedicine.

Bernard was a thoughtful and theoretically sophisticated scientist
who used the best science of his day to lay the foundations of
scientific physiology, biochemistry, and toxicology. He offered
detailed arguments for his views – after all, he was founding a
paradigm, not merely describing it. As Kuhn notes, revolutionary
scientists are usually more theoretically sophisticated than the
normal scientists who follow them. For these reasons we think it is
difficult to understand contemporary biomedicine without first
understanding Bernard. Indeed, much of the current paradigm
will be mysterious if we do not understand Bernard's influence. Put
differently, Bernard's view provides the relevant historical and
theoretical context within which to understand the current practice
of experimental biomedicine. In this chapter we lay out Bernard's
account of experimental medicine. Then in the following chapter
we describe the current paradigm.

THE PLACE OF ANIMAL RESEARCH IN
BIOMEDICINE

In defending biomedical research on animals, the AMA espouses
two crucial Bernardian tenets: (1) genuine biomedical science

must be conducted in the laboratory, and (2) laboratory experiments on animals are directly relevant to human biomedicine. Bernard asserts the primacy of interventionist laboratory science and denigrates observational, clinical medicine. He asserts not only that experiments on animals will yield significant biomedical truths about humans, but that, in principle, no other method (save immoral and illegal human experimentation) could yield the same results.

The primacy of lab science

Why did Bernard praise laboratory science and denigrate clinical medicine? Partly it was a matter of historical circumstance: clinical medicine in Bernard's time was little more than alchemy. Consider Sir Peter Medawar's description of the medicine of Bernard's day.

> The physician of a hundred and thirty years ago was confronted by all manner of medical distress. He studied and tried to cure his patients with great human sympathy and understanding and highly developed clinical skills, by which I mean that he had developed to a specially high degree that form of heightened sensibility which made it possible for him to read a meaning into tiny clinical signals which a layman or a beginner would have passed over or misunderstood. The physician's relationship to his patient was a very personal one, as if healing were not so much a matter of applying treatment to a "case" as a collaboration between the physician's guidance and his patient's willingness to respond to it. But there was so little he could do! The microbial theory of infectious disease had not been formulated, viruses were not recognized, hormones were unheard of, vitamins undefined, physiology was rudimentary and biochemistry almost non-existent (1984: 62).

However, to attribute Bernard's views simply to the sad state of mid-nineteenth century clinical medicine would be a mistake. Bernard had a grand vision for physiology: he wanted to place it on as firm a scientific footing as chemistry or physics. His view required, among other things, that the physiologist's scientific home be primarily in the laboratory, not at the patient's bedside.

When a chemist does laboratory experiments to determine the properties of potassium, the investigator reasonably assumes that the findings can be extended by induction to potassium outside the laboratory. A chemist can predict that if potassium reacts with sulfur one way in the lab, then it will react with sulfur similarly outside the laboratory (assuming, of course, that the other conditions remain constant). It would be silly for a chemist or physicist to claim to discover the "true" nature of the world in any other way. As Bernard put it:

> We cannot imagine a physicist or a chemist without his laboratory. But as for the physician, we are not yet in the habit of believing that he needs a laboratory; we think that hospitals and books should suffice. This is a mistake; clinical information no more suffices for physicians than knowledge of minerals suffices for chemists and physicists ([1865] 1949: 148).

Bernard wanted practicing physiologists to share the physicists' and chemists' commitment to controlled laboratory experimentation. That does not mean Bernard thought clinical investigation had no place in biomedicine. However, Bernard thought it crucial that scientists understood its limitations.

Bernard's understanding of the nature and role of clinical medicine and laboratory investigation was framed by the nineteenth century methodological debate between inductivists and hypothetico-deductivists. According to the hypothetico-deductivists, the distinction between the *context of discovery* and the *context of justification* marks a crucial methodological divide. When trying to frame hypotheses in the context of discovery, the scientist gives free rein to his or her imagination. Then, in the context of justification, the scientist first deduces predictions from these hypotheses and then tests the predictions in the laboratory. Hypothetico-deductivists claim that a hypothesis is confirmed – or at least made probable – if it explains and predicts a variety of scientifically significant phenomena. By the mid-nineteenth century, hypothetico-deductivists were part of the theoretical vanguard in physics and chemistry.

Inductivists claim it is not enough that the hypothesis accurately predicts the laboratory results. There must be an independent warrant between the hypothesis and the phenomenon it explains and predicts. Otherwise, the hypothesis may be no more than an artifact of the investigator's fancy. Put differently, hypothetico-deductivism is methodologically flawed, inductivists claim, since two conflicting hypotheses may be "confirmed" by the same evidence. That is why inductivists are loathe to frame hypotheses. As Sir Isaac Newton explained in a classic statement of inductivism:

> I frame no hypotheses [*hypotheses non fingo*]; for whatever is not deduced from the phenomena is to be called an hypothesis; and hypotheses, whether metaphysical or physical, whether of occult qualities or mechanical, have no place in experimental philosophy. In this philosophy particular propositions are inferred from phenomena, and afterwards rendered general by induction ([1687] 1962: 547).

Although hypothetico-deductivism is currently recognized in theoretical treatises as the best methodology, inductivism continues to shape the way science is *reported* in professional journals. Inductivism, so understood, has been parodied by Sir Peter Medawar.

> [S]cientific discovery ... starts with the unvarnished and unembroidered evidence of the senses ... and out of this sensory evidence, embodied in the form of simple propositions of declarations of fact, generalizations will grow up and take shape, almost as if some process of crystallization or condensation were taking place. Out of a disorderly array of facts, an orderly theory, an orderly general statement, will somehow emerge (1991c: 229).

The hypothetico-deductivist, as you might expect, denies that the scientist can discover facts simply by starting with the "unvarnished ... evidence of the senses." The scientist needs a well-formulated hypothesis to guide investigation. Moreover, the hypothesis itself is best understood from within a larger theoretical framework. Having formulated hypotheses in the *context of discovery*, the hypothetico-deductivist can evaluate that hypothesis before conducting any experiments. Those that lack the appropriate harmony and simplicity, and those that are grossly incompatible with the paradigm, can be rejected without ever being tested.

Bernard was a committed hypothetico-deductivist, and that placed him in the methodological vanguard of nineteenth century science:

> People who condemn the use of hypotheses and of preconceived ideas in the experimental method make the mistake of confusing invention of an experiment with noting its

results. We may truly say that the results of an experiment must be noted by a mind stripped of hypotheses and preconceived ideas. But we must beware of proscribing the use of hypotheses and of ideas when devising experiments or imagining means of observation. On the contrary . . . we must give free rein to our imagination; the idea is the essence of all reasoning and all invention. All progress depends on that. It cannot be smothered or driven away on the pretense that it may do harm ([1865] 1949: 24).

As a hypothetico-deductivist, Bernard recognized that hypotheses had a legitimate scientific role. However, he was also aware of their limitations. In the context of discovery, hypotheses arise from observation and creative imagination. Yet when the consequences of a hypothesis are to be tested, the investigator must exclude his imagination and preconceived ideas, and then rigorously test the hypothesis in the laboratory. If the hypothesis is not testable, it is useless. There is no other scientific way of testing it, except in the lab:

The experimental hypothesis . . . must always be based on prior observation. Another essential of any hypothesis is that it must be as probable as may be and must be experimentally verifiable. Indeed, if we made an hypothesis which experiment could not verify, in that very act we should leave the experimental method to fall into the errors of the scholastics and makers of systems ([1865] 1949: 33).

Consequently Bernard thought clinical medicine, based on observation and comparison, had a legitimate role: it could help frame hypotheses and it could provide an arena in which to apply laboratory findings. Nevertheless, on its own, it could never be a science. It could, at most, be physiology's handmaiden:

[W]e give the name observer to a man who applies methods of investigation . . . to the study of phenomena which he does not vary and which he therefore gathers as nature offers them. We give the name experimenter to the man who applies methods of investigation . . . so as to make natural phenomena vary . . . and to make them present themselves in circumstances or conditions in which nature does not show them ([1865] 1949: 15).

Bernard had a horror of so-called "observing physicians" who limited themselves to the mere observation of biomedical phenomena. For medicine so conceived:

> normal and pathological anatomy, vivisection applied to physiology, pathology and therapeutics – all would become completely useless. Medicine so conceived can lead only to prognosis and to hygienic prescriptions of doubtful utility; it is the negation of active medicine, i.e., of real and scientific therapeutics ([1865] 1949: 19).

We thus see the outline of Bernard's methodology: physiologists should frame their hypotheses by clinical observation, imagination, and previous experimentation. They should then test hypotheses in the laboratory and extend the results, by induction, to patients in hospitals. As Bernard explains:

> In a word, I consider hospitals only as the entrance to scientific medicine; they are the first field of observation which a physician enters; but the true sanctuary of medical science is a laboratory . . . In leaving the hospital, a physician . . . must go into his laboratory ([1865] 1949: 146–7).

By emphasizing the significance of the laboratory, "Claude Bernard . . . did indeed put scientific medicine on a new foundation. His philosophy *worked*" (Medawar 1984: 134). Following the lead of the best sciences of the day, Bernard claimed proper physiologists would observe the properties and behavior of matter in the laboratory and extend their results, by induction, to matter outside the laboratory. As Newton put it in his Third Rule: "The qualities of bodies, which admit neither intensification nor remission of degrees, and which are found to belong to all bodies within the reach of experiments, are to be esteemed the universal qualities of all bodies whatsoever" ([1687] 1962: 398).

Thus, if physiology was to be a genuine laboratory science, there must be subjects on which physiologists could conduct their controlled experiments. However, Bernard thought that conducting laboratory experiments on humans would be immoral. Non-human animals were the only option; they would be the physiologists' subjects. "[T]here in the laboratory by experiments on animals, he [the physiologist] will seek to account for what he has observed in his patients, whether about the action of drugs or about the origin of morbid lesions in organs or tissues" (Bernard

[1865] 1949: 147). Exactly *why* he though tests on animals would be directly applicable to man is another matter.

The primacy of animal experimentation

Laboratory experiments on animals are not merely relevant to the study of human biomedical phenomena, according to Bernard, they are scientifically essential for it:

> Experiments on animals, with deleterious substances or in harmful circumstances, are very useful and entirely conclusive for the toxicology and hygiene of man. Investigations of medicinal or of toxic substances also are wholly applicable to man from the therapeutic point of view; for as I have shown, the effects of these substances are the same on man as on animals, save for differences in degree ([1865] 1949: 125).

Bernard's belief that findings in animal experiments are straight-forwardly applicable to humans stems from his commitment to one side of another great scientific debate – the debate over determinism. Bernard was a causal determinist. He argued vociferously that if the living world was not deterministic, no science of life – and physiology in particular – would be possible. He was especially repulsed by the suggestion that medicine is an inherently statistical science:

> This false idea leads certain physicians to believe that medicine cannot but be conjectural; and from this, they infer that physicians are artists who must make up for the indeterminism of particular cases by medical tact. Against these anti-scientific ideas we must protest with all our power, because they help to hold medicine back in the lowly state in which it has been so long ([1865] 1949: 138–9).

And again,

> if based on statistics, medicine can never be anything but a conjectural science; only by basing itself on experimental determinism can it become a true science ... I think of this idea as the pivot of experimental medicine, and in this respect experimental physicians take a wholly different point of view from so-called observing physicians ([1865] 1949: 139).

Bernard accepted the then current statement of determinism: (1) all events have causes (principle of causality), and (2) for numerically distinct but qualitatively identical systems, same cause, same effect (*principle of uniformity*). The application of these principles to physiology was direct:

> If a phenomenon appears just once in a certain aspect, we are justified in holding that, in the same conditions, it must always appear in the same way. If, then, it differs in behavior, the conditions must be different. But indeterminism knows no laws; laws exist only in experimental determinism, and without laws there can be no science ([1865] 1949: 139).

Thus, if seemingly identical systems behaved differently, there must be a difference in initial conditions which accounts for this difference. A mature science should be able to account for these differences. Bernard believed experimental medicine could find deterministic laws akin to those of Newton. Then living systems would be like the planets. Although they may appear differently and their masses may vary, they nevertheless obey the same "universal" physiological laws. In Bernard's words:

> Physiologists ... deal with just one thing, the properties of living matter and the mechanism of life, in whatever form it shows itself. For them genus, species and class no longer exist. There are only living beings; and if they choose one of them for study, that is usually for convenience in experimentation ([1865] 1949: 111).

At first glance it seems physiology could never have laws akin to those of physics. After all, there are significant physiological differences between species. Bernard was well aware of species differences. However, since he was under the sway of the paradigm of the physical sciences, he assumed all laws were deterministic and uniform across nature. That paradigm specifically rejected the very idea of *fundamental* (or irreducible) species differences; it further rejected the idea of genuinely statistical laws. As Newton put it: "Therefore to the same natural effects we must, as far as possible, assign the same causes. *As to respiration in a man and in a beast;* the descent of stones in Europe and in America; the light of our culinary fire and of the sun; the reflection of light in the earth and in the planets" [emphasis added] (Newton [1687] 1962: 398). According to Bernard, the Newtonian view of causality is as applicable to biology as to physics. "All phenomena, to whatever order they belong, exist implicitly in the changeless laws of nature; and they show themselves only when their necessary conditions are actualized" ([1865] 1949: 85). Or, as it he puts it elsewhere:

> In living bodies, as in inorganic bodies, laws are immutable, and the phenomena governed by these laws are bound to the conditions on which they exist, by a necessary and absolute determinism ... Determinism in the conditions of vital phenomena should be one of the axioms of experimenting physicians ([1865] 1949: 69).

THE NATURE OF ANIMAL EXPERIMENTATION

Intact systems

If, as Bernard says, the laws of life are immutable and universal – the same everywhere – then why do we need to experiment on whole animals? Can't we simply do experiments on *parts* of animals, e.g., tissues, isolated organs, etc., and by that learn all we need to know?

Bernard thinks not. For animals are not simply collections of isolable parts that can be studied on their own, separate from the living organism. "[P]hysiologists ... must take account of the harmony of this whole" ([1865] 1949: 89). The intact animal "expresses more than the addition of their [the animals' parts] separate properties" (Ibid.: 91). That is why "We really must learn, then, that if we break up a living organism by isolating its different parts, it is only for the sake of ease in experimental analysis, and by no means in order to conceive them separately" (Ibid.: 89).

In short, animals are functionally integrated organisms. As such, "when we unite physiological elements, properties appear which were imperceptible in their separate elements" (Ibid.: 91). So, if we aspire to understand the workings of biological organisms, we cannot merely study their parts; we must also study the vital biological properties that arise from the organized unity of the whole.

This explains why the primary experimental tools will be whole, living animals, not isolated animal or human parts. However, the question now arises: if animals are organized wholes that exhibit properties greater than the sum of their parts, why should we assume that experiments on one species (usually non-human animals) can be legitimately generalized to another species (usually human)? To answer this question, we must delve further into Bernard's view of the nature of organisms, the nature of biological species, and the nature of species differences.

The nature of species differences

Bernard was not just an astute theoretician; he was also an accomplished bench scientist. Thus, he was well aware of species differences. "But aside from all the connections to be found between man and animals we must recognize that there are differences also" ([1865] 1949: 125). How, though, did Bernard conceive of these differences, and how, if at all, did he think they affected the researchers' ability to extrapolate results from laboratory animals to humans?

Crucial to understanding Bernard's view is his distinction between the *cause* of phenomenon and the *means* of producing that phenomenon.

> By the cause of a phenomena we mean the constant and definite condition necessary to existence; we call this the relative determinism or the *how* of things, i.e., the immediate and determining cause. The means of obtaining phenomena are the varied processes by whose aid we may succeed in putting in action the single determining cause which produces the phenomena. The necessary cause in the formation of water is the combination of two volumes of hydrogen with one of oxygen; this is the single cause which always determines the phenomenon ... Subordinate conditions or processes in the formation of water may be extremely varied; only all these processes reach the same result, viz., combination of oxygen and hydrogen in invariable proportions ... The determinism, i.e., the cause of the phenomenon, is therefore single, though the means for making it appear may be multiple and apparently very various ... But the real and effective cause must be *constant* and *determined*, that is unique; anything else would be a denial of science in medicine [emphasis his] ([1865] 1949: 83).

The basic idea is as follows: the commonality of life across species is to be explained by the common *causes* of biological phenomena, although the *means* of producing those phenomena may differ. As Bernard explains it,

> [D]etermining causes . . . in the phenomena of living beings . . . exist nevertheless in spite of the seeming diversity of means employed. Thus in certain toxic phenomena we see different poisons lead to one cause and to a single determinism for the death of histological units, for example, the coagulation of muscular substance ([1865] 1949: 84).

That idea springs from Bernard's understanding of the differences between animate and inanimate matter.

> A living being differs essentially from an inorganic body from the point of view of the experimenter. An inorganic body has no sort of spontaneity: as its properties are in equilibrium with outside conditions, it soon settles into physico-chemical indifference, i.e., into stable equilibrium with its surroundings ([1865] 1949: 96).

To put it differently, chemists and physicists need not concern themselves with the "interior" of the objects they study. The chemist is merely concerned with the ways chemicals interact, while the physicist is merely concerned with the mass, location, and movement of particles. Such investigators do not worry about the "inner state" of those particles. However, the biologist cannot ignore the inner state.

> To sum up, if we wish to find the exact conditions of vital manifestations in man and the higher animals, we must really look, not at the outer cosmic environment, but rather at the inner organic environment ([1865] 1949: 98).

The question for Bernard, though, was whether the need to look at the "inner organic environment" required abandoning a commitment to universal biological laws. He thought not.

The reason concerns Bernard's commitment to a reductionist methodology when it came to understanding the nature of that inner environment. As he put it:

> a created organism is a machine which necessarily works by virtue of the physico-chemical properties of its constituent elements. To-day we differentiate three kinds of properties exhibited in the phenomena of living beings:

45

physical properties, chemical properties and vital properties. But the term "vital properties" is itself only provisional; because we call properties vital which we have not yet been able to reduce to physico-chemical terms; but in that we shall doubtless succeed someday ([1865] 1949: 93).

Once the inner environment is understood in appropriate physico-chemical terms, analyzing its behavior using universal physico-chemical laws that are applicable to all biological species will be possible. Such laws of the inner environment will be the universal laws of biology.

Scaling

Since researchers are careful to distinguish between the cause and the means of producing a phenomenon, then neither the "inner organic environment" nor species differences are a bar to bio-medical research using animals. Nonetheless, Bernard was well aware many people thought species differences were biomedically significant.

Even to-day, many people choose dogs for experiments, not only because it is easier to procure this animal, but also because they think that experiments performed on dogs can be more properly applied to man than those performed on frogs ([1865] 1949: 123).

This belief, Bernard thought, occurs because some experimenters mistake quantitative differences in initial conditions for fundamental qualitative differences between species. Bernard disagreed. He thought the fundamental properties of vital units were the same for all species. Livers may come in different sizes and shapes, but they all respond to stimuli in basically the same way. In so far as there are species differences, these seem to consist in slightly different arrangements of essentially similar building blocks. This was simply another implication of the then current understanding of determinism:

Now the vital units, being of like nature in all living beings, are subject to the same organic laws. They develop, live, become diseased and die under influences necessarily of like nature, though manifested by infinitely varying mechanisms. A poison or a morbid condition, acting on a definite histological unit, should attack it in like circumstances in all animals furnished with it; otherwise these units would cease to be of like nature; and if we went on considering as of like nature units reacting in different or opposite ways under the influence of normal or pathological vital reagents, we should not only deny science in general, but also bring into zoology confusion and darkness ([1865] 1949: 124).

Bernard recognized that members of different species react differently to qualitatively identical stimuli. These "diversities" and "idiosyncracies" should not be ignored; they should be studied and eventually brought under universal deterministic physiological laws. "Only experimental studies of these diversities can furnish an explanation of the individual differences observed in man, either in different races or in different individuals of the same race" (Ibid.: 125–6).

The following analogy – of which Bernard was probably aware – may illuminate his proposal for dealing with idiosyncracies. In 1846, the French astronomer Leverrier explained the seemingly anomalous and idiosyncratic motions of the planet Uranus by predicting the existence of a previously unobserved planet, Neptune. When Neptune was subsequently discovered, within a degree of its predicted location, the idiosyncracies in planetary motions were explained, and order was restored to the universe.

Whether Bernard was aware of this case or not, he evidently thought we could find physiological "Neptunes" which would explain observed idiosyncracies – something yet unobserved which would explain the seeming violations of universal laws. Thus, observed differences between species were not physiologically irreducible; they were to be explained by more fundamental similarities.

Thus, species differences, though real, in no way undermine the work of physiologists. Species differences were not ultimately qualitative but quantitative. Once we make suitable mathematical adjustments for quantitative differences (e.g., body weight), we can straightforwardly apply experimental findings from one species to another. Bernard illustrates this reasoning in his discussion of a case that had initially puzzled him. Doses of toad venom that speedily stop the hearts of frogs, do not stop the hearts of toads. At first glance this is an example of same cause, different effect. Yet Bernard thought there was a better explanation.

Now, in logic, we should necessarily have to admit that the muscular fibers of a toad's heart have a different nature from those of a frog's heart, since the poison which acts on the former does not act on the latter. That was impossible: for admitting that organic units identical in structure and in physiological characteristics are no longer identical in the presence of a toxic action identically the same would prove that phenomena have no necessary causation; and thus science would be denied. Pursuant to these ideas, I rejected the above mentioned fact as irrational, and decided to repeat the experiments ... I then saw that toad's venom easily kills frogs with a dose that is wholly insufficient for a toad, but that the latter is nevertheless poisoned if we increase the dose enough. So that the difference described was reduced to a question of quantity and did not have the contradictory meaning that might be ascribed to it ([1865] 1949: 180).

Bernard, who had studied the physiological effects of poisons in great detail, lays down here a main principle of contemporary toxicology. Once purely quantitative differences have been allowed for (say, differences in body weight, metabolic rate, surface area, etc.), we may infer same effect from same cause, even when the test subjects belong to different species.

Choosing which animal to use

Although Bernard believed there were pervasive biological similarities across species, that does not mean that scientists have no reason to prefer some animals as test subjects. He thought important pragmatic factors would make the use of some species more suitable than others:

Some experiments would be impossible with certain species of animals, and intelligent choice of an animal offering a happy anatomical arrangement is often a condition essential to the success of an experiment and to the solution of an important physiological problem. Anatomical arrangements may sometimes present anomalies which must also be thoroughly known, as well as the variations observed between one animal and another ([1865] 1949: 121).

Thus, researchers may choose to use one animal because that

48

particular species has a physiological structure similar to that of humans. They may also choose it because its organs are so arranged as to make it a more convenient experimental tool. Or the reason for choosing one animal over another may be completely pragmatic:

> However, the animals most used by physiologists are those procured most easily, and here we must set in the front rank domestic animals such as dogs, cats, horses, rabbits, oxen, sheep, pigs, barnyard fowl, etc., but if we had to reckon up the services rendered to science, frogs would deserve first place ([1865] 1949: 115).

As noted by medical historian John Parascandola:

> Before the twentieth century, the frog played a major role in the history of research in the life sciences. The widespread use of frogs was due in part to their general hardiness for surviving severe operations and the excellent survival capacity for their isolated tissues. Frogs were experimented on so frequently that in 1845 Hermann Helmholz referred to them as "the old martyrs of science." His fellow physiologist, Claude Bernard, called the frog "the Job of physiology" (1995: 16).

As Parascandola goes on to note, in the twentieth century murid rodents have become the martyrs of science, amounting to some 80 to 90 percent of experimental subjects.

Reductionism

In many respects Bernard was well ahead of his times. He embraced the intact systems argument, and he recognized the importance of studying the organism's internal environment. Furthermore, he maintained that the animal's internal environment and the interactions of its systems could ultimately be reduced to their more basic physical and chemical components. Thus, physiology, as he conceived it, was deeply committed to an analytical approach. First the living machine must be broken down into its components:

> To succeed in solving these various problems, we must, as it were, analyze the organism, as we take apart a machine to review and study all its works; that is to say, before succeeding

in experimenting on smaller units, we must first experiment on the machinery and on the organs ([1865] 1949: 65).

Having taken the machine to pieces – ultimately down to physicochemical pieces, the phenomena of life may be understood in just those terms:

> [O]nly in the physico-chemical conditions of the inner environment can we find the causation of the external phenomena of life. The life of an organism is simply the resultant of all its inmost workings; it may appear more or less lively, or more or less enfeebled and languishing, without possible explanation by anything in the outer environment, because it is governed by the conditions of the inner environment. We must therefore seek the true foundation of animal physics and chemistry in the physico-chemical properties of the inner environment ([1865] 1949: 99).

Bernard was aware that organisms consist of mutually interdependent, interactive parts. He did not deny the interactive relational character of life, but he did assert that to understand the relations one had to understand the basic physico-chemical properties of the *relata*:

> The result is that physicists and chemists can reject all ideas of final causes for the facts that they observe; while physiologists are inclined to acknowledge an harmonious and pre-established unity in an organized body, all of whose partial actions are interdependent and mutually generative. We must really learn, then, that if we break up a living organism by isolating its different parts, it is only for the sake of ease in experimental analysis, and by no means in order to conceive them separately ... It is doubtless correct to say that the constituent parts of an organism are physiologically inseparable from one another, and that they all contribute to a common vital result; but we may not conclude from this that the living machine must not be analyzed as we analyze a crude machine whose parts also have their role to play in a whole ([1865] 1949: 89).

Finally, in comments that have an air of prescience about them, Bernard suggests that this analytical approach to physiology might involve the use of artificial models and tissue cultures:

With the help of experimental analysis we must transfer physiological functions as much as possible outside the organism . . . Thus we establish artificial digestion and fecundation, so as to know natural digestion and fecundation better. Thanks to their organic self-regulation, we can also detach living tissues, and by means of artificial circulation or otherwise, we can place them in conditions where we can better study their characteristics ([1865] 1949: 89).

On this view it might be possible to make biomedical discoveries using research methods that do not involve intact animal systems.

THE REJECTION OF EVOLUTION

Bernard's assumption that species differences were ultimately explicable using universal laws, is tied, in some important ways, to his rejection of the theory of evolution. He thought the theory of evolution, like the clinician's uncontrolled observations and case studies, did not have consequences that could be tested in controlled experiments. Therefore they were, in Bernard's eyes, purely speculative and not properly scientific. As medical historian Paul Elliot puts it:

Leading French biologists, such as Bernard himself . . . were resistant to the Darwinian theory of evolution . . . [he] resisted these ideas because he saw them as the results of speculation unsupported by proper experimental evidence. The emergence of experimental physiology based on vivisection was therefore an integral part of a general trend in French science away from anything that could be interpreted as speculation towards a science based rigidly, too rigidly perhaps, on laboratory work and experiment (1987: 73).

Perhaps his rejection of evolution is not surprising. Evolutionary theory was still in its infancy: it was not widely accepted, not even within biological circles. The evidence for the theory, though highly suggestive, was far from overwhelming. In fact, one reason Darwin delayed publication of *Origin of Species* was that the evidence was largely indirect. Thus, the theory of evolution was not entirely satisfactory to either inductivists or hypothetico-deductivists. There was no independent warrant that would satisfy inductivist methodologists – and inductivists represented the scientific orthodoxy of Darwin's day. Moreover, there were no clear laboratory tests for evolutionary hypotheses that would satisfy hypothetico-deductivists. Consequently, Bernard should not be faulted for rejecting the theory of evolution.

Nonetheless, it is important to understand that Bernard rejected evolutionary biology, and that his rejection of the theory springs from his methodological commitments. This Bernardian paradigm was shaped by the deterministic, "bottom-up" approach of the nineteenth century physical sciences. This commitment to determinism helps explain his rejection of evolution, and, consequently, his belief that species differences could be safely ignored. He believed that once we understand the physico-chemical underpinnings of biological phenomena, physiology would have found its Neptune that explained all those seeming species differences.

According to evolutionary biologist Ernst Mayr, although physiology's commitment to nineteenth century determinism was productive in its day, "it left a vast number of phenomena in the living world totally unexplained" (1988: 9). In succeeding chapters we will explain why Bernard's theoretical commitments, including his commitment to determinism, create serious problems for the current biomedical paradigm. That paradigm cannot account for many biological phenomena; moreover, it is at odds with the now well-confirmed insights of evolutionary theory.

THE MORAL ARGUMENT

Although Bernard was most interested in laying out the parameters of scientific investigation, he was quite aware of the moral questions about the use of animal experimentation. It would be a mistake, therefore, not to mention his understanding of the moral problem. For Bernard was not an evil man: he recognized there were moral problems with doing controlled experiments on humans:

> The principle of medical and surgical morality, therefore, consists in never performing on man an experiment which might be harmful to him to any extent, even though the result might be highly advantageous to science, i.e., to the health of others. But performing experiments and operations exclusively from the point of view of the patient's own advantage does not prevent their turning out profitably to science ([1865] 1949: 101).

Nonetheless, biomedicine must continue. Experimentalists must have subjects if biomedicine is to be a science. Given his belief that biological organisms were "vital units," experiments on inanimate objects or parts of an organism would not be productive. Rather, experiments must be on whole, living organisms. His subjects would have to be whole, intact, laboratory animals. There was, by his lights, no other option:

> [As for vivisection on animals, no] hesitation is possible; the science of life can be established only through experiment, and we can save living beings from death only after sacrificing others. Experiments must be made on either man or on animals ... the results obtained on animals may all be conclusive for man when we know how to experiment properly ([1865] 1949: 102).

It is intriguing, that although Bernard claims "no hesitation is possible" in deciding to experiment on animals, he himself had moral qualms about experiments on chimpanzees (Schiller 1967: 255). This suggests that even Bernard thought animals had some moral worth. Moreover, he also thought that worth could be sufficiently great to call certain forms of experimentation into question.

4

THE CURRENT PARADIGM

In this chapter we set out the basic structure of the current biomedical paradigm. This paradigm's indebtedness to Bernard will be quickly apparent. We do not claim to provide a comprehensive accounting of all its variations. We do, however, capture its central features. Then, in Chapters 9–12, we discuss refinements and modifications to the basic paradigm.

THE PLACE OF ANIMAL RESEARCH IN BIOMEDICINE

The primacy of lab science

Scientific hypotheses may arise from a variety of sources. However, bare hypotheses are scientifically worthless; they must be tested by observation or experiment. This cornerstone of modern science is stated by Hempel:

> In his endeavour to find a solution to his problem, the scientist may give free rein to his imagination, and the course of his creative thinking may be influenced even by scientifically questionable notions . . . Yet, scientific objectivity is safeguarded by the principle that while hypotheses and theories may be freely invented and *proposed* in science, they can be *accepted* into the body of scientific knowledge only if they pass critical scrutiny, which includes in particular the checking of suitable test implications by careful observation or experiment (1966: 16).

However, not just any experiment will be suitably rigorous. Many scientists think that an experiment is a reliable test of a hypothesis only if it is tightly controlled. Suppose, for instance, that a scientist wants to test a hypothesis of the following form: "Agent X causes biomedical phenomenon Y." How should she proceed?

The preferred research method of achieving the appropriate controls is the randomized (blind or double blind) experiment. Researchers randomly select experimental subjects from the population at large (human or non-human), and then randomly divide those subjects into an experimental and a control group. The researcher conducts tests on members of these two groups and compares the results. Suppose, for instance, that experimenters are interested in the effect of phenol on a given type of organism. The investigator administers phenol to members of the experimental group, and (through the same route) an inert substance to members of the control group. The researcher observes the reactions in each group to determine if there is a statistically significant difference in response.

Moreover, the researcher must carefully exclude all extraneous causal factors. For instance, to ensure that no genetic differences influence the outcome of the study, the investigator may use genetically homogeneous strains of experimental subjects. Furthermore, the researcher will keep both groups of subjects in similar environmental conditions before and during the experiment. Finally, the experimenter should include sufficiently large numbers of subjects in each group to ensure statistically significant results. Taken together these procedures will guarantee, so far as is possible, that any statistically significant findings are caused by the suspect factor – in this case phenol.

However, not all research methods permit the experimenter to control relevant variables appropriately. There are other scientific methodologies, methodologies widely used in human research. Many biomedical researchers think these human methodologies are poor substitutes for fully controlled, randomized experiments. If these alternative methods are so inferior, then why do scientists studying humans use them? As we stated earlier, the answer is that it is generally considered immoral to do fully randomized controlled experiments on humans, especially when the experiment is dangerous. So human researchers resort to what are generally thought to be less rigorously controlled forms of experimentation. Although we briefly mentioned these methodologies, we must discuss them further.

One methodology often used in humans is the prospective

epidemiological study. For instance, the famous Framingham study investigated the possible connection between smoking and coronary heart disease. Researchers divided the subjects – residents of Framingham Massachusetts – into two groups, according to lifestyle: smokers comprised the experimental group while non-smokers comprised the control group. Initially, members of neither group had coronary heart disease. Membership in the groups was not assigned randomly; their environments were not strictly controlled; and members were genetically heterogeneous. That explains why, according to the current paradigm, its results were not wholly reliable; after all, the experiment was inadequately controlled.

The second method of human experimentation is the retrospective epidemiological study. This method provides even fewer controls than prospective studies. An experimenter using this method identifies people who have the symptom or effect being studied (cancer, heart disease, etc.), and then seeks to isolate the cause of the condition by identifying any commonalities in the subjects' histories. The problem, of course, is that of knowing what other causal factors may be at work. Thus, although these studies may identify significant correlations, they cannot establish causality. That is why many contemporary biomedical researchers share Bernard's fear of "observing physicians."

The current methodological reliance on controlled experiments is closely tied to an underlying (though not completely recognized) commitment to classical causal determinism. According to that doctrine, all events have causes, and for qualitatively similar systems, same cause, same effect. The role of this principle is apparent in many branches of scientific inquiry. When a chemist or physicist conducts a laboratory experiment, the investigator manipulates some substance, X, and records the results. For instance, when the researcher may combine hydrogen with oxygen in the lab, water is produced. The investigator infers that when similar elements combine outside the lab, water will likewise be formed. It is a sound inductive inference. After all, *ceteris paribus*, we have no particular reason to believe that hydrogen will behave differently outside the lab than in it. Nor do we have any reason to think any two molecules of hydrogen or oxygen are relevantly different.

Consequently, it is not surprising that many scientists embrace classical determinism. Deterministic, universal laws allow researchers to predict future events if they currently know the initial conditions. That is why "the controlled experiment was considered the only respectable scientific method, whereas observation and comparison were viewed as considerably less scientific" (Mayr 1988: 9).

The primacy of animal experimentation

Current biomedical researchers assume not only that experiments on animals will yield results directly applicable to man, but that those experiments are, for many purposes, the only way to obtain the desired results. That is why animal research is the centerpiece of the current biomedical paradigm. As the AMA expresses it, there is "no alternative to using animals for most types of health related research" (1992: 27). Or, as Franklin Trull, President of the Foundation for Biomedical Research puts it: "[E]very major medical advance of this century has depended on animal research" (1987: 327).

Some defenders of research claim that these public policy documents perhaps overstate the role of animal experimentation. They claim animal research, properly understood, is part of a "quadrumvirate of techniques: Clinical studies, epidemiological studies, in vitro studies, and animal studies. All complement each other and none should be considered 'alternatives' to any other" (Willis and Hulsey 1994: 216).

Although the view of Willis and Hulsey is defensible, it is not the view articulated by the AMA. According to the authors of the AMA White Paper, animal experimentation is the first among unequal components. They praise the role of research on intact animals, but do not make similarly laudatory remarks about clinical studies and cell cultures. Moreover, the authors of the White Paper chronicle what they see as the drawbacks of these methods; they do not go to great lengths to explain and identify the drawbacks of animal experimentation.

Similar sentiments are expressed in the "Sigma Xi Statement on the Use of Animals in Research", referred to in Chapter 1. The limitations of cell and tissue cultures, and the centrality of animal experimentation, are likewise echoed by contemporary neuroscientists:

> Although tissue culture is certainly a valuable and widely used tool in biomedical research, isolated cells do not respond as whole systems do. This is apparent for investigations of the

outcome of activity within complex neural networks. For example, tissue cultures are unlikely to reveal the interactions among the thalamic reticular nucleus, thalamic nuclei that project to the cortex, and the cortex itself that lead to production of the rhythms of the electroencephalogram (Nonneman and Woodruff 1994: 4).

Thus, although public policy documents and some contemporary researchers portray the other elements of the Willis–Hulsey quadrumvirate as members of the family of modern biomedicine, they clearly portray these elements as weak relatives of the patriarch. As the Sigma Xi "Statement" explains it: "virtually all of these alternative methods are now adjuncts to the use of animal subjects in research, not replacements for such subjects" (1992: 75).

THE NATURE OF ANIMAL EXPERIMENTATION

What is a model?

What do researchers mean when they speak of "animal models"? Before we can explain exactly what a scientific model is, we must explain what it is not. Scientific models are not models in two ordinary senses of the term. For instance, we sometimes speak of a model as a design – a model of how something is supposed to be done. If an architect makes a scale model of a building, then the job of the contractor is to complete the structure following that design. Or, if an education specialist designs a model curriculum, then the job of the teacher (or the school system) is to implement that curriculum. However, this is clearly not the relevant sense of "model." We do not assume human diseases aspire to resemble the corresponding animal condition.

On other occasions we may speak of models as representations. For example, a model Boeing 747 is supposed to represent, to resemble, a real Boeing 747. However, this sense of "model" also fails to capture the relationship between an animal model and the phenomena it is intended to explain or illuminate. Yet both sides of the debate sometimes talk as if it were. For instance, the AMA claims "No other method of study can exactly reproduce the characteristics and qualities of a living intact biological system or organism" (AMA 1992: 27). And animal activists often decry animal research because human systems and diseases are not exactly like those in animals (Reusch 1978). Yet neither activists nor researchers should demand or expect that animal models be representations of human biomedical conditions. For if animal models were mere representations, then they would be useless to the scientific enterprise. Since a model Boeing 747 is manufactured to embody the details of a real Boeing 747, then we cannot learn anything new about the real plane by looking at its model – it is a model only because we made it similar to the thing it models.

Animal models are not models in either of these ordinary senses; but then, they don't try to be. However, although animal models are not designs or representations, they can serve scientifically valuable functions. According to biomedical researchers, animal models reveal significant information about human biomedical phenomena. How can animal models serve this purpose? To elucidate the relationship between animal systems and the human biomedical phenomena they presumably model, we must explain in some detail the central argument for the use of animals in biomedical research.

Intact systems

In defending the importance of animal experimentation, researchers typically cite the "intact systems argument" in one of its many guises. According to this argument, animal models are a special type of causal model of human biomedical phenomena. "Animals are important in research precisely because they have complex body systems that act and interact with stimuli much as humans do" (AMA 1992: 5). This explains why many biomedical researchers make animal experiments the focus of their work. As the AMA states in explaining why, for example, cell cultures cannot replace experiments on whole animals:

> Cells in isolation, however, do not act or react the same as cells in an intact system . . . isolated systems give isolated results that may bear little relation to results obtained from the integrated systems of whole animals (1992: 18).

The AMA similarly explains the limitation of computer simulations – limitations only animal experiments can overcome.

> Both computers and computer simulations have inherent limitations that make it unlikely that they will ever totally

replace animals in experiments. One of these limitations is the nature of simulation. The validity of any model depends on how closely it resembles the original in every respect . . . Until full knowledge of a particular biological system is developed, no model can be constructed that will in every case predict or accurately represent the reaction of the system to a given stimulus (1992: 18).

And more generally,

No other method of study can exactly reproduce the characteristics and qualities of a living intact biological system or organism. Therefore, in order to understand how such a system or organism functions in a particular set of circumstances or how it will react to a given stimulus, it becomes necessary at some point to conduct an experiment or test to find out. There simply is no alternative to this approach (1992: 19).

The centrality of the intact systems argument, though, is not restricted to public policy documents. It is part of the scientific paradigm as articulated by practitioners. As Nomura *et al.* claim "It is essential to develop animal models for human diseases with disease onset mechanisms the same as those for humans to study the causes" (1987: 337). These animal models must use whole, intact systems. As Patton argues:

[I]t is the whole organism in particular that gives us our greatest chance of seeing the unexpected. It alone contains all the mechanisms, known and unknown, that we seek to understand . . . It is because of this that the whole animal has to be used for experimenting with a new drug or exploring the physiological action of some newly discovered body constituent or investigating the function of a newly identified gland or cluster of nerve cells in the brain (1993: 117).

Patton uses a variation on this general argument specifically to defend the use of animals in toxicology. "This is the fundamental reason why toxicity testing must involve whole animals . . . It is only then that the full range of genes and gene products is available for the showing-up of any toxic effect" (Ibid.: 170). Patton's argument is echoed by R.D. Hood, who says not only that the laboratory subject must be an intact *animal* but that for many purposes it had to be an intact *mammal*:

Also it is widely accepted that although submammalian species may eventually be shown to have utility in prescreens or for testing low priority chemicals, only an intact mammal has the numerous characteristics needed to mimic the human situation when more definitive answers are required (1990: 185).

Indeed, researchers claim we should use whole animals not only to find those things we are specifically investigating, but to discover things we do not expect: "To be prepared for unusual discoveries in scientific research, we must continue testing the biological effects of compounds in whole animals" (Clarke 1973: 3). As Comroe and Dripps argue throughout their essay, the indirect benefits of research are often more important that the direct, expected benefits (1974).

In short, the "intact systems argument" claims there is a class of biomedically significant data that cannot be extracted from cell and tissue cultures, computer simulations, clinical studies, or epidemiological investigation, but only from the study of intact biological systems. Experiments on whole non-human animals can tell us much about humans, since non-human animals are thought to be similar to humans in relevant, though perhaps unknown and unexpected, biomedical respects. That is, researchers assume there is no ontological problem of relevance, only an epistemological problem. That is why they think animal models are useful.

Animal models as causal analogs

Researchers claim carefully selected non-human animal models are causal analogs of human biomedical phenomena. Indeed, they think the central role of animals in biomedical research is as *causal analog models* (CAMs). Their aim, in selecting models, is to find animal systems which "resemble the original [the human condition] in every respect" (AMA 1992: 27). Otherwise, researchers say, we cannot make causal inferences from the former to the latter:

> Animals are important in research precisely because they have complex body systems that react and interact with stimuli much as humans do. The more true this is with a particular animal, the more valuable the animal is for a particular type of research (AMA 1992: 5).

In short, researchers aim to find what we term *strong models*; that is, animal models in which the "etiology [is] mechanistically identical to that of human diseases" (Nomura *et al.* 1987: 352). Doubtless some researchers think they need not use strong models; they think weak models will suffice. We discuss this option later in the book. However, the following comments from *Casarett and Doull's Toxicology* – where the two principles underlying animal toxicity testing are identified – suggest that researchers seek and expect strong models:

> The first [principle] is that the effects produced by the compound in laboratory animals, when properly qualified, are applicable to man. This premise underlies all of experimental biology and medicine (Klaassen and Eaton 1993: 31).

(By "proper qualification" they mean primarily that experimenters should make allowances for quantitative differences in body weight. This is discussed in some detail in the next section on "Scaling" – see pp. 65–6.)

> The second main principle is that exposure of experimental animals to toxic agents in high doses is a necessary and valid method of discovering possible hazards in man. This principle is based on the quantal dose-response concept that the incidence of an effect in a population is greater as the dose or exposure increases (Klaassen and Eaton 1993: 31).

That is, since experimental animal populations are small relative to the human population, experimenters infer that they should give animal subjects large doses of potentially toxic agents to increase the (possibly low) incidence of deleterious effects, the appearance of which are assumed to be relevant to human populations of interest.

Researchers study non-human animals to determine how they react to drugs, poisons, food additives, surgical intervention, etc. They then infer (by analogical reasoning) that humans will react similarly. The aim is to design experiments that reveal relevant causal mechanisms. The researchers can then infer, by analogy, that the mechanisms in humans are similar. If the inference is reliable, then scientists can probably prevent or treat the conditions being studied. That is why causal analogical models (CAMs) are thought to be the primary engines of biomedical advance.

When they reason from models to subjects modeled, researchers employ *causal analogical arguments*. Such arguments have the following general structure:

> X (the model) is similar to Y (the subject being modeled) with respect to properties {a, . . ., e}. X has additional property f. While f has not yet been observed directly in Y, likely Y also has the property f.

Researchers assume that systems in laboratory animals are analogous to human systems of interest (i.e., they presuppose ontological relevance), and therefore that the results of experiments on the former will be relevant to the latter.

Crawley *et al.* explicitly state the researchers' hope: "Ideally, a laboratory-based animal model should be the same as the human disorder in (1) symptoms, (2) postulated etiology, (3) neurobiological mechanism, and (4) treatment response" (1985: 300). Nevertheless, one might ask why researchers would assume that systems in laboratory animals are, in fact, ontologically analogous to systems in humans. Moreover, the epistemological problem of relevance also stares researchers square in the face. Researchers aim to choose animals which "resemble the original in every respect" (AMA 1992: 18). However, they perform experiments on animals because they are ignorant of the causes of human biomedical phenomena – randomized, controlled experiments on humans are ethically objectionable. Consequently, it is difficult to know how to select a model that resembles humans "in every respect."

Especially since, *pace* Crawley *et al.*, modern biologists are unlikely to believe that the systems in humans and laboratory animals are exactly alike (after all, they wouldn't be different, if they were exactly alike). Nonetheless, although most acknowledge that there are genuine differences between species, they do not see this as undermining the legitimacy of animal experimentation. For, besides the differences between species, they also believe: (a) that there are broad commonalities across species, and (b) any differences are primarily quantitative and can be accounted for by the appropriate scaling formulae.

The belief in the broad biological commonalities across species is clearly stated by Patton:

> But one should not over-estimate these differences. We have only to look at an account of evolution or at textbooks in

63

comparative anatomy to see how much we have in common: hearts, lungs, kidneys, brains, endocrine glands, nerves, muscles, digestive systems, all *built* on the same plan. This homology goes back still further as one moves down to the biological elements like the nucleus, the mitochondria, or the cell membrane, out of which the higher organisms are *built*. The only differences [in drug actions] that appear are in dose required, duration of action, sometimes in the way the action manifests itself, and sometimes in side-effects [emphasis added] (1993: 166).

Discoveries in biochemistry suggest that there are pervasive bio-chemical similarities between organisms. All organisms with which we are familiar are constructed out of the same chemical building blocks. Some biochemists refer to these similarities as evidence of *the unity of biochemistry*. According to biochemist A.G. Cairns-Smith, all life on earth reflects this fundamental unity.

There is a SYSTEM common to all life on Earth, not just a set of molecules. The unity of biochemistry applies, for example, to the ribosome technique of protein synthesis; to the idea of using proteins for catalysts, and of making membranes from proteins and lipids. It applies too to more particular manu-facturing procedures: to the sequencing of operations in the making and breaking of molecules. These "central metabolic pathways" are extraordinarily similar in all forms of life that we know of (1985: 38).

For instance, in discussing the similarities between whales and bats, Cairns-Smith claims, in a manner reminiscent of Claude Bernard's discussion of species differences:

the design similarities may be far greater than the differences that catch the eye. Whales and bats are each of them mammals derived from a common ancestor not all that far back, and sharing most of the design ideas on which their survival depends. The machinery for breathing, digesting, excreting; the lay-out of nerves and circulation; the means of making skin and bone; the kinds of protein molecules – all these, and many more, are more similar than different between the whale and the bat. *These two animals might also be said to be the same animal dressed up differently*; even if this time you would have to go a bit deeper to see it. You would have to go deeper still to see what is the same between a herring and a hamster, but the similarities are still not that deep. Still there are more similarities than differences [emphasis added] (1985: 50).

These commonalities across species have led researchers to believe that we could safely extrapolate findings in laboratory animals to humans, if only we knew some way to eliminate or discount extraneous species differences. Many scientists think scaling formulae can serve this scientific purpose.

Scaling

According to the standard (classical) view of causal analogical reasoning, analogical inferences are reasonable only if the similarities between two systems are great and the differences are small and insignificant. However, although toxicologists find many similarities across species, they find many differences as well. This leaves toxicologists with a problem, a problem well-stated by Calabrese:

Evolutionary theory certainly explains the continuity of life on earth, but it also explains the diversity as well. The observer of nature may not know what is the most impressive phenomenon – the marvelous unity and similarity of life as tied together by a common genetic code or the striking diversity of sizes, shapes, forms and functions. For while the predictive toxicologist may want to emphasize the phylogenetic continuity of life as the basis of animal extrapolation, he or she must also successfully deal with the diversity issue as well. Thus how is it possible to predict a human response from a mouse, when the human is about 3500 times larger or the mouse takes 14 breaths for every 1 human breath or the metabolism of the mouse is seven times faster than the human's ... While there are similarities between humans and mice, are the differences so great that any predictions are of little practical value? (1983: 499).

Most researchers think not. They think scaling provides the answer. That is, researchers assume that once they adjust for purely quantitative differences between species (say, differences in body weight, metabolic rates, surface area, etc.) that they may infer the same effect from the same cause. Since, in the words of Cairns-Smith, members of different species are just "the same animal dressed up differently," scaling is thought to provide a mechanism to disrobe members of different species and to treat them as if they were conspecifics.

For some biological characteristics this is surely a reasonable assumption. Doubtless the strength of an animal's supporting structures or the weights of its organs can often be estimated in this quantitative way. Moreover, the rates at which some physiological functions are achieved are likely related to body weight or surface area. However, many biomedical researchers go further. They think most (if not all) inter-species differences are not fundamental differences, but relatively superficial ones that can be adjusted for by using scaling formulae. This is a central principle of modern toxicology. For instance, in carcinogenicity tests, surface area (calculated as body weight $^{2/3}$) is the scaling factor of choice. As Klaassen and Eaton explain:

> scaling factors implicitly consider two independent physiological processes: (1) differences in pharmokinetics, which determine the actual dose delivered to target tissues, and (2) differences in tissue sensitivity between species to an identical delivered dose. In practice scaling factors seldom incorporate such considerations explicitly but rather use dose adjustments across species based on some normalizing factor such as body weight or surface area (1993: 43).

In summary, most researchers assume species differences do not undermine the utility of animal experimentation.

Choosing the proper animal: the Krogh principle

Since scaling factors are generally thought to eliminate (or lessen) the significance of biological differences between species, contemporary physiologists are inclined to embrace the Bernardian claim that animals should be selected primarily because they are convenient test subjects. While there is no non-human animal on which all biomedical experiments can be conducted, the Krogh principle (named after Danish physiologist August Krogh) states that for each problem of interest there is an animal upon which it can be most conveniently studied. Thus, biologists Burggren and Bemis note:

> animals are usually chosen for comparative physiological experimentation either on the basis of extreme physiological

characters or because the animal is conducive to a certain physiological technique (i.e., squid axons 1mm in diameter can be punctured relatively easily by microelectrodes). This manner of choosing animals, known as the Krogh principle, is not concerned with whether a species occupies a key position (or any position!) within a putative evolutionary sequence (1990: 205).

That is, since researchers assume that scaling formulae account *compensate* for relevant differences between humans and non-human animals, then test species can be selected for non-scientific reasons. As Palmer states in a discussion of teratological methodology:

> Species are rarely chosen for scientific reasons but are used because they are available, economical and easy to manage ... These practical considerations often legitimately outweigh more theoretical ones (1978: 219–20).

This theme recurs frequently in the experimental literature, as in Hood's discussion of the criteria for the selection of species:

> In practice, such selection seems to be dominated by factors based on practicality. Animal models are selected on the basis of how many criteria they possess, such as: ready availability, low cost, ease of handling, high fertility, ease of breeding, large litters, short gestation length, ease of mating time determination, low rates of spontaneous deaths and developmental abnormalities, ease with which their fetuses can be examined, and the amount of information available on their reproduction, development, and response to developmental toxicants ... The rationale for using such criteria is that none of the animal models tested is an obvious counterpart of humans in response to developmental toxicants. This leaves the issue of practicality foremost in the selection process (1990: 184–5).

The widespread use of the Krogh principle shows that contemporary physiologists, following Bernard, are inclined to think all vertebrates (and especially mammals) are biologically the same. For them, species differences are simply a complicating factor that can be accommodated by scaling formulae. Researchers thereby indicate that they reject the current best understanding of biological phenomena as expressed in the theory of evolution.

REJECTION OF EVOLUTION

Evolution is currently the unifying theory in modern biology. However, the modern physiologists' paradigm fails to understand or appreciate the implications of biological evolution for the practice of physiology. That should not be surprising since the current physiological paradigm was established by Bernard who, as you may recall, rejected evolution. This paradigm continues to be wedded to biological reductionism. Even scientific luminaries such as Francis Crick are still under its sway. As he states it, "the ultimate aim of the modern movement in biology is in fact to explain all biology in terms of physics and chemistry" (1966: 10). However, *pace* Crick, reductionism is no longer acceptable to most evolutionary biologists. As Ernst Mayr, a father of the New Synthesis in evolutionary biology, explains it:

> Physiology lost its position as the exclusive paradigm of biology in 1859 when Darwin established evolutionary biology. When behavioral biology, ecology, population biology, and other branches of modern biology developed, it became even more evident how unsuitable mechanics was as the paradigm of biological science . . . more and more biologists recognized that all processes in living organisms are consistent with the laws of physics and chemistry, and that the differences which do exist between inanimate matter and living organisms are not due to a difference in substrate but rather to a different organization of matter in living beings (1988: 12).

Biological reductionism ignores the existence and significance of emergent biological properties. As Mayr puts it:

> Recognition of the importance of emergence demonstrates, of course, the invalidity of extreme reductionism. By the time we have dissected an organism down to atoms and elementary particles we have lost everything that is characteristic of a living system (1986: 57).

Typically this extreme reductionism is best seen as "property reductionism" which Gould explicitly rejects:

> The general alternative to such reductionism is the concept of hierarchy – a world constructed not as a smooth and seamless continuum, permitting simple extrapolation from

the lowest level to the highest, but as a series of ascending levels, each bound to the one below it in some ways and independent in others. Discontinuities and seams characterize the transitions; "emergent" features not implicit in the operation of the processes at lower levels, may control events at higher levels. The basic processes – mutation, selection, etc. – may enter into explanations at all scales . . . but they work in different ways on the characteristic material of divers levels (1982: 132).

Theorists under the influence of a mechanistic paradigm are also apt to downplay the significance of species differences for their research. They will focus on similarities between species while overlooking or downplaying their differences. Specifically, to anticipate a theme discussed in Chapter 6, these researchers will overlook the ways that the systems and sub-systems of biological organisms are organized. According to contemporary evolutionists, that is a serious error. Contemporary evolutionary biologists recognize species differences are genuine discontinuities in nature. Thus, there is a profound tension between mechanistic physiological theory and the other biological sciences. In one way this is highly surprising since one would have expected comparative physiology to be the branch of physiology most sensitive to evolved species differences. Not so. According to Burggren and Bemis:

Unfortunately, comparative physiology traditionally has been, and continues to be, outside the framework of contemporary evolutionary biology, often embracing theories, positions or approaches that contemporary morphologists, evolutionary biologists, and geneticists have abandoned (1990: 193).

The tendency to treat species differences as quantitative is reflected in the scaling principles discussed earlier. Many physiologists also ignore the biological significance of interspecific variation. This is a mistake. For example, although the hearts of mice are similar at the level of gross anatomy, they have widely varying heart rates. As Burggren and Bemis note:

While comparative physiologists have made an art of avoiding the study of variation, such heritable variation nonetheless is the source for evolutionary changes in physiology as well as for all other types of characters (1990: 201).

Because they ignore interspecific and intraspecific differences, comparative physiologists focus on paradigm "model" species. But these models usually have two significant deficiencies: (1) they do not reflect intraspecific variation; (2) they are frequently "atypical" species. Burggren and Bemis remark:

> Yet the use of "cockroach as insect", "frog as amphibian", or "the turtle as reptile" persists, in spite of clear evidence of the dangers of this approach. Not surprisingly, this type of comparative physiology has neither contributed much to evolutionary theories nor drawn upon them to formulate and test hypotheses in evolutionary physiology (1990: 206).

Contemporary physiologists are also inclined to embrace Bernard's belief that test animals should be chosen primarily because of their convenience as test subjects. While there is no non-human animal – no panacea species – on which all human biomedical phenomena can be conveniently studied, the Krogh principle states that for each problem of interest there is an animal upon which it can be most conveniently studied. As we have suggested, this ignores the significance of evolved differences between the species. This tension between physiology and evolutionary biology will become more apparent after the discussion of the theory of evolution in the following chapter.

MORAL ARGUMENT

Before leaving this chapter, we should briefly summarize the current paradigm's understanding of the moral propriety of animal experimentation. Like Bernard, most modern physiologists claim it would be morally inappropriate to do controlled invasive laboratory experiments on humans, especially non-consenting humans. Therefore, by their lights, the only choice is using non-human animals.

However, that does not mean there are no constraints on using animals. Non-human animals do have some moral worth; we cannot treat them just anyway we please. "[A]nimals should be treated with respect ... animals should be used only for legitimate purposes ... and (within the limitations of the experiment) every reasonable effort should be made to minimize or reduce pain or discomfort" (Sigma Xi 1992: 75).

Likewise, Carl Cohen, in offering what many researchers take as the definitive ethical defense of animal experimentation:

It does not follow from this, however, that we are morally free to do anything we please to animals. Certainly not. In our dealings with animals, as in our dealings with other human beings, we have obligations that do not arise from claims against us based on rights . . . In our dealings with animals, few will deny that we are at least obliged to act humanely – that is to treat them with the decency and the concern that we owe, as sensitive human beings, to other sentient creatures (1986: 866).

In short, even researchers acknowledge that animals have some moral worth – that non-human animals count for *something* even if they to not count for much.

CONCLUSION

The paradigm governing the practice of contemporary biomedicine is deeply influenced by the work of Claude Bernard. Those working under the paradigm prefer controlled laboratory experiments and downplay the role of other research methodologies. These methodological biases are shaped by a deep commitment to causal determinism. This commitment led Bernard – and contemporary biomedical researchers – to believe that the only route to biomedical knowledge is by using intact animal systems. They, and Bernard, assumed that members of different mammalian species are really "the same animal dressed up differently." That is, species differences are purely quantitative and may be accommodated by using scaling formulae. Finally, many contemporary biomedical researchers have inherited Bernard's disregard for the subtleties of evolutionary biology. Indeed, most of the flaws in Bernard's views, and in the current paradigm, are traceable to their rejection of evolutionary theory. Evolutionary biology has a direct relevance to the scientific (and moral) assessment of animal experimentation. As we argued in Chapter 2, the battle over animal experimentation cannot be waged using bare examples. We must interpret those examples in the light of our best biological theory. That is the theory of evolution, which we discuss in the next two chapters.

5

EVOLUTION I
Species and species differences

But the chief cause of our natural unwillingness to admit that
one species has given birth to clear and distinct species, is that
we are always slow in admitting great changes of which we do
not see the steps. The difficulty is the same as that felt by many
geologists, when Lyell first insisted that long lines of inland
cliffs had been formed, the great valleys excavated, by the
agencies which we see still at work. The mind cannot possibly
grasp the full meaning of the term of even a million years; it
cannot add up and perceive the full effects of many slight
variations accumulated during an almost infinite number of
generations (Darwin [1859] 1972: 116–17).

Biology is the study of the causes and effects of evolution. As
Futuyma puts it: "Evolution . . . is the central unifying concept
of Biology. By extension it affects almost all other fields of knowledge and must be considered one of the most influential concepts
in Western thought" (1986: 16). The aim of this chapter is to
present the central concepts of evolutionary biology, specifically
those concepts relevant to an understanding and assessment of the
practice of animal experimentation. Evolutionary biology has
important implications for our understanding of the nature of
organisms, species, and species differences. This will, among other
things, help illuminate several "problems of relevance" discussed
in Chapter 2.

Evolutionary theory also has implications for moral debates over
animal experimentation. This is not to say that what *is* the case
determines or logically implies what *should* or (morally) *ought* to
be the case. Rather, we claim that what we know about the world –
e.g., our current best biological theory – is *relevant*, as evidence, to

the assessment of animal experimentation (Rachels 1990: 91–8). Having traced the implications of evolution for a scientific assessment of animal experimentation, we will, in the final chapters, morally assess the practice.

We do not pretend to provide a thorough introduction to the theory of evolution. Readers who want a general introduction should consult Miller and van Loon (1982), Berra (1990), or Edey and Johanson (1989). Those who want a more detailed discussion should consult Futuyma (1986) or Mark Ridley (1993), who provide extensive references to primary research literature. In this chapter we focus on contemporary evolutionary biology, most especially, the New Synthesis. In the next chapter we discuss more recent developments in evolutionary biology and then trace their significance for the practice of biomedical experimentation.

We are less directly concerned with Darwin's original theory of evolution. Darwin did not know much about biochemistry or the mechanisms of inheritance. More generally, he lacked the stock of theoretical concepts available to contemporary evolutionary theorists – concepts that inform our understanding of organisms, species, and species differences. Nonetheless, we should briefly outline Darwin's theory of evolution. Just as Bernard's theory illuminates the current biomedical paradigm, Darwin's theory likewise illuminates contemporary evolutionary biology.

DARWIN'S THEORY OF EVOLUTION

Darwin's *Origin of Species*, originally published in 1859, was hardly the first publication to suggest that biological evolution had occurred. Many components of Darwin's theory were shaped by the works of others (Depew and Weber 1995). That is not to say that Darwin was bereft of original ideas. However, his grandest achievement was the novel synthesis of ideas. His theory unified seemingly fragmentary biological phenomena and explained those phenomena without resorting to metaphysical or supernatural forces.

Darwin adopted Charles Lyell's uniformitarian geological theory. He believed that the world had undergone slow, continuous, and systematic changes, over vast periods of time. These changes were produced by forces still operative today: erosion by wind and water, vulcanism, glaciation, etc. Small, often imperceptible, changes accumulated over eons, resulting in significant environmental changes. As Darwin explained it:

73

As Lyell has well remarked, the extent and thickness of our sedimentary formations are the result and the measure of the denudation which the earth's crust has elsewhere undergone. Therefore a man should examine for himself the great piles of superimposed strata, and watch the rivulets bringing down mud, and the waves wearing away the sea-cliffs, in order to comprehend something about the duration of past time, the monuments of which we see all around us ([1859] 1972: 97).

Darwin was convinced environmental change affects biological life. Evidence suggested that plants and animals adapted to environmental changes ([1859] 1972: 26). However, before Darwin no one knew how to explain these biological changes (Rachels 1990).

Darwin offered the first plausible naturalistic explanation. Here is the gist of that explanation. A species is a cohesive population of individual organisms bound together by reproductive ties. However, members of these populations have varied *heritable* traits. Animal breeders had long exploited intraspecific variation to "create" new varieties. Varieties, though, are not just an artifact of intentional design; they also pervade nature. Darwin wanted to explain these natural varieties without appealing to a supernatural or metaphysical breeder:

Again, it may be asked, how is it that varieties, which I have called incipient species, become ultimately converted into good and distinct species which in most cases obviously differ from each other far more than do the varieties of the same species? ([1859] 1972: 39).

Darwin's answer: the fecundity of nature leads to an unremitting

struggle for existence ... [which] inevitably follows from the high rate at which all organic beings tend to increase. Every being, which during its natural lifetime produces several eggs or seeds, must suffer destruction during some period of its life, and during some season or occasional year, otherwise, on the principle of geometrical increase, its numbers would quickly become so inordinately great that no country could support the product ([1859] 1972: 41).

Some creatures will have traits that make them more likely to survive and reproduce than other members of their species. These advantaged (more "fit") creatures are thus likely to have more

74

offspring than conspecifics. If the beneficial trait is heritable, then their offspring will inherit the fitness advantages conferred by such trait(s).

> Owing to this struggle, variations, however slight and from whatever cause proceeding, if they be in any degree profitable to the individuals of a species, in their infinitely complex relations to other organic beings and to their physical conditions of life, will tend to the preservation of such individuals, and will generally be inherited by the offspring ([1859] 1972: 39).

Darwin claims this mechanism is the primary engine of evolution.

> This preservation of favourable individual differences and variations, and the destruction of those which are injurious, I have called Natural Selection, or the Survival of the Fittest. Variations neither useful nor injurious would not be affected by natural selection, and would be left either a fluctuating element, as perhaps we see in certain polymorphic species, or would ultimately become fixed, owing to the nature of the organism and the nature of the conditions ([1859] 1972: 44).

Natural selection exploits intraspecific variation. When teamed with Lyell's gradualism, it also explains how even small changes could be amplified over succeeding generations to lead to even greater diversity within the species:

> As each species tends by its geometrical rate of reproduction to increase inordinately in number; and as the modified descendants of each species will be enabled to increase by as much as they become more diversified in habits and structure, so as to be able to seize on many and widely different places in the economy of nature, there will be a constant tendency of natural selection to preserve the most divergent offspring of any one species. Hence, during a long continued course of modification, the slight differences characteristic of varieties of the same species, tend to be augmented into the greater differences characteristic of species of the same genus ([1859] 1972: 108).

This process of adaptive radiation explains what happens when animals from an ancestral species move into a multiplicity of ecological niches. Each niche is characterized by a particular complex of features that affect an animal's flourishing: nature and availability of food, nature and number of predators and pathogens, climates, etc. Natural selection favors populations adapted to their respective niches. This further accentuates existing intraspecific variation. Darwin thought this process, carried out over a long enough time, would eventually create new species. That is, if these small differences accumulate over many generations, then the "invisible hand" of natural selection would produce populations of individuals so distinct as to be designated as distinct species. Biology is replete with examples – Darwin's finches in the Galapagos Islands and the diversification of Australian marsupials are but two.

Summarizing Darwin's theory

We can extract five points from Darwin's account which set the stage for our discussion of contemporary evolutionary biology:

1 Evolution can occur by natural selection, but it is not the only route to evolution. In the 6th edition of *Origin of Species*, Darwin gives the following caution:

> [I]n the first edition of this work, and subsequently, I placed in a most conspicuous position – namely, at the close of the introduction – the following words: "I am convinced that natural selection has been the main but not the exclusive means of modification." This has been to no avail. Great is the power of misrepresentation ([1859] 1972: 115).

Some Darwinists appear to have forgotten these words. Panselectionists, for example, have argued that every trait of an organism is an adaptation that confers some fitness advantage. However, adherents of the New Synthesis have acknowledged the Darwinian claim that evolution occasionally results from means other than natural selection. However, unlike Darwin, later evolutionists can describe these other means.

2 Although Darwin knew there was some mechanism for the inheritance of traits (he speculated about the existence of "gemmules" – basic units of heredity), he did not understand that mechanism. This is the main hole in Darwin's theory, a hole nicely plugged by the New Synthesis.

3 Any two species are ultimately descended from a common ancestor species (the principle of phylogenetic continuity). No serious biologist rejects this principle.

4 Since phylogenetically related species, say, mammals, have all evolved from the same ancestral species, we would expect them to be, in some respects, biologically similar.

5 Nonetheless, evolution also leads us to expect important biological differences between species; after all, the species have adapted to different ecological niches. However, Darwin's theory does not tell us how pervasive or significant those differences will be. This again brings the ontological problem of relevance to the fore. Will the similarities between species be pervasive and deep enough to justify extrapolations from animal test subjects to humans? Or will the biological differences be quantitatively or qualitatively substantial enough to make such extrapolations scientifically dubious? The answer to these questions emerges more clearly from later evolutionary developments.

EVOLUTION AND THE NEW SYNTHESIS

The New Synthesis refers to the development of theoretical biology from the 1930s to the 1960s. The main figures associated with the New Synthesis were: R.A. Fisher, J.B.S. Haldane, Sewell Wright, Julian Huxley, Ernst Mayr, G. Ledyard Stebbins, George Gaylord Simpson, and Theodosius Dobzhansky. These theorists reshaped evolutionary biology in two general ways. First, they made the theory compatible with existing discoveries in genetics, systematics and paleontology. Second, they provided a framework for the unification of the disparate branches of the biological sciences. These developments helped explain (a) the diverse routes to evolution, (b) the nature of species, (c) the importance of developmental processes, and (d) the hierarchical nature of biological phenomena.

Routes to evolution

Darwin understood that any population of organisms will manifest variation in heritable traits. When any two members of a species breed, their offspring will differ not only from other members of the species but also from each parent. Sexual reproduction thus produces novel traits that can be exploited by the animal breeder, or that can be preserved or eliminated by natural selection. As we suggested earlier, Darwin assumed this was the main source of variation in traits on which natural selection can operate.

Darwin was right that this is an important source of heritable traits. However, he did not understand the genetic underpinnings of observable phenotypic traits. By wedding genetics and evolutionary theory, advocates of the New Synthesis explained this process. More generally, they showed that evolution should be understood as changes in gene (allele) frequencies over time.

This more general explanation allowed them to understand that evolution was more than just natural selection working on traits produced by recombination during sexual reproduction. For instance, they showed that variation in heritable traits can also emerge from germ line mutations: most mutations are harmful, but in a given environment some are adaptively neutral and some confer fitness advantages upon their bearers.

The insights of the New Synthesis also help us see and explain non-adaptive evolution. For instance, gene flow (the exchange of genes within and between populations) – and the cessation of gene flow – can dramatically change gene frequencies within a population. It has been proposed that non-adaptive evolution can also occur as the result of random genetic drift, mutation pressure, Kimura's neutral mutation, and what Ernst Mayr called the "founder effect."

To explain this latter, suppose a few individuals, perhaps even a single pregnant female, split(s) off from a parent population. The gene pool in the new population will differ from that found in the parental population by virtue of its being an incomplete sample of the parental gene pool. Gene frequencies will differ between the two populations, but not because of the effects of natural selection. Chance will have eliminated some genes from the new gene pool. Due to intense inbreeding early in the new population, there will be increased homozygosity, with recessive alleles exposed to selection. Genes rare in the parental population may become common in the new gene pool. Mayr believes that such genetically unbalanced populations may be ideally suited to shift into new niches.

What the New Synthesis emphasized, in short, was that changes in gene frequency, however produced, drive evolution. Many of these changes are produced by natural selection; but some are produced by other processes mentioned above. However, since all products of evolution are ultimately subject to selection pressures, then all changes will eventually be eliminated from the gene pool if they are grossly maladaptive. What is important for present purposes, though, is to note the genetic basis of intraspecific variation, and ultimately of speciation. Now we must ask how speciation occurs. And what is a species anyway? How, precisely, does the category of "species" help us understand the biological world?

Speciation and the Biological Species Concept

What is a biological species? Biologists disagree over the precise definition of "species." Perhaps more than one definition is needed given the complexity and diversity of life on earth. What is clear is that most biologists view the concept species as crucial to our understanding of the biological world. Mayr points out:

> Modern biologists are almost unanimously agreed that there are real discontinuities in organic nature, which delimit natural entities that are designated as species. Therefore the species is one of the basic foundations of almost all biological disciplines. Each species has different biological character-istics, and the analysis and comparison of these differences is a prerequisite for all other research in ecology, behavioral biology, comparative morphology and physiology, molecular biology, and indeed all branches of biology (1988: 331).

The dominant species concept in contemporary biology is the Biological Species Concept (BSC) – sometimes called the isolation species concept. Templeton writes:

> Mayr defined the isolation species concept as "groups of actually or potentially interbreeding natural populations which are reproductively isolated from other such groups." Similarly, Dobzhansky states that "Species are systems of populations: the gene exchange between these systems is limited or prevented by a reproductive isolating mechanism or perhaps by a combination of such mechanisms." As White has emphasized, the isolation concept species "is at the same time a reproductive community, a gene pool and a genetic system." It is these latter two attributes that make this con-cept of species particularly useful for integrating population

genetic considerations into the problem of the origin of species (1989: 5).

It would be a mistake to think that the BSC is a species concept with universal applicability. Most notably, it fails to explain how asexual species can be species. Nevertheless, the concept does illuminate the differences between mammalian species – and these are the species with which we are primarily concerned in this book.

Biologists may disagree not only about the concept of species, but also about the processes by which species are formed. Most biologists think the main mechanism of speciation is "allopatric speciation." Here is a simplified account: a population of inter-breeding animals becomes divided by some geographic barrier. The barrier impedes gene flow between the two sub-populations. Additionally, the population that has become separated from the parent population may be subject to different environmental conditions (not just the physical environment, but also different prey, predators, pathogens and parasites). Some will have traits that make it more likely that they will survive and reproduce. Those individuals best adapted to prevailing conditions are more likely to leave behind more offspring, who in turn will inherit the favorable traits, and so on. Succeeding generations will be sub-ject to natural selection and all other factors affecting gene frequencies. In time, the genetic differences between the two populations will become more profound. This divergence may manifest itself morphologically, anatomically, behaviorally, physio-logically, or biochemically.

These divergences may become so great that the populations become reproductively isolated. When that happens, then even if the geographical barriers separating the two populations become traversable, individuals within the groups can no longer successfully interbreed. Speciation has occurred.

Allopatric speciation is generally recognized as the primary engine of speciation. However, many theorists recognize speciation can occur by different means, although there is considerable disagreement about their nature or frequency (see Futuyma 1986: 227–42). Since there is considerable debate about the existence and scope of such means, and since their precise relevance to an assessment of animal experimentation is unclear, we will not consider them further. What all adherents of the BSC acknowledge is that every means of speciation involves some form of reproductive isolation, whether it is behavioral, mechanical (anatomical) isolation, or physiological isolation.

We should note that reproductive isolation is not the same thing as interspecific sterility. Sometimes it is possible for members of different species to produce fertile hybrids. Some biologists (e.g., Templeton 1989), have taken this to be a mark against the adequacy of the BSC. However, other biologists think the existence of fertile hybrids is compatible with the BSC:

> [T]his usually happens under artificial or disturbed con- ditions and may mean that the two parental species are very closely related, that they are relatively recent derivatives of a common ancestor, or that their isolating mechanisms are incomplete and still evolving ... Partial isolation, known as hybrid breakdown, may result in reduced hybrid fitness, whereby the hybrids ... leave fewer offspring than the non- hybrids do and tend to be eliminated from the population. Many of the viable hybrids that are produced in laboratories of biologists never occur in nature (Berra 1990: 16).

Consequently, the existence of fertile hybrids is not a clear reason to reject the applicability of the BSC to sexual species.

In summary, speciation occurs when genetic differences between two populations (usually geographically isolated) lead them to become reproductively isolated. Once a new species has emerged, the same processes that produced speciation will lead to further genetic changes within that species.

The New Synthesis and biomedical phenomena

Genetic differences between individuals and populations are not just relevant to the theoretical understanding of speciation and species differences, they are also practically important. They are central to the understanding of three biological phenomena that have practical biomedical significance: balanced polymorphism, phylogenetic inertia, and host–parasite coevolution.

Balanced polymorphism

Every person gets two "copies" (i.e., alleles) of a gene, one from each parent. Occasionally, possession of one mutant allele is beneficial (confers a fitness advantage), whereas two mutant copies are damaging or even lethal. For instance, individuals who have the "sickle cell trait" have one normal allele and one mutant allele of the gene that controls the development of hemoglobin, the protein that carries oxygen in red blood cells. This trait most often appears in West Africa where humans are also exposed to malaria. Since individuals with the sickle cell trait are partially resistant to malaria, the trait is highly beneficial in that environment. However, mutations in both alleles of the gene lead to sickle cell anemia, frequently a fatal disease.

If the parents of a child both have the sickle cell trait (one normal allele, one mutant allele), then there is a probability of 1/4 that they will have a normal child (two normal alleles). There is a probability of 1/4 that they will have a child with sickle cell anemia. However, there is a probability of 1/2 that their child will have the sickle cell trait, with the advantage it confers in that environment. Therefore the presence of this mutant allele, although it occasionally leads to a deadly disease, will tend to be preserved in populations living in that environment. After all, traits are not advantageous *simpliciter*; rather, they are advantageous relative to certain environmental contexts. For instance, individuals with the sickle cell trait are more fit in an environment where they are exposed to malaria, but disadvantaged at high altitudes due to decreased oxygen levels in body tissues.

Additionally, some mutations are not dangerous unless the individuals possessing these mutant alleles are exposed to specific environmental factors. Diet sodas carry warnings for persons with a condition known as phenylketonuria (PKU). This condition results from a specific genetic mutation that is not, in itself, dangerous. If, however, an individual with PKU is exposed to a chemical called phenylalanine (a substance found in diet sodas and some other foodstuffs), that person may suffer adverse medical reactions, including severe mental retardation. By avoiding exposure to this substance, individuals can live normal lives.

Phylogenetic inertia

Evolution does not always produce the most fit or the best designed physiological traits (Gould 1980). Some traits are functionally serviceable, although seemingly ill "designed." Other traits or biological structures may become, through evolutionary time, functionally useless. However, biological organisms are historical objects that retain genetic "memories" of their evolutionary pasts. Thus, organisms may retain anatomical structures simply because of "phylogenetic inertia." That is, if these old structures have little overall affect on an individual's reproductive fitness, then evolutionary processes may "ignore" these functionless structures. Occasionally, however, these vestiges of earlier evolutionary processes may become harmful to the organism.

For example, the human appendix once had some biological function (the presence of lymphatic tissue suggests it was part of the immune system). Now, though, it serves little function: an individual whose appendix has been removed can live a normal life. Normally we just ignore the appendix since, under most circumstances, its presence is not detrimental. However, if the appendix becomes inflamed, surgery is often required (if left untreated, it may rupture, causing peritonitis). It is not surprising, however, to find structures that are vestigial in one species yet fully functional in another After all, evolution has different consequences for members of distinct species.

Phylogenetic inertia also explains the presence of different causal routes to similar functional ends – a theme we discuss in more detail in the following chapter. Neese and Williams note:

> Many design features, while not maladaptive, are functionally arbitrary and explicable only as historical legacies. In mammals, the right side of the heart circulates the blood to the lungs, the left side to the rest of the body. In birds it is the other way around, for no better reason than that birds and mammals came from different reptilian ancestors that took arbitrarily different routes to cardiac specialization. Either way works equally well (1994: 133).

Organisms are historical objects and their current structural and functional properties reflect the contingencies of history.

Host–parasite coevolution

The emergence of drug-resistant strains of bacteria illustrates the phenomenon of host–parasite coevolution. When antibiotics were first introduced, they were considered wonder drugs. These new drugs effectively combated diseases that killed many; those the diseases did not kill were often forced to spend weeks recovering in infectious disease wards. The bacteria that caused these diseases were not well suited to survival in this new environment: they were vulnerable to the antibiotics of the day. Humans substantially benefited from this vulnerability. However, bacteria, like everything else in the biological world, evolve. A random mutation in a bacterium (or the appearance of new genes introduced by plasmids) may permit that organism to survive in a human host, even in the presence of given antibiotics. This bacterium will thus be better able to survive and reproduce *in that environment* than other members of the population. As Neese and Williams note:

> Wars between hosts and parasites initiate escalating arms races that require extravagant, harmful expenditures and create extraordinarily complex weapons and defenses. Just as political powers sometimes put more and more of their energies into weaponry and defenses to keep from being dominated by opponents, hosts and parasites must both evolve as fast as they can to maintain their current levels of adaptation ... We are in a relentless all-out struggle with our pathogens, and no agreeable accommodation can ever be reached (1994: 50).

These biological arms races are sometimes described using what is called the *Red Queen Hypothesis*. This hypothesis is inspired by Lewis Carroll's Red Queen, who remarks to Alice, "Now, here, you see, it takes all the running you can do, just to keep in the same place." The assumption is that each species must evolve just to keep pace with other species – who are also evolving.

Thus, in the current world of antibiotics, some bacteria will survive because they have "drug-resistant genes" – genes that confer a fitness advantage in that environment. Eventually these genes will become widespread in the bacterial population. That is why we now have strains of bacteria that are relatively unaffected by (certain types of) antibiotics. Some strains of bacteria have evolved so that they actually feed on antibiotics.

Of course, while the parasite evolves, the human host evolves as well. Can the hosts evolve new defenses to combat these new bacteria? In principal, yes. But it must be remembered, however, that evolutionary effects result from the differential reproduction of genetic variants. New generations of bacteria may appear roughly every twenty minutes, while new generations of humans appear roughly every twenty years. Bacteria can thus evolve more quickly than humans. As Neese and Williams point out:

84

Some of our defenses against disease, such as sickle cell hemoglobin, have evolved markedly in the last ten thousand years, during which we have had perhaps three hundred generations. The species as a whole has evolved significantly higher resistance to a few epidemic diseases such as smallpox and tuberculosis in the last few centuries, perhaps a dozen generations. Compare this to a bacterium's three hundred generations in a week or two and the even faster reproduction of a virus. Bacteria can evolve as much in a day as we can in a thousand years . . . We cannot evolve fast enough to escape from microorganisms (1994: 51).

This explains why drug-resistant bacteria are becoming a special problem, not just for patients being treated in hospital, but for the population at large. The reappearance of drug-resistant tuberculosis in our inner cities is particularly disturbing. In our hospitals, drug-resistant infections are becoming a serious nuisance. This burgeoning health care crisis is an expected, but unwelcome, consequence of evolution.

Drug companies try to outwit the consequences of bacterial evolution by coming up with new antibiotics. However, we cannot be confident that these efforts will be successful. There are already many strains of bacteria our current antibiotic arsenals cannot destroy. We cannot yet determine if drug companies can continually develop new "magic bullets" to battle evolving bacteria, or whether the ongoing war between humans and microorganisms will revert to older, deadlier, and costlier forms.

Doubtless there are other applications of the Red Queen Hypothesis lurking in the wings. One, specifically relevant to the current discussion, is that to sustain our current advantage in the war against microorganisms we must intentionally develop curative and preventive measures at least as swiftly and effectively as evolution unintentionally develops new strains of bacteria. It will be interesting to see if this biomedical arms race is scientifically and economically sustainable.

One especially potent weapon humans have evolved is an extremely complex and versatile immune system. As Neese and Williams point out:

From an immunological perspective, an epidemic may change a human population dramatically. Those individuals who have contracted a disease and recovered will likely be immune to reinfection because they harbor vastly increased concentrations of the lymphocytes that make the antibodies that are most destructive of that particular pathogen. Adult immunity to childhood diseases such as mumps depends not on changing human gene pools but on changing the concentrations of different kinds of antibodies within each individual (1994: 52).

Of course, this is not to say that epidemics do not have effects on gene frequencies. However, their effects are likely to be relatively small, especially when gauged against the speed at which bacteria evolve.

In the next chapter we discuss other developments in evolutionary biology that are relevant to an assessment of biomedical research using non-human animals.

6

EVOLUTION II
The widening synthesis

In physics, there is no great difference between a why question and a how question. How does the earth go around the sun? By gravitational attraction. Why does the earth go around the sun? Because of gravity. Evolution, however, causes biology to be a very different game because it includes contingent history (Mark Ridley 1993: 17).

The New Synthesis merged Darwinian evolutionary theory with genetics and molecular biology. In the last two decades, biologists have gone further and tried to unify all their disparate fields. Evolutionary theory has played a central role in these efforts. There are now pervasive ties between divergent fields of biological inquiry, and evolution is the common thread.

One of the most significant features of the expanding synthesis is the effort to incorporate developmental biology into evolutionary theory. The processes that guide the development of genotypes (genes) into phenotypes (organisms) are central to an adequate understanding of biological phenomena. However, we are only now beginning to understand the details of ontogenesis. As evolutionary biologist John Maynard Smith explains it:

> When Weismann formulated his theory of the independence of germ line and soma ... he was in effect saying that it is possible to understand genetics without understanding development. He thus set the stage for the growth of the science of genetics during this century; sadly we still do not understand development. It follows that our understanding of evolution is necessarily partial, because genes are selected through their effects on development (1992: 189).

87

The difficulties in understanding the process of development are enormous. We know the mechanisms of development are themselves the products of evolution. Nevertheless, the precise details remain somewhat mysterious. We know that many physiological and anatomical changes would, in some ideal sense, provide a fitness advantage to an organism, for instance, if zebras evolved machine guns to protect themselves from predators they would be more fit. Yet we do not expect zebras to evolve machine guns. Indeed, most of these "ideal" changes could not be the products of evolution. Some could not be realized because they are incompatible with some aspect(s) of the organism's developmental processes. However, the nature of these constraints are only beginning to be understood.

STRUCTURAL VERSUS REGULATORY GENES

Consider the differences between humans and chimpanzees. Lewis Wolpert asks what really distinguishes members of these species.

> Compare one's body to that of a chimpanzee – there are many similarities. Look for example, at its arms or legs, which have rather different proportions from our own, but are basically the same. If we look at the internal organs there is not much to distinguish a chimpanzee's heart or liver from our own. Even if we examined the cells in these organs we will again find that they are again similar to ours. Yet we are different, *very* different from chimpanzees ... We possess no cell types that the chimpanzee does not, nor does the chimpanzee have any cell types that we do not have. The difference between us and chimpanzees lies in the spatial organization of the cells (1991: 31).

Kauffman (1993: 412) and Gould (1977: 9) have been puzzled by the same phenomenon. Although chimps and humans are virtually identical genetically, they manifestly differ in morphology and behavior.

One way to explain this phenomenon is by focusing on the different roles of structural and regulatory genes. Structural genes control the synthesis of the proteins in the body. Regulatory genes, by contrast, control development and physiology by regulating the switching behavior ("on" or "off") of the structural genes. When we focus simply on the structural genes, the similarities between humans and chimps are striking. As Gould puts it:

> Yet King and Wilson . . . have found that the average human polypeptide is more than 99 percent identical with its counterpart in chimps. Moreover, much of the difference can be attributed to redundancies in the genetic code or to variation in nontranscribed regions. For 44 structural loci, the average genetic distance between chimps and humans is *less* than the average distance between sibling species barely, if at all, distinguishable in morphology – and far less than the distance between *any* measured pair of congeneric species (1977: 405).

However, we can see the likely explanation for manifest differences between humans and chimps if we focus on differences in regulatory genes. As King and Wilson explain:

> Small differences in the timing of activation or in the level of activity of a single gene could in principle influence considerably the systems controlling embryonic development. The organismal differences between chimpanzees and humans would then result chiefly from genetic changes in a few regulatory systems, while amino acid substitutions in general would rarely be a key factor in major adaptive shifts (1975: 114).

Kauffman seconds this explanation.

> The general idea is that a single regulatory mutation can cause very large alterations in patterns of gene expression by disrupting the coordinating behavior of the genomic regulatory system (1993: 412).

Indeed, the evidence suggests that even a few differences in regulatory genes have significant developmental consequences. As John Maynard Smith puts it:

> [F]rogs are, as a group, about twice as ancient as placental mammals, and the range of differences between their proteins is correspondingly about twice as great. Yet in morphological structure the differences between mammals are far greater. This presumably reflects a more rapid change in their "regulator" genes, although we have no direct evidence (1992: 190).

These findings are crucial to a proper understanding of biological phenomena. First, they focus our attention not merely on structural similarities and differences between organisms but also on the similarities and differences in regulatory mechanisms. Second, they illustrate an important fact about complex, evolved animal systems: very small differences between them can be of enormous biological significance (Depew and Weber 1995: 437–40). Profound differences between species need not indicate any large quantitative genetic differences between them. Instead, even very small differences, allowed to propagate in developmental time, can have dramatic morphological and physiological consequences.

ORGANISMS AND HIERARCHICAL COMPLEXITY

Evolved biological organisms differ from rocks and stars because of their *structural organizational complexity*. As Dawkins explains it:

> We animals are the most complicated things in the known universe . . . Complicated things, everywhere, deserve a very special kind of explanation. We want to know how they came into existence and why they are so complicated. The explanation, as I shall argue, is likely to be broadly the same for complicated things everywhere in the universe; the same for us, for chimpanzees, worms, oak trees and monsters from outer space. On the other hand, it will not be the same for what I shall call "simple" things, such as rocks, clouds, rivers, galaxies and quarks. These are the stuff of physics. Chimps and dogs and bats and cockroaches and people and worms and dandelions and bacteria and galactic aliens are the stuff of biology (Dawkins 1987: 1).

Humans are not "essentially" different from rats, nor are we "higher" life forms. Nevertheless, we are differently complex. DNA exhibits this complexity and, in concert with environmental influences, helps produces phenotypic complexity in biochemistry, anatomy, and physiology. For the most part, genes do not do their work one by one – most traits are not monogenic. Rather genes "cooperate" among themselves and with the environment to produce polygenic effects at all levels of the biological hierarchy. Thus, biological effects are produced not only by individual genes, but also by evolved complex relations between the genes and between the environment with which they interact.

Thus, many biomedically significant properties of evolved organisms (mammals in particular) are relational properties – properties that emerge from the complex interactions between an organism's sub-systems. Biological entities at lower levels in the biological hierarchy are compounded to produce biological entities at higher levels of the hierarchy (macromolecules to cells, cells to tissues, tissues to organs, organs to organisms, organisms to populations, populations to ecologies). As Mayr puts it:

> Systems at each hierarchical level have two properties. They act as wholes (as though they were a homogeneous entity), and their characteristics cannot be deduced (even in theory) from the most complete knowledge of the components, taken separately or in combinations. In other words, when such a system is assembled from its components, new characteristics of the whole emerge that could not have been predicted from a knowledge of the constituents . . . Indeed, in hierarchically organized biological systems one may even encounter downward causation (1988: 15).

What is the biological significance of the appearance of emergent properties? Most importantly for the current discussion, if biological systems manifest causally significant emergent properties, similarities in properties at lower levels of the hierarchy will not guarantee similarities in properties at higher levels. Two such systems may be similar at lower levels in the biological hierarchy, yet differ at higher levels in causally relevant respects. Put differently, whole organisms may be intact systems, albeit differently intact.

This emergence of biomedically significant properties at higher levels of complexity is crucial for a proper scientific understanding of animal experimentation. Physiologists claim that experiments on animals are a rich source of important information about humans. Physiologists acknowledge that species may appear different. However, in a manner reminiscent of Bernard, they claim that despite these seeming differences, species are fundamentally similar. In one sense, they are undoubtedly correct. Biochemical (and metabolic) evolution has been very conservative. We know that all life is based on DNA and RNA and that metabolic pathways are roughly similar across species. As A.G. Cairns-Smith expresses it:

Surely there is a deep significance in the observation that of the millions and millions of possible organic molecules, all life that has been discovered so far is based on a mere one or two hundred units – molecules of the size of amino acids or nucleotides that contain from 10 to 100 atoms. "The molecules of life" they have been called (1985: 35).

Yet physiologists tend to make too much of these similarities in basic substrate and structure. We should not conclude that these similarities imply more general similarities higher up the biological hierarchy. The organizational complexity of biological organisms makes this inference questionable. We shall discuss this issue in some detail in the following chapters. Here, it is sufficient to illustrate the biological significance of complexity as seen in the phenomenon of phylogenetic compromise.

Phylogenetic compromise

Mammals are functionally organized, complex, intact biological systems. Their sub-systems are highly interdependent; there are complex, evolved, internal relationships between organs and biochemical processes, and indeed, between systems at all levels of the hierarchy. However, if these systems are so tightly interlocked, how could evolution occur? The problem is well stated by Gould:

How can evolution occur if parts cannot alter separately, or at least with some degree of independence? If each tiny modification requires a redesign of absolutely every other feature, then inertia itself must debar evolution. How can we imagine a coordinated change of all parts every time some minute advantage might attend a slight alteration in one feature? (1993: 254).

The answer, as Gould explains, is that evolution occurs, "by dissociating complex systems into parts, or modules made of a few correlated features, and by altering the various units at different rates and times" (1993: 255). This process is known as mosaic evolution. Futuyma comments:

The term MOSAIC EVOLUTION refers to differences among the characters in their rate of evolution within a lineage ... Humans (*Homo sapiens*) and chimpanzees (*Pan troglodytes*) differ strikingly in morphology, but their DNA and proteins are extraordinarily similar, suggesting that morphological and biochemical evolution have proceeded at different rates. Mosaicism of evolution is the rule rather than the exception; higher taxa emerge not by coherent transformation of all or even most of their features, but by sequential changes in various traits (1986: 293).

Nevertheless, when evolution causes a change in any structure or process, compromises must be made with other structures and processes that interact with the changed system. As Futuyma notes:

[E]ven if we restrict attention to evolution by natural selection, there are numerous selective factors besides those imposed by the external ecological world. Chief among these are the internal relationships among biochemical and developmental pathways, and among different organs, that impose selection by requiring that new features be compatible with the rest of the organism's internal organization (1986: 19).

This is a likely source of biomedically significant differences between members of distinct species. As the physiologists correctly note, members of each species may have the same basic biochemical building blocks. However, members of species who insinuate themselves into different niches will face different selection pressures that may result in different adaptive changes. These differences may be associated with different internal compromises elsewhere in the organism. Such compromises, appearing in evolutionary time, represent the ripple effects – the indirect consequences – of natural selection.

For instance, humans derive a fitness advantage from having large brains. However, large brains must be "housed" in large heads. Consequently, humans have unusually difficult births compared with other mammals because their skulls (that house large brains) barely fit through the birth canal (itself an evolved structure).

Phylogenetic compromise is a pervasive feature of evolving, complex, interactive biological systems, and its presence is central for understanding biomedical phenomena. In *Why We Get Sick: The New Science of Darwinian Medicine*, Neese and Williams (1994) claim the phenomenon explains much that we find mysterious about human disease, including myopia (Ibid.: 102–4) and Huntington's disease (Ibid.: 97–8). We tend to forget, they say, that "the body is a bundle of compromises" (Ibid.: 4). Features that may serve some evolutionary advantage, may also be the source, at least in certain environmental contexts, of disease.

Biological organisms are complex dynamical systems

Biologists acknowledge that mammals are hierarchically organized, intact biological systems. Such systems, they claim, exhibit bio-medically significant phenomena that differ from what we would expect in more simple systems. Although biologists cannot yet explain the source and precise nature of this complexity, many biologists now think that these phenomena can best be understood as the dynamical characteristics of nonlinear, complex systems (Depew and Weber 1995: 429–96). This is a comparatively recent conceptual innovation. As Ivan Dvořák put it:

> Until the mid-sixties, however, mathematical modeling in the biosciences was still in its infancy ... This situation was caused mostly by the overwhelming complexity of biological and physiological systems. Even the simplest mathematical model designed not to lose touch with reality leads almost surely to serious problems in solving model equations. In every physiological system there are very many quantities that can be measured, that exhibit complicated internal bonds between them. A realistic model inevitably yields a set of complex nonlinear equations. Sophisticated mathematical means for their investigation either had not been discovered by the mid-1960's [sic] or were not in the theoretical equip-ment of the biomedical researcher (1989: 90–1).

What, however, is a complex system? Depew and Weber offer the following account:

> The structure of a snowflake ... persists unchanged, and crystalline, from the first moment of its existence until it melts, while complex systems change over time. It is true that a turbulent river rushing through the narrow channel of a rapids changes over time too, but it changes chaotically. The kind of change characteristic of complex systems lies some-where between the pure order of crystalline snowflakes and the disorder of chaotic or turbulent flow. So identified, complex systems are systems with a large number of com-ponents that can interact simultaneously in a sufficiently rich

number of parallel ways so that the system shows spontaneous self-organization and produces global emergent structures (1995: 437).

The full import of conceiving of biological organisms as non-linear, dynamical systems is unclear. Nonetheless, we can identify some profound implications. For two systems whose dynamics are described by linear equations, small differences in initial conditions will be amplified (at most) linearly in time. In contrast, in nonlinear dynamical systems, small differences in initial conditions may lead to radical and unpredictable changes. In this latter context, we have no reason to expect that identically stimulated dynamical systems will behave in similar (or even only slightly different) ways. Even small evolved differences between members of distinct species may profoundly affect the way they react to the same stimulation. This, of course, is just an aspect of the ontological problem of relevance we first mentioned in Chapter 2, and discuss further in Chapter 7.

Although biologists do not yet agree how complex systems theory is best used in explaining biological phenomena, some biologists have offered proposals that have generated considerable interest. Stuart Kauffman (1993) has employed insights from dynamical systems theory to help explain the nature of adaptive evolution, the emergence of life, the evolution of a connected metabolism, and to help solve some puzzles in developmental biology. Kauffman has focused attention on the order and self-organization that can spontaneously appear in complex systems. The emergence of self-organizing systems provides a rich space of biological possibilities that can be co-opted by adaptive evolution for various functional ends. And, if Kauffman is right, the dynamics of evolutionary biology are not exhausted by the effects of natural selection:

It is not that Darwin is wrong, but that he got hold of only part of the truth. For Darwin's answer to the sources of the order we see all around us is overwhelmingly an appeal to a single singular force: natural selection. It is the single-force view which I believe to be inadequate, for it fails to notice, fails to stress, fails to incorporate the possibility that simple and complex systems exhibit order spontaneously. That spontaneous order exists, however, is hardly mysterious. The nonbiological world is replete with examples, and no one would doubt that similar sources of order are available to living things. What is mysterious is the extent of such spontaneous order in life and how such self-ordering may mingle with Darwin's mechanism of evolution – natural selection – to permit or, better, to produce what we see (1993: xiii).

Ongoing research suggests Kauffman is headed in the right direction. Consider the Belousov–Zhabotinski (BZ) reaction. This chemical reaction exhibits, under appropriate conditions, non-linearity (as unexpected behaviors), and self-organization (as the spontaneous crystallization of macroscopic ordered states) (Nicolis 1989: 321).

In the BZ reaction, four reactants (malonic acid, potassium bromate, cerium sulfate, and sulfuric acid) interact in non-equilibrium chemical conditions. If the chemical mixture is spread in a thin layer and parameters are varied to alter the non-equilibrium state of the system, then various wave types form, e.g., propagating circular and spiral waves. Moreover, under appropriate conditions far from equilibrium, the BZ reaction manifests oscillatory behaviors that are asymptotically stable.

Like the BZ system, biological systems are open, dissipative chemical systems far from equilibrium. Nonlinear chemical behaviors (manifested as propagating wave forms), akin to those observed in the BZ reaction, have been observed in intracellular biochemical reactions, for instance, those in microtubule assembly. As Tabony explains:

> The assembly process can show nonlinear kinetics, and the system is hence capable of manifesting various complex nonlinear phenomena. Some microtubular solutions show spontaneous macroscopic space ordering, a phenomenon attributed to chemically dissipative mechanisms (1994: 245).

Tabony concludes:

> The reorganization of the cellular microtubular system involves the disassembly and reassembly of microtubules. As a result, cell biologists have invested considerable effort into understanding the process of microtubule assembly, mainly in terms of linear phenomena. The present results show that complex biological phenomena occur as a result of nonlinear mechanisms. Identifying and understanding such processes are a pre-requisite to investigating their possible role in living organisms (1994: 248).

These results suggest that the internal chemical dynamics of a cell are nonlinear. Historically, however, many mechanistically inclined physiologists have ignored nonlinear biochemical phenomena. That is a serious mistake since, as Steinbock *et al.* explain:

> Propogating waves are observed in living organisms and biological tissues as well as excitable chemical systems. The familiar rotating spiral waves and expanding target patterns of the Belousov–Zhabotinski (BZ) reaction are also observed in thin slices of heart tissue, in the cytoplasm of frog oocytes, and in animal retinas. Three-dimensional scroll waves, extensively studied in the BZ reaction, have now been characterized in migrating slugs of the slime mold *Dictyostelium discoideum*, and it is likely that these waves are precursors to ventricular fibrillation in mammals (1995: 1857).

We return to these matters in Chapter 9.

EVOLUTION AND THE CAUSAL/FUNCTIONAL ASYMMETRY

The theory of evolution has inevitable and important implications for our understanding of biomedical phenomena. Evolution shows us that biomedical phenomena are not as simple as Bernard thought. Bernard had a narrow, mechanistic view of biological function. He did not appreciate the richness of the notion, or understand its full significance for biomedicine. However, as we argued in Chapter 3, we should not fault him for that; after all, he was merely relying on the best science of his day. In the remainder of this chapter we will explore the notion of *biological function* that plays so central a role in understanding biomedical phenomena.

The evolution of functional properties

In Bernard's time it was scientifically suspect to speak of biological function as anything more than shorthand for some underlying physical process. Such talk was thought to imply the need for a "cosmic designer," or to imply that there were irreducible "vital forces." After Darwin, all that changed (Sober 1993: 82–6). Although, as Sober points out, there is more than one concept of "function" at work in biological discussions, in evolutionary theory the central concept is an etiological one. Sober explains this concept of function as follows:

> There are those ... who treat biological function the way I have characterized adaptation ... to ascribe a function to some device is to make a claim about why it is present. For traits of organisms, assignments of function make reference to evolution by natural selection (1993: 85).

He then characterizes "adaptation" as follows:

> Characteristic c is an adaptation for doing task t in a population if and only if members of the population now have c because ancestrally there was selection for having c and c conferred a fitness advantage because it performed task t (1993: 84).

To use Sober's example, to say that "the function of the heart is to pump blood" is to say that the organ was selected because this trait conferred some fitness advantage upon our (distant) ancestors. The heart also has the property of making a "lub-dub" noise. This is not a functional property but an indirect effect of selection for a blood-pumping organ. As Sober puts it, "this property evolved as a spin-off; there was *selection of* noise makers, but no *selection for* making noise" (1993: 83). Thus, we can distinguish a functional property from a property that is merely a spin-off of selection, only by tracing their histories, by seeing how they emerged.

More generally, evolved functional properties are different from purely physical properties of objects: whereas physical properties are ahistorical, biological functional properties are distinctly historical; that is, they emerge in evolutionary time. Put differently, macroscopic objects have ahistorical physical properties such as position, momentum, energy, and mass. Most, however, do not have any biological functional properties. That explains why we cannot predict that biological functional properties will arise simply by knowing (a) the purely physical properties of these objects and (b) the laws governing the way physical properties change. Still less can we specify the character of these functional properties. The emergence of functional properties reflects the historical contingencies of evolution.

As Wilson and Sober explain it, an important feature of adaptive explanations is that they:

can be employed with minimal knowledge of the physiological, biochemical and genetic processes that make up the
organisms under examination. For example, imagine studying the evolutionary effects of predation on snails, seeds and
beetles. Suppose you discover that for all three groups, species
exposed to heavy predation have harder and thicker exteriors
than species not so exposed. The property "hard exterior"
can be predicted from knowledge of the selection pressures
operating on the populations. Since the exteriors of snails,
beetles, and seeds are made of completely different materials,
there is a sense in which these materials are irrelevant to the
prediction. That is why Darwin was able to achieve his
fundamental insights in almost total ignorance of the mechanistic processes that make up organisms. Adaptationist explanations have the power to unify phenomena that are
physiologically, biochemically and genetically quite different
(1994: 588).

In short, the same biological functions can be achieved through
different causal (biochemical, genetic and physiological) routes.
Ernst Mayr calls this the *principle of multiple pathways* (1986: 56). This
principle undergirds what we call the causal/functional asymmetry.

The causal/functional asymmetry

Before Darwin, scientists noticed that humans and non-human
mammals often achieved similar biological functions. Since they
assumed similarity of biological function implied similarity of
causal mechanisms, they understandably thought they could safely
generalize experimental results in animals to humans. (As we saw
in Chapter 3, Sir Isaac Newton had made the "same effect, same
cause principle" one of his rules of reasoning, and illustrated it with
the physiological example of respiration.) This assumption, though,
overlooks the inferential gap between an organism's underlying
causal mechanisms and its functional properties.

Evolution leads us to expect this gap. Vertebrates achieve many
similar functions: they obtain nourishment, exchange gasses with
the environment, oxygenate the blood, excrete wastes, reproduce,
and maintain an adequate bodily temperature. However, as
members of different species adapt to their particular ecological
niches, they will likely "find" different mechanisms to achieve
these common biological functions.

Since an organism's biological sub-systems are tightly interlocked, these differences in mechanisms may be biomedically significant. In fact, we should expect that they will often be significant, sometimes profoundly so. For example, humans have evolved amino acids (biochemical adaptations) that permit oxygen to bind more firmly to fetal hemoglobin than it does in non-primate mammals. It appears this evolved difference has important biomedical ramifications. "[T]he emergence of such a unique fetal hemoglobin may have been a precondition for the developmental changes that lengthened gestation and intrauterine fetal life in simian primates" (Goodman 1990: 886).

The ability of differently evolved creatures to achieve common biological functions through different causal means is ubiquitous. For example, evolutionary theory leads us to expect that members of distantly related species may employ different mechanisms to achieve the common function of gas exchange with the environment. These differences are most apparent when we contrast fish with mammals. However, even two organisms with lungs (mammals and birds) may have substantially different underlying causal mechanisms for exchanging gases with the environment. As noted by Burggren and Bemis:

> The peribronchial lungs of birds, ventilated in a unidirectional fashion using a series of air sacs, and the alveolar lungs of mammals, ventilated in a tidal fashion using a diaphragm, differ considerably in structure and mechanism. Yet, both ultimately produce the same effect – full oxygen saturation of the arterial blood (1990: 193).

Therefore, evolutionary biology has some important consequences for our understanding of functional properties and the relations of functional properties to underlying causal properties and mechanisms:

Consequence 1: from similarity of biological function we cannot infer similarity of underlying causal mechanism.

Conversely, from differences in causal biological mechanisms we cannot infer differences in function. To use a previous example, fish have gills and mammals have lungs. Evolutionary pressures determined that a common biological function (exchange of gases with the environment) is achieved by different causal mechanisms. Thus:

100

Consequence 2: from differences in causal mechanisms we cannot infer differences in functional properties.

However – and this is crucial – similarity of causal mechanism *does* imply similarity of biological function. Why should this be so? Think, for a moment, about even purely mechanical systems. A collection of springs and gears, if suitably organized, will produce an analog watch. An electrically powered quartz and suitably organized gears will also yield an analog watch. Even in purely mechanical systems, similarity of function does not imply similarity of mechanism. However, exactly similar components, organized in exactly the same way, will produce the same function.

This is true not only for mechanical systems, but for biological systems as well. Two organisms with identical properties at all levels of complexity, subject to identical environmental stimulation, would exhibit identical functional properties. This is nothing more that the Principle of Uniformity, which is a presupposition of all science. That principle states that for qualitatively identical systems, "same cause will be followed by same effect." Thus,

Consequence 3: from similar causal mechanisms (and values of causally relevant parameters) we can infer similar functional properties.

These three consequences, taken together, yield the causal/ functional asymmetry:

Causal/functional asymmetry: although we cannot infer similarity of causal properties from similarity of functional properties, we can infer differences in causal properties from differences in functional properties.

This causal/functional asymmetry helps give shape to a moral dilemma for researchers – a dilemma we develop in Chapter 14. For the present, we need only note that the causal/functional asymmetry captures the fact that adaptive explanations work even if we do not know an organism's precise physiology and biochemistry. For instance, as Wilson and Sober noted above, natural selection can bring about the same functional property, "hardness of exterior" in a range of organisms faced with certain types of predators. Conversely, the asymmetry also captures the fact that similar adaptations (functional properties) can result from different physiological and biochemical causal mechanisms.

Homology, analogy and biological function

Evolutionary biologists distinguish homologies from analogies. Roughly speaking, features of two species are homologous if they are evolutionary descendants of features in a common ancestor. Features of two species are analogous if they have evolved from different ancestral species yet have similar functional properties.

The arms of a human, the flippers of a porpoise, the forelegs of a horse and the wings of a bat are homologous structures: they are all evolutionary descendants of anatomical features of a common reptilian ancestor. Yet these homologous structures serve different functional ends. In contrast, the wings of butterflies and birds are analogous structures: they serve the same functions although these traits are not evolutionary descendants of features in a common ancestor. Or, again, the eye of the octopus and the eye of vertebrates serve similar functions, but evolved from different ancestors. They are similar, not because they are descendants from a common ancestor but because they serve similar functions. These common features are products of convergent evolution: they evolved in unrelated organisms facing similar selection pressures in the same niche, or in similar niches in geographically distinct regions. Butterflies, birds, and bats evolved wings in their aerial niche, while sharks and whales independently evolved a streamlined shape in their aquatic niche.

Biochemical homologies

Scientists can identify biochemical, as well as morphological, homologies. In fact, biochemical analysis has become a powerful tool in determining phylogenetic trees. Biochemists examine the primary structure of proteins – the sequences of their constituent amino acids – to determine the relationships between different species. Proteins in different species may be descended with modification from proteins in a common ancestor species. As Stebbins puts it:

> Evidence from biochemistry strongly supports the Darwinian conception of evolution as a continuous succession of forms. When either proteins or DNA are compared, a complete spectrum is found, from species that are exactly alike with respect to some of their proteins but show slight differences with respect to others, through species that are progressively

more different, to species that are separated by so many biochemical differences that no relationship could be recognized between them were it not for the existence of intermediate forms (1982: 129).

Researchers have shown that the DNA sequences of closely related animals are quite similar: 89 percent of the sequences of cows and sheep, 84 percent of the sequences of humans and New World monkeys, and 97.5 percent of the sequences of humans and chimpanzees. Yet even when comparing chimpanzees and humans, we see evidence of descent with modification. As Stebbins comments:

> The same kinds of proteins can be isolated from the cells of chimpanzees as from human cells. Some of these proteins are identical; others are different with respect to immunological affinities, electric charges, or amino acid sequences (1982: 130).

Moreover, although homologous proteins may serve similar functions, they need not. If they do serve similar biological functions, that is a contingent fact about these proteins. Other proteins may serve quite different functions, although they are homologous. For instance, horse proinsulin and mouse nerve growth factor are homologous: the probability that their similarities in amino acid sequence could have arisen by chance is about four in 10 million. Nonetheless, these proteins serve quite different functions.

Likewise other proteins are analogous: that is, although they are not derived from a common ancestor protein, they serve similar biochemical functions. As Smith *et al.* explain it:

> The wings of insects and birds operate by distinct mechanisms and possess entirely different structures, but they both serve the same function. There are many types of enzymes catalyzing reactions that utilize molecular oxygen but perform these reactions by different mechanisms, and the enzymes are not structurally related. Thus it cannot be assumed, without additional evidence, that proteins performing the same or a similar function are homologous in structure (1983: 827).

For instance, the subtilisins have a serine-histidine-aspartic acid charge-relay system that is essentially the same as that of the pancreatic proteases. Nonetheless, these enzymes have distinct amino acid sequences and differences in three-dimensional structure; in short, they are not homologous (Ibid.).

In summary, evolution does not merely influence gross anatomical development. Rather, it creates and shapes systems and subsystems throughout the biological hierarchy. In this sense, the causal/functional asymmetry has a long biological reach. Most mammals have pervasive biochemical functional similarities. However, the causal properties and structural features of their biochemical constitution may well differ even when they serve similar functional purposes. This feature of evolved biological systems exacerbates the problems of relevance mentioned earlier. In the following three chapters we discuss this problem of relevance. Specifically, we investigate the nature and extent of causal disanalogies between members of different species.

Part II

EVALUATING ANIMAL EXPERIMENTATION: THE SCIENTIFIC ISSUES

7

CAUSAL DISANALOGY I
Strong models and theoretical expectations

In the previous two chapters we examined the theory of evolution. We focused specifically on those elements of the theory that have significant implications for our understanding of the practice of biomedicine. Here we further clarify the standard view of the use of animals in biomedical research, namely, their use as *Causal Analog Models* (CAMs) of human biomedical phenomena. Then, using insights gleaned from the theory of evolution, we will spell out its theoretical implications for the use of animals as CAMs. In this chapter we specifically focus on CAMs as *strong* models, models that are supposed to be causally isomorphic to the human systems they model. While strong models are generally recognized to be *ideal* models, some researchers have asserted the actual existence of causal isomorphisms, and this is part of a tradition extending back to the writings of Claude Bernard.

In connection with strong models, we explain how a proper understanding of the theory of evolution leads us to expect evolved causal disanalogies (failure of causal isomorphism) between members of different species. Then, in the following chapter, we summarize some relevant empirical findings, findings that are consistent with these theoretical expectations. The existence of causal disanalogies between members of different species does not establish that animal research is worthless. However, it does suggest that apologists' grand claims about the direct and substantial benefits of such research are exaggerated. In Chapter 9 we consider *weak models* – CAMs in which there is a partial breakdown of causal isomorphism. While such models represent many instances of the real-world experimental situation, they turn out nevertheless to be problematic.

The presence of causal disanalogies undermines the claim that

107

animal research is of immediate and direct relevance to human biomedical phenomena. More specifically, these disanalogies will undercut claims about the direct benefits of applied research – like predictive toxicology and teratology – which aims to make *predictions* about human biomedical phenomena. These arguments will *not* show that findings in animals invariably differ from findings in humans. Rather, they show that we do not know, before tests on humans, if there are causally relevant disanalogies between humans and animal test subjects with respect to the phenomenon under study. Thus, the predictive value of these tests is, at best, uncertain. That is, any benefits of applied research to humans will be much more indirect.

As we explain in Chapter 12, the existence of causal disanalogies does not undermine the scientific legitimacy of basic research in the same way or to the same extent that it undermines applied research. Some types of basic research may be relatively insensitive to causal disanalogies between the species; indeed, they may even exploit these differences. However, the *reason* these forms of research may be less adversely affected by the existence of causal disanalogies is that any benefits of this research are themselves indirect. Understanding that any benefits of animal experimentation are relatively indirect is important when we evaluate public policy documents. For, as you may recall from Chapter 1, such documents proclaim that animal experimentation is immediately and directly beneficial to humans.

A word of caution: we do not think that a hard and sharp distinction can be drawn between basic and applied research. In reality there will be a spectrum of cases. However, this does not mean that no distinction can be drawn. Moreover, some research programs have both applied and basic aspects. For such programs, the existence of causal disanalogies will be of variable importance: likely they will have less of an impact on the basic research, but will be more directly relevant to evaluation of the applied aspects of that research.

THE RESEARCHER'S EXPECTATIONS

As we explained in Chapter 4, biomedical researchers claim there is significant biomedical information about humans that can be discovered only by experiments on intact animals (AMA 1992: 2). Although epidemiological studies, computer simulations, clinical investigation, and cell and tissue cultures have become important weapons in the biomedical scientist's arsenal, these are primarily adjuncts to the use of animals in research (Sigma Xi 1992: 76). The researchers claim controlled laboratory experiments on animals are the core of scientific medicine. After observing the effects of various stimuli in non-human subjects, we can legitimately infer the likely effects of these stimuli in humans. Perhaps what is more important, we can understand the biomedical condition's causal mechanisms.

That is, tests on animal subjects are supposed to uncover the causal mechanisms that produce and direct the course of a disease or condition in animals. These results can then be extended by analogy to humans, enabling physicians to prevent or treat the disease or condition under investigation. There are other uses of experiments on animals, most especially, their use as *Hypothetical Analog Models* (HAMs). We shall discuss HAMs in Chapter 12. Here we shall focus on the primary use of animal models as CAMs.

THE LOGIC OF CAMs

When conducting a laboratory experiment, a chemist or physicist manipulates some substance X and records the results. Then, using the principles of causal determinism ((a) all events have causes, and (b) for qualitatively identical systems, same cause, same effect), the investigator infers that, other things being equal, similar manipulations of X outside the laboratory will have similar effects. It is a sound inductive inference.

However, this model cannot quite capture most biological phenomena which are best described probabilistically. That is, an experimenter observes some phenomenon in a certain percentage of the laboratory subjects of species X and infers that a similar percentage of creatures of that species will react similarly outside the laboratory (all other things being equal). Although some people think probabilistic reasoning cannot be genuine causal reasoning, since it fails to satisfy the requirement of Humean "constant conjunction" (according to which events of type A are to be invariably followed by events of type B, if the A-type events are to stand as causes of B-type events). But, we see no reason to embrace this restricted view of causality. Probabilistic causal reasoning in the biological sciences is ubiquitous, even if there are debates about how the phenomenon is to be explained. Most reasonable people accept that smoking causes lung cancer, even though not all smokers develop lung cancer – a case of A-type events not invariably being followed by B-type events. Some claim that the element of probability arises from researchers' ignorance of initial conditions; others claim it reflects the fundamentally probabilistic nature of the universe.

Those who claim it arises from ignorance note that small, often imperceptible, differences in initial conditions can, even in deterministic systems, lead to probabilistic outcomes, especially if the differences are unknown to the investigator. That, they say, is why researchers are so concerned to control experimental variables: they want to limit the effects of any differences in initial conditions. However, we can never completely control all relevant variables. In complex biological systems, there will generally be some causally relevant differences between experimental subjects (and their environments) – differences that lead subjects to respond differently to similar experimental stimuli.

Other philosophers of science claim that probabilities describe significant strands of the fabric of the universe. *Probabilistic causality*, according to Wesley Salmon, is a "coherent and important scientific concept" (1984: 190). In fact, according to Salmon, there is "compelling (though not absolutely incontrovertible) evidence that cause–effect relations of an ineluctably statistical sort are present in our universe" (1984: 188). Whether Salmon is right, we need not decide here. All we need note is that most biomedically significant data are statistical in nature.

Researchers do not see this as a bar to extrapolating results from animals to humans. They assume their research methods rely on either deterministic or straightforwardly probabilistic reasoning; that is, they think inferences from non-human CAMs to humans exhibit normal causal reasoning. However, animal experimentation is neither deterministic nor probabilistic in either of the senses discussed above. In both standard methodologies, experimenters make inferences from what happens to Xs in the lab to what will happen to Xs outside the lab. Not so with animal experiments. Here researchers make predictions from what happens to Xs (some non-human CAM) in the lab to what will happen to Ys (humans) outside the lab. This cannot be straightforward causal reasoning, not even probabilistic causal reasoning.

Biomedical experiments on animals are doubly probabilistic: experimenters discover that some percentage of laboratory animal subjects react in some particular way and conclude that it is probable or likely that a similar percentage of humans will react similarly outside the lab. There is probabilistic behavior within the (non-human) lab population, probabilistic behavior within the human population outside the lab, and also a *probabilistic (epistemological) uncertainty* about whether the results observed in the non-human animal population will be (statistically) relevant to humans.

That is why, contrary to many researchers' expectations, they are not engaged in normal causal reasoning but in some form of analogical reasoning. The basic idea of analogical reasoning, according to David Hull is that:

> the behavior of a poorly understood system is assimilated to the behavior of a well-understood paradigm system. Hopefully the principles that govern the behavior of the paradigm system can be extrapolated to the poorly known system (1974: 105).

To the extent that either of these systems is poorly understood, we can never be confident that these systems are relevantly similar. If they are different, they may be different in ways that undermine our ability to extrapolate from one species to the other.

At first glance it appears the theory of evolution would guarantee that there would be no relevant differences that would undermine our ability to extrapolate from one species to another, especially phylogenetically close species. After all, the theory of evolution suggests that there exist important biological similarities between members of distinct species.

Certainly such causal analogical inferences would be legitimate if experimenters were merely concerned with gross toxicological effects. For example, if injecting a rat with concentrated sulfuric acid destroys its tissues, it is reasonable to expect a similar result in humans. Unfortunately, that expectation is grounded more in the antecedently known effects of such an acid on organic compounds rather than in any detailed knowledge about the organization and evolution of biological organisms. However, it is these latter details that are especially relevant to the practice of biomedicine. For instance, if we are interested in the long-term effects of exposure to low levels of sulfuric acid (perhaps from acid rain), we cannot know that the results of such exposure in rats can be extrapolated to humans. At least that is something scientists cannot assume without argument and evidence.

Reformulating the logic of CAMs

In Chapter 4 we stated the following schema for causal analogical arguments:

> X (the model) is similar to Y (the subject being modeled) with respect to properties $\{a, \ldots, e\}$. X has additional property f. While f has not yet been observed directly in Y, it is likely that Y also has the property f.

However, we can now see why that first statement of the logic of CAMs is inadequate. Since CAMs are a sub-species of analogical arguments in which (some of) the premises and conclusions involve *causal analogical* claims, the CAMs must satisfy two further conditions:

> (1) the common properties $\{a, \ldots, e\}$ must be causal properties which (2) are causally connected with the property $\{f\}$ we wish to project – specifically, $\{f\}$ should stand as the cause(s) or effect(s) of the features $\{a, \ldots, e\}$ in the model.

These are rigorous requirements. But not yet rigorous enough. Animal researchers insist that only properly controlled experiments are scientifically acceptable; that is why they think epidemiological studies are poor cousins of properly controlled animal experiments. These researchers want to ensure that there are no differences in conditions that might skew test results. Differences between the causal mechanisms of the model and the object modeled could skew experimental results.

Hence, we can be confident that extrapolations from animal test-subjects to humans are highly probable only if we are confident that the relevant causal mechanisms in the non-human animal are relevantly similar to those in the human animal. For the investigators who followed Bernard, that assumption was innocent enough. Bernard thought "all animals may be used for physiological investigations, because with the same properties and lesions in life and disease, the same result everywhere recurs . . ." ([1865] 1949: 115). However, evolutionary theory tells us that assumption is anything but innocent. Hence, it should not be an unstated assumption: it should be an explicit condition of causal analogical reasoning.

That is, if animal subjects are to be good CAMs of human biomedical phenomenon, then, in addition to conditions (1) and (2), we must also require that, (3), *there must be no causally relevant disanalogies between the model and the thing modeled.* Some researchers are aware that CAMs should ideally satisfy condition (3). As Nomura *et al.* explain it: "the most useful animal models are those with an etiology mechanistically identical to that of human diseases" (1987: 352). Models that satisfy condition (3) will be called *strong models.*

To the extent that there are no (or insignificant) causal disanalogies between the test subjects and humans, then the additional layer of probability or uncertainty mentioned earlier will be minimal. To the extent that there are important disanalogies, then this additional layer of probability will attenuate our confidence in animal test subjects as CAMs of human biomedical phenomena of interest. To the extent that we do not *know* the extent and significance of disanalogies, we should be less confident that the results found in the model are relevant to humans.

There is scope for at least two kinds of evolved disanalogy in biological systems. First, we may find *intrinsic disanalogy* at any level in the biological hierarchy. As a result of evolution, causal properties (and structures and mechanisms) found in the systems of members of one species may be absent in members of another species; for example, rats lack gall bladders. Furthermore, because many biological systems are intact systems, systems composed of mutually interacting sub-systems, we may find *systemic disanalogy*; that is, evolved differences in the relations between an organism's systems. Phylogenetic compromise is an especially likely source of systemic disanalogy.

Besides evolved disanalogies, researchers must also be concerned with what we call *intervention disanalogies*. These disanalogies may arise from any causally relevant differences in the environments of animal subjects and human populations, especially differences caused by experimental intervention. For example, experimental rats will almost certainly be exposed to suspect toxins in a different way than humans will be. These different routes of administration might be relevant to the way animals and humans react to the substance. If so, this will be a source of *intervention disanalogy*. These disanalogies can arise in at least two ways: (a) in experiments to uncover the causes of biomedical phenomena of interest, the means of inducing the condition in the animal subjects may not correspond to the way(s) in which these phenomena are caused in humans; and (b) in experiments to treats a condition (however caused), the investigator may be aware that the mechanisms of induction are different in model and humans, but may assume (erroneously) that similarities in observable symptoms and deficits imply that what is causally efficacious in ameliorating symptoms and deficits in the model will thereby be causally efficacious in humans. Examples of both types of intervention disanalogy will be discussed in the next chapter.

We now have a precise way to formulate the epistemological problem of relevance first mentioned in Chapter 2: even if researchers could be confident that both conditions (1) and (2) were satisfied for any particular animal model, condition (3) would remain a substantial stumbling block. That is, researchers cannot assume, without presentation of evidence, that there are no causal disanalogies. They can be confident there are no causal disanalogies only if they know the model and subject modeled are *causally isomorphic*, i.e., only if they know the model is a *strong* model.

Some animal investigators have asserted the existence of just such isomorphisms. This claim, which seldom receives any justification, forms part of a tradition going at least as far back as Claude Bernard. Many researchers see causal isomorphism as an ideal to be approximated. As Nonneman and Woodruff state it, "If every aspect is fully isomorphic between the animal model and human condition, including cause and mechanism, the model is *homologous*. Most would agree that such a model represents the ideal" (1994: 9). (Notice this is a different use of the word "homologous" than that occurring in evolutionary biology. In the present context, homologous models are models where there is complete isomorphism. Thus, Nonneman and Woodruff contrast homologous models with analogous models (models where there is only partial isomorphism). These in turn are contrasted with correlational models, models where issues of isomorphism are irrelevant.)

However, causal isomorphism is an incredibly strong condition, even *within* a species. Genetic, developmental, and environmental factors may undermine the hope of causal isomorphism even within the human species. Similar factors often lead to intraspecific variation within laboratory animals: that is why researchers seek genetically homogeneous test animals. More importantly for our current discussion, however, are failures of inter-specific causal isomorphism.

WHY CONDITION (3) IS NOT SATISFIED: THE IMPLICATIONS OF EVOLUTION

There are powerful theoretical reasons to expect that condition (3) will not be satisfied. Humans and non-human animals have been subject to divergent evolutionary pressures. Their responses to these pressures differ, not merely at the level of gross morphology, but also in terms of their underlying biomedically significant causal mechanisms. Members of a species may change over time through the gradual accumulation of changes resulting from natural selection. And, through the process of "adaptive radiation" organisms insinuate themselves into a myriad of ecological niches. This leads to specialization of organic function.

While no organ is an island, the collection of organs in a viable organism interact so as to constitute an entity capable of surviving in some finite (often quite restricted) range of environmental conditions. As the zoologist Richard Dawkins has pointed out, not only is there a niche to be filled by being a multi-cellular organism, there are also advantages from specialization of organic function:

> The advantage of being in a club of cells doesn't stop with size. The cells in the club can specialize, each thereby becoming more efficient at performing its particular task. Specialist cells serve other cells in the club and they also benefit from the efficiency of other specialists (1989: 258).

And the evolution of specialization, with the associated advantages arising from mutual cooperation between the "specialist" organs, will also be accompanied by many and various phylogenetic compromises elsewhere in the organism – further differences and potential sources of disanalogy.

In organisms like mammals, adaptive specialization has had consequences especially relevant to animal researchers. As we explained in the previous chapter, biological systems exhibit enormous complexity. Moreover, the organism's sub-systems are tightly interlocked. This is true not just at the level of organs, tissues and cells, but also at the biochemical level. As Cairns-Smith points out:

> Subsystems are highly interlocked . . . [P]roteins are needed to make catalysts, yet catalysts are needed to make proteins. Nucleic acids are needed to make proteins, yet proteins are needed to make nucleic acids. Proteins and lipids are needed

to make membranes, yet membranes are needed to provide protection for all the chemical processes going on in a cell ... The whole is presupposed by all the parts. The interlocking is tight and critical. At the centre everything depends on everything (1985: 39).

It is this interlocking of sub-systems, which makes even small changes potentially so important. Nowhere is this better seen than in the relationship between structure and function discussed in the previous chapter.

Differently organized complex systems can achieve many of the same functional ends. Biological organisms are usually "built" from similar parts – they share many of the same biochemicals, many of the same metabolic pathways, etc. However, these organisms are faced with different evolutionary pressures. Over evolutionary time ways were "found" to organize their parts so that they can achieve similar functional ends by different causal means. In short, the fact that two species have similar biological functional properties will give us no reason to think they have relevantly similar underlying causal mechanisms.

Yet researchers think animals are good models of human biomedical conditions precisely because human and their non-human CAMs achieve similar biological functions. However, since the same biological function may be achieved in a variety of causal ways, mere functional similarity does not give us a reason to think condition (3) is satisfied. The process of convergent evolution – which undergirds the evolution of analogous structures (e.g., the wings of bats and butterflies, the dorsal fins of sharks and dolphins) – unquestionably illustrates that functional similarity does not show that condition (3) is satisfied.

Even where underlying structures are homologous, we cannot assume condition (3) is satisfied. The phenomenon of phylogenetic compromise makes that evident. An adaptive change one place in an organism often requires a wide range of changes, ripple effects if you will, elsewhere in that organism. The parts of organisms did not evolve on their own. Any changes in one part of an organism must be accommodated with other changes elsewhere. For instance, if evolutionary pressures "encourage" faster animals, those pressures cannot be accommodated simply by developing larger leg muscles. The animal may also need a more efficient heart to get more blood to those muscles – or perhaps the animal needs a different skeletal structure.

116

For another example, if some organisms evolve the capacity for flight, that capacity will not come into being simply through the evolution of wings, there will also have to be metabolic and other changes. In humans ammonia is excreted in the form of urea in urine, via the kidneys. However, this will not suffice for organisms in arid or aerial niches. Lehninger *et al.* note:

> Excretion of urea into urine requires simultaneous excretion of a relatively large volume of water; the weight of the required water would impede flight in birds, and reptiles living in arid environments must conserve water. Instead, these animals convert amino nitrogen into uric acid, a relatively insoluble compound that is extracted as a semisolid mass of uric acid crystals with the feces (1993: 521–2).

Consequently, humans, birds, and reptiles achieve a similar function – excretion of ammonia – by different causal routes. That is exactly what the discussion of the causal/functional asymmetry would lead us to expect. Generally, then, since the organism's parts did not evolve on their own, any change one place in an organism must be accommodated by, and reflect, other changes elsewhere. This is what renal physiologist Homer Smith had in mind when he remarked of the kidneys:

> Only because they work the way they do has it become possible for us to have bones, muscles, glands and brains. Superficially, it might be said that the function of the kidneys is to make urine, but in a more considered view, one can say that kidneys make the stuff of philosophy itself (1961: 3).

In addition to phylogenetic compromise, host–parasite co-evolution may also be a source of evolutionary causal disanalogy between members of different species. Consider vegetarian primate species. They have evolved relationships with intestinal flora that are different from those found in humans, and yet are relevant in drug metabolism (Mitruka *et al.* 1976: 342). As Sipes and Gandolfi note:

> An aspect of *in vivo* extrahepatic biotransformation of xenobiotics frequently overlooked is modification by intestinal microbes. It has been estimated that the gut microbes have the potential for biotransformation of xenobiotics equivalent to or greater than the liver. With over 400 bacterial species

known to exist in the intestinal tract, differences in gut flora content as a result of species variation, age, diet, and disease states would be expected to influence xenobiotic modification (1993: 109).

Once again, differences with respect to evolutionary history may lead to causal differences which result in violations of condition (3).

Thus, even a seemingly small change in an organism will almost certainly be associated with a variety of other changes – changes that may be biomedically significant. Perhaps occasionally these accompanying differences are not biomedically significant. However, this is not something we can know in advance. Certainly we cannot merely assume these differences will not be significant.

In summary, species differences may come in at two levels: there may be evolved differences in sub-systems at any point in the hierarchy and there may be evolved differences in the relationships between these sub-systems. Thus, there will be scope for causal disanalogy, not only from the species-specific manner in which the individual sub-systems have evolved, but also from the mutual interactions that have evolved between these sub-systems.

Hence, evolutionary theory tells us that animal models cannot be *strong* models of human disease: thus, we are theoretically unjustified in assuming that results in test animals can be extrapolated to humans. We have a theoretical expectation that there is an ontological problem of relevance. Although humans are not "essentially" different from rats, nor are we "higher" life-forms, we are differently complex. Species differences, even when small, often result in radically divergent responses to qualitatively identical stimuli. Evolved differences in biological systems between mice and men cascade into marked differences in biomedically important properties between the species.

Minimally, we should not assume, *a priori,* that condition (3) is satisfied. Whether it is satisfied (and if not, the extent to which it is not) must be established empirically. That is, we could be confident that condition (3) is satisfied only after we have conducted extensive, controlled tests on humans – tests that show that the systems are not disanalogous. However, as we pointed out in Chapter 2, animal tests are deemed desirable primarily because they are thought to eliminate the need for such tests on humans.

8

CAUSAL DISANALOGY II
The empirical evidence

Evolutional theory leads us to expect that we will find causally relevant disanalogies between species. That expectation is substantiated by empirical findings in fields as diverse as toxicology, teratology, endocrinology, virology, and stroke research. Taken collectively, researchers' findings provide evidence that condition (3) is frequently not satisfied in much animal research. Consequently, the empirical evidence and evolutionary theory show us that animal models of human disease are not, in fact, strong causal analogical models.

Before we continue, we wish to make it clear that the citations in this section, and throughout the book, are usually from scientists who favor biomedical research on animals. We use the citations simply to show that animal researchers recognize the pervasiveness and importance of causal disanalogy. Furthermore, we do not claim to know, for arbitrarily selected research programmes, exactly when and where causally relevant disanalogies between species will appear. However, we do believe researchers cannot simply assume there are no disanalogies without rigorous investigation of both animal and human systems. To the extent that human systems are not examined (for moral/legal reasons) or are examined only using questionable human research methodologies, then claims about the direct relevance of animal research for human biomedical phenomena will be empirically unsubstantiated. (The extent to which we know that the systems are analogous – because we have extensive knowledge of the human system – to that extent we have undercut one principal reason for doing animal experiments: that they will tell us something we do not know about humans.) Put differently, the problem facing researchers is that they simply do not know when and where causally relevant

disanalogies will be found. In fact, since causal disanalogies between species are ubiquitous, then we should expect such disanalogies will be present, and we should not be surprised when they
undermine the utility of animal models.

THE EMPIRICAL EVIDENCE OF CAUSAL DISANALOGY

Toxicology

As noted early in the book, some drugs are safe for animals but
toxic for humans; others are detrimental to animals yet valuable for
humans. As Caldwell points out, researchers are well aware of
species differences in response to chemical stimulation:

> It is a matter of common experience that the actions of the
> major classes of drugs, which in the main work by interfering
> with the normal function of physiological systems, are the
> same throughout mammals and most other living organisms
> ... Despite this commonality of fundamental mechanisms
> of drug action, it is now appreciated that there are numerous
> situations where the effects of a drug or a chemical on the
> body depend on the animal species in question (1992: 652).

Even small differences cannot safely be ignored since they can
yield biomedically significant differences. For instance, small differences in:

> Metabolic pathways and rates play a major role in carcino-
> genesis. That is one basis for individual, inter-strain, or
> interspecies differences in susceptibility. For such reasons,
> man cannot be expected to react to DDT the way mice do.
> After all, if a man had exactly the same metabolism as a mouse,
> he would be a mouse (Freedman and Zeisel 1988: 12).

In short, species' specific adverse reactions to xenobiotics are
ubiquitous:

> The occurrence of major quantitative and qualitative dif-
> ferences between animal species in the metabolism of xeno-
> biotics is well documented. Interspecies differences in meta-
> bolism represent a major complication in toxicity testing,
> being responsible for important differences both in the

nature and magnitude of toxic responses . . . these differences represent probably the single greatest complicating factor in the use of animal toxicity data as an indication of potential human hazard (Caldwell 1992: 651).

As the International Agency for Research on Cancer summarizes the evidence, and its implication for extrapolation: "At present, no objective criteria exist to interpret data from studies in experimental animals or from short-term tests directly in terms of human risk" (IARC 1983: 13).

A consensus report, issued more than a decade later by the same group, still contends that we can gain some information from animal experiments. However, they recognize that animal models of cancer are not, using our language, strong: "Understanding of mechanisms of carcinogenesis is based primarily upon molecular and cellular analysis of the effects of particular agents in the laboratory. This is a reductionistic approach that simplifies a complex reality" (IARC 1992: 12).

In short, toxicological studies show that causally relevant disanalogies between species are pervasive. In this field of biomedical research, it cannot be assumed that condition (3) is satisfied.

Teratology

The findings in toxicology are repeated in the field of teratology – the scientific study of abnormal development. The marked species differences in teratologic response are related to differences between both structural and regulatory genes – after all, regulatory genes play a central role in an organism's development. As teratologist J. Wilson puts it:

In simple terms, genetic makeup of the developing organism is the setting in which induced teratogenesis occurs, the genes and the extrinsic influences interacting to various degrees. Differences in the reaction to the same potentially harmful agent by individuals, strains or species are presumed to depend on variations in biochemical or morphological makeup that are determined by genes (1977: 49).

Consider the following species-specific reaction: mice are more likely than most other mammals to develop cleft palate after exposure to glucorticoids.

121

This susceptibility could relate to such features as the rates at which the hormone is absorbed, eliminated or transformed by the maternal animal; its rate of passage across the placenta; or the nature of its interactions within the cells and tissues of the embryo. Whatever it is that allows the hormone to get to the mouse embryo in larger amounts, for longer periods, or to have a more disruptive effect, it is at least to some extent genetically determined (Wilson 1977: 49).

The connections between teratogenesis and developmental considerations, first mentioned in Chapter 6, are made explicit by Nishimura and Shiota. They present data on ten mammalian species, ranging from rodents to primates and conclude:

it is evident that most of organogenesis and other developmental events are similar in their sequence in all ten species. However, the actual age of their occurrence varies from species to species, almost independently from length of gestation (1978: 123).

These differences will be biomedically significant. For instance, some significant features of development occur prenatally in humans but postnatally in other species: the richer intrauterine lives of humans reflect the evolution of brains larger than that of other primates, relative to body size.

Moreover, the developmental differences are not merely a matter of timing. Nishimura and Shiota (1978: 123–5) list four qualitative species differences. First, some mammals do not develop organs found in other mammals. For instance, rats do not have gall bladders; mice lack palatine tonsils; and rabbits do not have lingual tonsils. Second, the same organ may develop from different tissues in different species. While the mouse vagina originates from both the Muellerian epithelium and the urogenital sinus, in humans it originates primarily from the sinus epithelium. Third, there are different modes of morphogenesis: primates primarily have eccrine sweat glands while other mammals have apocrine sweat glands. Fourth, there are varying degrees of morphogenetic progress. For instance, the Muellerian ducts fuse differently in different species. This produces the duplex uterus in marsupials, the bipartite uterus in some rodent species, the bicornuate uterus in carnivores, and the simplex uterus in primates.

Given the pervasiveness of developmental differences, we should not be surprised by the dramatic differences in species in response to potential teratogens. Such differences are pervasive:

> False positives and false negatives abound. Once one has established that a drug is a teratogen for man, it is usually possible to find, retrospectively, a suitable animal model. But trying to predict human toxicity – which is after all what the screening game is about – is quite another matter. Cortisone is a potent dysmorphogen in the rabbit and mouse, but does not produce malformations in the rat. Azathioprine is not a teratogen in the rat, but is highly dysmorphogenic in the rabbit. Carbutamide produces malformations in the eyes of rats and mice, but facial and visceral malformations in rabbits (Lasagna 1984: 15).

In fact, the differences are so profound that we cannot safely generalize findings in animals to humans, not even for drugs within the same chemical or pharmacologic class.

> One hypoglycemic sulfonylurea may cause a high percentage of malformations in animals while another may have little or no dysmorphogenic activity. The same applies to antiemetics and cytotoxic drugs (Lasagna 1984: 15).

Again, the evidence suggests condition (3) is not satisfied in CAMs using non-human animals.

Endocrinology

Findings in endocrinology likewise reveal the pervasiveness of causally relevant disanalogies. Consider, for example, the actions of the thyroid. The systemic effects of the thyroid are very widespread:

> The list of organs, organ systems, and metabolic processes affected by thyroid hormones is longer by far than that for any other hormone. If one seeks to find some unifying pattern or principle among these diverse functions of T4, in the present state of our knowledge this proves impossible (Gorbman *et al.* 1983: 240).

Moreover, the structure of the gland is similar across species:

> The thyroid in all adult vertebrates is follicular. With few exceptions it would be difficult to differentiate among species

on the basis of thyroid histology. Even on the level of electron microscopy, parallelism of thyroid structure has been found between lower vertebrates and mammals (Gorbman *et al.* 1983: 43).

Yet there are clear and substantial species differences in the action and pathology of this all-important gland.

> The marked species' differences between rodents and primates in thyroid gland physiology, the spontaneous incidence of thyroid gland neoplasia and the apparent susceptibility to neoplasia secondary to simple hypothyroidism support the conclusion that thyroid gland neoplasia secondary to hormone imbalance is species specific (McClain 1992: 401).

In fact, the endocrine system not only exhibits systemic disanalogy, it is a biological microcosm of the effects of evolutionary forces. For instance, we know that evolution is conservative in the sense that it "uses" the same biochemical building blocks across species lines. Yet it is radical in that it uses those blocks to serve very different functional ends:

> The comparative anatomy of endocrine glands also shares a fairly conservative evolution, so that it can be said that generally the same or very similar hormones are produced by corresponding glands of different vertebrates. Despite the general similarities, hormones do many different things in different vertebrates. The diverse functions of the pituitary hormone prolactin is perhaps one of the most extreme examples (Gorbman *et al.* 1983: 33).

Since prolactin is instrumental in the production of milk, it is not unreasonable to speculate that this may be related to developmental differences between species. Furthermore, this hormone has been co-opted to serve a "large number of uses" in the organism, largely because of large numbers of "tissues have frequently become responsive to this hormone during evolution" (Ibid.).

In fact, the endocrine system generally illustrates common evolutionary processes. According to Russell and Nicholl ubiquitious species differences evolved to help organisms cope with their specific environmental conditions:

> How could such hormone and species' specificities have evolved, and how is it that some members of the family have

both activities? The ancestral hormone may have had only one activity: with divergence, one line lost it and gained a new one. Or, the ancestor may have had both activities: with evolution, one line lost one and the other line lost the other. Both alternatives require postulating that members of the two diverging subfamilies occasionally acquired or reacquired the activities of the other (1990: 168).

In fact, these differences are often best explained by each animal's insinuation in its particular ecological niche, and these affect the way the organism must live, including its diet:

> The sensitivity of different species to insulin may be related to their dietary habits. It has been noted that herbivorous mammals withstand an absence of insulin far more readily than carnivorous ones. Carnivores only eat periodically so that they may have a sudden large intake of nutrients which must be stored for utilization during the fast between meals (Shambaugh 1986: 185).

Thus, we can see how the endocrine system is closely connected to an organism's metabolism, and species differences in the endocrine system may be the source of previously identified differences in metabolism.

> Hormones play an important role in regulating the interconversions of nutrients to metabolic substrates and their stored forms. The endocrine secretions may help to regulate the levels of nutrients by contributing to the control of their absorption from the gut, their levels in the blood, the nature and rate of their storage, their release from tissues, and their assembly into the structural elements of the body (1986: 173).

In short, the pervasiveness of these endocrinal differences is doubly relevant to the current discussion. Not only is it another particular instance of causal disanalogy between species, it is especially relevant to what we called *systemic disanalogy*. The endocrine system plays a central role in bodily function – recall, for instance, the first quotation in this section on the wide ranging role of the thyroid. Given this pervasive role, small changes in the system may cause ripples throughout the organism. Arguably it is the source of much systemic disanalogy.

In toxicology in general, there has been an over-emphasis on biotransformation to toxic metabolites. It has proved heuristically useful in studies on estrogens, in contrast, to adopt the unifying concept that species differences in estrogen toxicity mirror species differences, not in pharmacokinetics, but in estrogen endocrinology. The poor predictiveness of animal studies for humans thus becomes comprehensible in terms of interspecies variations in endocrinology (Hart 1990: 213).

So, in the field of endocrinology, condition (3) appears to be an unattainable ideal. Evolutionary theory and empirical evidence suggest we will find, across species lines, relevant causal disanalogies with respect to endocrine systems.

Virology: a closer look at a historical case

A close reading of the history of poliomyelitis – often cited as a flagship case for the benefits of animal experimentation – shows the dangers of ignoring causal disanalogy. Flexner and Lewis intranasally infected rhesus monkeys with the simian strain of the polio virus and concluded that the virus entered the body through the nose, traveled to the brain via the olfactory nerves, and eventually migrated to the spinal cord. We will call this causal claim the *nasal hypothesis*. Physicians, relying on this animal model, developed various preventive and therapeutic strategies. For instance, Flexner had discovered that placing alum, zinc sulfate and picric acid into the nasal passages of monkeys had blocked absorption of the simian polio virus. However, nasal sprays that were developed from this idea, e.g., the "Schultz–Peet Prophylactic Spray," were useless. The problem here is the first form of *intervention disanalogy*, first mentioned in the previous chapter. The researchers assumed that because they could infect rhesus monkeys intranasally, that humans must be infected by the same route.

Researchers' allegiance to this animal model led them to ignore compelling clinical evidence. For instance, clinicians had long known that the polio virus was present in the intestines and excreta of infected persons. They also knew the virus affected the lymphatic system and the spleen. There was no good explanation for these clinical manifestations if the disease was essentially neurotropic, migrating swiftly from the nose to the brain.

However, experimentalists' inability to explain these findings did not shake their faith in the "nasal hypothesis." After all, it was derived from animal experimentation. For them, the clinical data were anomalies, perhaps the result of backswallowing nasal secretions, which they thought the nasal hypothesis would eventually explain. As Paul put it:

> So strong was this theory fixed in the minds of the medical profession that it imparted the erroneous idea that poliovirus had such an intimate and special tropism for nervous tissue that it became locked away in the cells of the brain and cord almost at once, at the very start of the acute disease, making it difficult to access any form of therapy directed toward destroying the virus ... So the theoretical experimentalists, like so many who have immured themselves in their laboratories before and since, drifted further and further away from the human disease in their attempts to use experiments in the monkey for interpretations of the disease in man (1971: 224–5).

Only after researchers ceased relying on these misleading animal studies, and heeded evidence uncovered by human clinical virological studies, could they identify the pathogenesis of polio. For besides intervention disanalogy mentioned earlier, there was also systemic disanalogy between humans and rhesus monkeys. That is, there appears to be more than one kind of disanalogy at work here. Sabin eventually discovered intrinsic disanalogies between specific systems (susceptibility to infection in the central nervous system in rhesus monkeys and the alimentary tract of humans). Flexner got lucky. His experimental intervention produced polio in rhesus monkeys using a route by which they were especially susceptible. Yet his intervention, coupled with biological luck, led him to believe this was the primary route of infection in humans. As Paul explains:

> Of great importance was Sabin's discovery by quantitative studies that the central nervous system of lower primates (rhesus and cynomolgus monkeys) was more susceptible to polioviruses than that of higher primates (chimpanzees) – and by epidemiologic analogy, man. The reverse was true for the alimentary tract particularly in rhesus monkeys; whereas the susceptible human intestinal tract was readily infected by doses of virus that were ineffective in monkeys (1971: 451).

In particular, the development of polio vaccines was spurred by the work of Enders and his colleagues who, in the late 1940s, showed that polio viruses could be cultured in non-neural human tissue, and in particular in human embryonic intestinal tissue. In short, despite similarities between human and rhesus monkey polio, the causal mechanisms of infection were very different.

Likewise for many "new" viruses. For instance the Marburg virus is most lethal in guinea pigs and is often deadly in velvet monkeys and humans, but has no obvious effect at all in mice (Garrett 1994: 44–5). On the other hand, the Reston Ebola virus is lethal in rhesus monkeys, but has no detrimental effects on humans, although it does multiply in human hosts (Preston 1994: 252–3).

Models of ischemic stroke

Scientists have attempted to use animals to model stroke in humans for more than a century. Since ischemic stroke in humans is common and often devastating, good animal models of this phenomenon would be highly desirable. Ideally it could help us understand the causes of stroke, and help us develop potential therapies. However, animal studies clearly fail to illuminate strokes in humans. As Wiebers *et al.* point out:

> A large proportion of patients with ischemic stroke have underlying multifocal atherosclerosis which has developed over many years or decades. Such individuals may have numerous associated risk factors which predispose to this disease process . . . Some attempts have been made to model atherosclerosis in some animal species and to account for hypertension and increasing age, but it is clear that these circumstances do not reproduce the human situation. In fact, most models of ischemic stroke are derived from young animals with no underlying chronic disease or any genetic predisposition to such diseases (1990: 1).

Wiebers *et al.* make it clear that the failure of animal models stems from systemic disanalogy:

> Many variations, both within and between species, have been recognized, not only in the vascular anatomy, but also in histopathologic responses to identical ischemic insults and treatment responses to cerebral ischemia (1990: 1).

In fact, since the non-human animals lack certain higher cognitive

128

functional properties and lack a language then the effects of strokes on these cognitive abilities cannot be measured in laboratory animals. In this regard, if in no other, non-human animals will fail to be good models of stroke in humans.

Moreover, not only do we have systemic disanalogies in animal models of stroke, we will also find further intervention disanalogies. The condition is induced in animals entirely by the researchers' intervention. Moreover, the methods of inducing stroke will be biomedically relevant. Wiebers *et al.* explain:

> With some ligation techniques, craniotomy introduces several variables unlike the human disease situation. These include skull trauma, external blood vessel injury, and changes in intracranial pressure. While most of the embolic techniques avoid the invasive features of craniotomy, they provide less control over the location and extent of the resulting cerebral infarction. Foreign body techniques also fail to mimic many observable features of human emboli, including the tendency for human clots to undergo lysis, migrate into distal portions of the arterial system, or recanalize over time (1990: 2).

These models may be further compromised by using anesthetics that change important metabolic parameters – changes which, as we have seen above, may vary in quality and quantity from species to species. These changes may be evaded by not using general anesthesia. Nevertheless, as Wiebers *et al.* explain:

> this introduces animal stress, another undesirable variable, which has the potential for altering other parameters, including the release of endogenous corticosteroids (1990: 2).

In summary, the empirical evidence from stoke research suggests we have further reason to think condition (3) will not be satisfied.

IMPLICATIONS OF CAUSAL DISANALOGY

There is abundant empirical evidence that animal models of human disease will typically violate condition (3), that non-human animal models are not strong models of human biomedical phenomena. This should not be surprising since that is exactly what the theory of evolution, our current best theory of biological phenomena, predicts. Thus, our current best theory, coupled with laboratory evidence, suggests that non-human models of human biomedical phenomena are at best partially isomorphic. Whether such models are nonetheless valuable research tools will be discussed in Chapters 9 and 10. For the moment, though, we want to spell out in more detail the ramifications of this finding. Specifically, we want to state how the presence of causal disanalogies affects the standard arguments for animal experimentation, arguments that are part of the current paradigm.

Intact systems

As we explained in Chapter 4, according to the current paradigm researchers must conduct tests on whole, intact animals since whole animals respond differently than isolated parts of animals. In an important sense the current paradigm is correct: evolutionary theory does tell us that most biomedically significant properties arise from complex biological systems with mutually interactive subsystems. However, the same theory that undergirds the researchers' claim that they need to study whole intact systems, comes back later to haunt them. Since the phenomena of interest are results of the interactions of biological sub-systems, then any causal disanalogies between species may undermine the reliability of intact animals used as CAMs of human biomedical phenomena. Systemic disanalogy, supervening on intrinsic disanalogy, will always be lurking in the wings.

How can animal researchers avoid these effects of systemic disanalogy? – only by studying systems which are unlikely to be causally disanalogous with the human phenomenon under study. If our only concern were good science, then, since we want to know about biomedical phenomena in humans, we should use human subjects. This would overcome some concern about systemic disanalogy between species. However, other difficulties would remain. We also have strong evidence of intraspecific variation. Moreover, as Schardein notes in the context of teratology:

> It is unlikely that testing of chemicals (even drugs) in the pregnant woman will ever be acceptable. Testing agents for teratogenicity only in impending therapeutic abortions may be more desirable, but since vast numbers of subjects would have to be treated, even this method would not necessarily determine a chemical's teratogenic potential. To establish at the 95% confidence level that a given agent changes by 1%

the naturally occurring frequency of congenital deformity would require a sequential trial involving an estimated 35,000 patients ... One study also indicated that there are even difficulties encountered in distinguishing teratogenic effects due to chemicals from those caused by other factors, such as disease states like influenza (1985: 27–8).

Additionally, since fully randomized controlled experiments on humans are morally odious, researchers must find other test subjects. They choose non-human animals. Ideally they will want to find some species whose members satisfy condition (3), and who also satisfy pragmatic criteria. Thus, in teratogenic testing, this would require that test subjects satisfy the following conditions outlined by Schardein (1985: 19):

• Absorbs, metabolizes, and eliminates test substances like man.
• Transmits test substances and their metabolites across the placenta like man.
• Has embryos and fetuses with developmental and metabolic patterns similar to those of man.
• Breeds easily and has large litters and short gestation.
• Is inexpensively maintained under laboratory conditions.
• Does not bite, scratch, kick, howl or squeal.

However, as Palmer notes:

a great deal of time and effort has been expended discussing the most suitable species for teratology studies, and it is time that a few fallacies were laid to rest. First, there is no such thing as an ideal test species, particularly if the intent is to extrapolate the results to man. The ideal is approximated only when testing veterinary products or new food materials in the domestic species for which they are intended ... Even then, the value of using the ultimate recipient of the test material may be severely limited by practical difficulties of obtaining sufficient numbers of animals and sufficient background information to interpret the results (1978: 219).

Finally, even if we were to find some species that did satisfy condition (3), we would still be plagued by the specter of intervention disanalogies. Animal researchers have long recognized that laboratory intervention may skew experimental results. To give just one example:

131

The effects were observed of moving male, adult Han Sprague rats ... Heart rates (telemetrically recorded), packed cell volume, haemoglobin and plasma protein content were 10–20% elevated 2–10 minutes after cage movement, or 2–10 minutes after ether confrontation, over those of controls sampled within 50 seconds, indicating circulatory and micro-circulatory shock reactions. Serum glucose, pyruvate and lactate concentrations rose by 20–100% 2–5 minutes after cage movement and 1–15 minutes after ether exposure (Gartner 1980: 267).

Other factors, such as diet, lighting, noise, and bedding chips, to list but a few, are known to affect experimental outcomes. These intervention disanalogies will affect extrapolation from lab to lab, and from the lab to the human world, even if the model satisfied condition (3). Since models typically do not satisfy condition (3), the effects of intervention will provide additional uncertainty about our extrapolations from animal models to humans.

Biological reductionism

The current biomedical paradigm suggests that if experimental work were pursued with sufficient reductionist vigor, then infer-ences from mammal CAMs to humans would come close to satisfying condition (3). That is, since humans and other mammals are all formed from the same biochemical building blocks, then we may assume condition (3) to be satisfied at the molecular/ biochemical level, notwithstanding differences higher up the bio-logical hierarchy. Thus, species differences, which currently appear to be a bar to extrapolation from animals to humans, are thought to be ultimately explicable in terms of the fundamental units of life – which are the same across species. This reductionist view under-standably emphasizes molecular studies: these studies currently get the lion's share of available research resources. Researchers hope that by focusing on what is highly similar across species we may simultaneously explain species differences further up the hierarchy and find a common biochemical currency to undergird extra-polations across species.

Following in Claude Bernard's footsteps, researchers think reductionist analyses of biological phenomena will discover funda-mental commonalities of all species. If humans and rats are the same animals dressed up differently, then biological reductionism can disrobe members of these different species. Having suitably disrobed animals, researchers can make legitimate causal inferences from members of one species to members of the other.

This response, though, clashes with the latest developments in evolutionary theory. The "New Biology" does not countenance reductionism – neither reductionism of biology to physics and chemistry, nor the reductionism of all biology to molecular biology and biochemistry. As Mayr notes:

> Attempts to "reduce" biological systems to the level of simple physico-chemical processes have failed because during the reduction the systems lost their specifically biological properties. Living systems ... have numerous properties that are simply not found in the inanimate world (1988: 1).

Nor, Florkin and Schoffeneils argue, can we reduce the biological to the biochemical:

> If animals are generally endowed with motility (function of organism), this is related to the fact that certain cells biosynthesize macromolecules of contractile proteins (molecular structures related to function considered at the level of the organism). In fact, molecular biology, in spite of the concentration of its studies at the molecular level, brings us back to the organismic viewpoint too often neglected in biochemical studies (1970: 162).

Evolved biological systems are complex, hierarchically organized systems whose causally significant features typically arise from the causal interactions between its sub-systems *at all levels in the biological hierarchy*. Such systems have emergent properties at higher levels in the biological hierarchy that cannot be predicted and explained in terms of even a complete knowledge of the properties of systems at lower levels in the biological hierarchy.

These interactive relations cannot be reduced or eliminated. Moreover, since whole organisms, and not just their components, face selection pressures, then there is no way to explain the effects of natural selection, either by looking at the physical and chemical properties of that organism or by just knowing the organism's genetic composition. The complete phenotype matters too. This is a point recognized even by selfish-gene theorists, who represent the reductionist wing of evolutionary thinking.

Moreover, even though many philosophers of science have historically been ready to embrace reductionistic programs, most philosophers of biology reject reductionism in biology. After discussing the relatively high-level attempts to reduce all of biology to molecular biology, Philip Kitcher notes, "the examples I have given seem to support both anti-reductionistic doctrines ... [Despite] the immense value of the molecular biology that Watson and Crick launched in 1953, molecular studies cannot cannibalize the rest of biology" (1994: 398). Elliott Sober, who suggests he rejects any strong form of reductivism, notes that "the thesis of reducibility in principle does not seem to have any direct methodological consequences for current scientific practice" (Sober 1993: 26). Put simply, reductionistic hopes do not appear reasonable, either on biological or philosophical grounds.

MODELERS' FALLACIES

The previous analysis explains why researchers cannot be confident that non-human animal models are strong causal analogs of human biomedical phenomena. Researchers who nonetheless contend non-human animals are strong CAMs of human biomedical phenomena are frequently guilty of either or both of two fallacies. In fact, defenders of animal experimentation often commit these fallacies explicitly.

The modeler's functional fallacy

Some researchers claim non-human animals are strong CAMs of human biomedical phenomena because both species are functionally similar. Lungs oxygenate the blood, while livers remove impurities from it, whether the animal is a rat, a bird, or a human. As Lubinski and Thompson explain:

> Darwin's work suggested that to gain biological insight into human beings it may be more illuminating to study non-human animate systems rather than the inanimate models of da Vinci and Descartes. Claude Bernard (1885) [sic], the founder of experimental medicine, used dogs in laboratory preparations as models of human physiology, assuming basic continuity in physiological functions across species. Both Darwin and Bernard argued that anatomy, physiology, and

134

behavior not only look similar in different animals but often share common evolutionary origins and current regulatory mechanisms (1993: 628).

This view of the commonality of species originates with Bernard:

> Physiologists . . . follow a different conception; instead of proceeding from the organ to the function, they start from the physiological phenomenon and seek its explanation in the organism ([1865] 1949: 111).

According to some biomedical researchers, the connection between function and causal mechanisms is so tight that, for their purposes, humans and non-human animals are virtually interchangeable. Other researchers might claim that the distinction between causal mechanisms and functional properties is just a matter of description and, hence, that similarity of physiological function implies similarity of causal mechanism. Such a view, at least historically, seemed quite reasonable. After all, functional properties are effects of underlying causal mechanisms. Sir Isaac Newton put it this way: "Therefore to the same natural effects we must, as far as possible, assign the same causes. As to respiration in a man and in a beast; the descent of stones in Europe and in America" ([1687] 1962: 398).

However, as the preceding arguments show, we should not infer that functionally similar systems share the same underlying causal mechanisms. This point is well recognized by most bench scientists. They are primarily interested in an organism's causal mechanisms – even when the effects of the mechanism can be described, for other purposes, in functional terms. For instance, they are more interested in the liver's mechanisms for purifying blood than in the simple functional fact *that* it purifies blood. Both interventionist and preventive medicine hinge on a proper understanding of a disease's or condition's causal mechanisms:

> Pragmatists have argued that a machinist is able to repair an engine without understanding the theory behind its operation. But teratology is concerned with more than repair. One of the major objectives is to anticipate risks before they materialize. The anticipation of teratic risks in today's rapidly changing environment becomes an endless succession of screening tests unless a knowledge of mechanisms can lead to extrapolations, generalizations and shortcuts that will simplify

135

the task. Furthermore the use of animal tests for evaluation of human risk will become more than empirical only when the degree of comparability of mechanisms between test animal and man is understood. Finally, with a better knowledge of mechanisms, unknown causes may be more easily recognized (Wilson 1977: 72).

When discussing the causal/functional asymmetry in Chapter 6, we saw that functional similarity does not imply underlying causal similarity. Consider the metabolization of phenol. Phenol is metabolized by a conjugation reaction with either glucuronic acid or sulfate. The purpose of this reaction is to enhance its water solubility and thereby ease excretion. Cats, rats, pigs, and humans are functionally similar: they can all metabolize phenol. However, the precise mechanism of phenol metabolism varies widely from species to species. The ratio of conjugation with sulfate to conjugation by glucuronidation in humans is 80:12 percent; in rats is 45:40 percent (percent excreted in 24 hours). By contrast, pigs cannot conjugate phenol with sulfate, and cats cannot metabolize phenol via glucuronidation. Wide species variation in the mechanisms of metabolism is also seen in other compounds, like amphetamines and the benzodiazephines (Caldwell 1980: 94–106).

In short, functional similarity does not guarantee underlying causal similarity, nor does it make such similarity "probable." To assume it does is to commit what we term the *modeler's functional fallacy*.

The modeler's phylogenetic fallacy

Some researchers also claim that since non-human animals and humans are phylogenetically continuous, we can legitimately assume condition (3) is all but nearly satisfied, at least for phylogenetically close animals. However, even when species are phylogenetically close – as are the rat and the mouse – we cannot assume that the two species will react similarly to similar stimuli. Tests for chemically induced cancers in rats and mice yield the same results (non-site specific concordance) for 70 percent of the substances tested (Lave *et al.* 1988). The figure drops to 51 percent for site-specific cancers (Gold *et al.* 1991: 245).

Likewise, primates, our "closest" biological relatives (and presumably nearly ideal as test subjects), have some biological

136

sub-systems that are significantly disanalogous from those in humans:

> Nonhuman primates offer the closest approximation to human teratological conditions because of phylogenetic similarities ... However, a review of the literature indicates that except for a few teratogens (sex hormones, thalidomide, radiation, etc.) the results in nonhuman primates are not comparable to those in humans (Mitruka *et al.* 1976: 467–8).

Phylogenetic continuity, even relative phylogenetic "closeness," does not guarantee that relevant sub-systems are relevantly similar causally. Still less does it guarantee that the interactions between those sub-systems are identical. For, as Caldwell points out, relatively small biological differences between test subjects can produce substantially different experimental outcomes:

> It has been obvious for some time that there is generally no evolutionary basis behind the particular drug metabolizing ability of a particular species. Indeed, among rodents and primates, zoologically closely related species exhibit markedly different patterns of metabolism (1980: 106).

Moreover, it sometimes happens that members of phylogenetically more distant species show more similar reactions to similar stimulation than do members of phylogenetically closer species. For example, the carcinogenic effect of aflatoxin B is more similar in rats and monkeys than in (phylogenetically closer) rats and mice (Vainio, *et al.* 1992: 20). And pigs, phylogenetically more distant from humans than rats, are nevertheless more similar from a physiological point of view. As transplant surgeon Michael Bewick described pigs, "physiologically they are horizontal men – or men are vertical pigs" (1988: 20). Thus, to reason that phylogenetic closeness implies underlying causal similarity is to commit what we term the *modeler's phylogenetic fallacy*.

CONCLUSION

We have seen that there are good reasons to think animal CAMs of human biomedical phenomena typically do not satisfy condition (3), and, thus, are not strong models. Darwinian descent with modification all but guarantees that condition (3) will not be completely satisfied. However, Darwinian descent with modification also means that there will be many points of similarity between members of different species. Thus, condition (3) will be partially satisfied. CAMs that partially satisfy condition (3) we call *weak models*. Can weak models still serve researchers' experimental purposes? That we discuss in the next two chapters.

9

CAUSAL DISANALOGY III
Weak models

Evolutionary theory leads us to expect broad functional and biochemical similarities across mammalian species. However, as the arguments in the previous chapters show, evolutionary theory also explains why we cannot assume that species which are broadly similar will have identical causal mechanisms. So, although researchers can reasonably expect that animal CAMs of human biomedical phenomena will partially satisfy condition (3), they cannot expect CAMs to completely satisfy condition (3). That is, at best, an ideal they may hope to approximate in the laboratory. As Nonneman and Woodruff explain:

> [T]he assumption is that to be useful a model must be completely isomorphic with that being modeled in all relevant relationships. Biomedical scientists are well aware that this is generally not the case with models they use. Indeed, there are many types of models, and their usefulness varies with the degree to which they are isomorphic with the human system or disease being modeled (1994: 7).

Researchers (as opposed to some of their public policy advocates) openly acknowledge the lack of causal isomorphism between animal systems and the human phenomena they supposedly model. They acknowledge the pervasiveness of causal disanalogy, even in phylogenetically close species. Commenting on primate research in teratology, Schardein notes:

> It is the actual results of teratogenicity testing in primates which have been most disappointing in consideration of these animals' possible use as a predictive model. While some nine subhuman primates (all but the bushbaby) have demonstrated the characteristic limb defects observed in humans

when administered thalidomide, the results with 83 other agents with which primates have been tested are less than perfect. Of the 15 listed putative human teratogens tested in nonhuman primates, only eight were also teratogenic in one or more of the various species ... The data with respect to the "suspect" or "likely" teratogens in humans under certain circumstances were equally divergent. Three of the eight suspect teratogens were also not suspect in monkeys or did not induce some developmental toxicity (1985: 20–3).

Nonetheless, many researchers claim animals are useful CAMs of human biomedical phenomena. They believe the biomedically significant causal mechanisms of animals and humans, although different in some respects, are sufficiently similar to justify inferences from the former to the latter. As Nonneman and Woodruff put it:

If a model is strictly homologous (complete isomorphism in all respects) then validity is guaranteed. But the converse is not true. A model that is not homologous with the human condition it represents may still have some validity. The key to validity rests in the choice of the right model for the right reason, not necessarily in homology (1994: 10).

(Notice that these researchers use "homologous" to indicate causal isomorphism, while evolutionary biologists use it to describe traits and structures in species descended from a common ancestor. As we have seen, "homology" in the evolutionary sense will not guarantee "homology" in these researchers' sense, i.e., complete satisfaction of condition (3).)

Nonneman and Woodruff think that, at least for some purposes, partial causal isomorphism provides "the right reason":

In most cases, models represent a compromise. A relatively simple experimental system is used to represent a more complex and less readily studied system. The model may represent only one aspect of a biological or behavioral system, but it is used because of the complexity of the natural system or because we believe we are modeling the most relevant component(s) of the problem, and the model allows a test of that belief (1994: 10).

Or, as the same experimenters express it later:

It is typically assumed that the more closely a species is related to humans the better the model it will provide. In some cases, this likely is true ... But presumed similarity of relationship to humans is not the only, and not necessarily the best, consideration in developing an animal model. Sometimes species that appear very dissimilar to humans in some respects share particular characteristics that suit them especially well to answer specific questions (1994: 11–12).

What does this mean? We can formalize their point in the following way: begin with two systems, S_1 and S_2. S_1 has causal mechanisms {a,b,c,d,e}, S_2 has mechanisms {a,b,c,x,y}. When we stimulate sub-systems {a,b,c} of S_1 with s_f, response r_f regularly occurs. We can therefore infer that were we to stimulate sub-systems {a,b,c} of S_2 with s_f, r_f would *probably* occur.

Under what conditions would this inference be likely? All other things being equal, the probability will be high only if the common mechanisms {a,b,c} are causally independent of the differing mechanisms ({d,e} and {x,y}). If any of the common mechanisms causally interact with the different mechanisms, as they typically do in intact biological systems, then these interactions may produce divergent responses to qualitatively identical stimuli. We have no *a priori* reason to think there will be no such divergence, or that any divergence will be insignificant. Unless we know that the different mechanisms are causally independent of the similar mechanisms, then we can never be confident, before observing the behavior of both systems, that these divergences will not undermine the extrapolation from S_1 to S_2.

The point is well illustrated by studies on hypertension. Even while advocating animal research, Sassard shows he is aware that condition (3) is partially violated:

> The fact that there are so many models for hypertension and atherosclerosis indicates that none of them is completely satisfactory. Thus experiments using several models must always be done requiring a larger number of laboratory animals. Identical observations can be made for the other severe cardiovascular pathologies: coronary ischemia, cerebral ischemia, cardiac insufficiency and rhythm disorders (1990: 83).

Despite these partial disanalogies, many researchers maintain

141

animal models are useful CAMs of human biomedical conditions. Thus, Ganten *et al.* point out:

> Each strain of genetically hypertensive rats displays unique pathophysiological features linked to the development of hypertension which then often resemble disorders found in subgroups of hypertensive patients. Thus the cause of hypertension in an individual hypertensive patient may closely resemble the disturbances found in one or more of the rat strains (1990: 92).

However, as our previous analysis showed, this is a sound expectation only if the mechanisms of hypertension in the test animals and the relevant subgroups of humans are independent of these organisms' differing causal mechanisms. Without further argument and evidence, this cannot be assumed.

Ganten *et al.* suggest that since human hypertension is often caused by a variety of factors, then by identifying the distinct ways that genetically homogeneous rats develop hypertension, we can better understand the phenomenon in humans. It is not clear, however, how this is to be done. Do these researchers assume we can somehow add the distinct ways in which distinct strains of rodent develop hypertension, to understand how these factors interact to cause hypertension in humans? This seems highly unlikely. In humans, these different causal factors interactively conspire to cause hypertension. The complex interactions between these factors cannot be understood simply by observing how each of these factors, in isolation, causes hypertension in distinct strains of rat. Certainly we cannot assume, *a priori*, that merely summing these causal factors will explain the phenomenon in humans.

Given the centrality of causal analogical reasoning for understanding and assessing animal experimentation, we must now examine the logic of analogical arguments more deeply.

THE NATURE OF ANALOGICAL REASONING

Many researchers, and especially those engaged in applied research, assume animal CAMs of human systems straightforwardly reveal significant information about human biology. However, since we cannot be confident that the model and the subject modeled are causally isomorphic, then, as the earlier arguments show, researchers must assume that the models, though weak, are nonetheless revealing. This is not a crazy assumption. Indeed, it is entirely reasonable – on the classical view of causal analogical reasoning.

Researchers who make predictions about what will happen in humans based on findings in animals (as in toxicology and teratology) rely on causal analogical arguments. That is, researchers using animal CAMs employ analogical arguments of the following form:

> Members of species A have properties a, b, c, z.
> Members of species B have properties a, b, c.
> Therefore, with probability P, members of species B will have property z.

Let z be the property of developing cancer when exposed to substance Z. We will want the probability P to be as high as possible since a mistake – either way – can have enormous economic and social costs. So how do we evaluate analogical arguments proceeding from weak models that partially violate condition (3)?

John Stuart Mill stated the classical view more than a century ago:

> it follows that where the resemblance is very great, the ascertained difference very small, and our knowledge of the subject-matter tolerably extensive, the argument from analogy may approach in strength very near to a valid induction. If, after much observation of B, we find that it agrees with A in nine out of ten of its known properties, we may conclude with a probability of nine to one, that it will possess any given derivative property of A. If we discover, for example, an unknown animal or plant, resembling closely some known one in the greater number of the properties we observe in it, but differing in some few, we may reasonably expect to find in the unobserved remainder of its properties a general agreement with those of the former, but also a difference corresponding proportionately to the amount of observed diversity (Mill 1961: 367).

Mill's model precisely articulates the reasoning of many researchers. For instance, toxicologists test a chemical on animals to determine whether that chemical will be dangerous for humans. They assume that if we have a tolerably extensive knowledge of the model and the object modeled, and that we find many similarities and few differences between them, then we can safely extrapolate findings in the former to the latter.

Toxicologists would likely note that the theory of evolution tells us there are relatively few biochemical and metabolic differences between species. Thus, following Cairns-Smith, they might claim that humans and other mammals are just the same animals dressed up differently. (Perhaps, though, in a discussion of weak models, we should say that we are *very nearly* the same animals dressed up differently.) These conservative features of evolution are widely acknowledged by prominent theorists:

> [N]ew biochemical pathways seldom come into existence. As every biochemist knows, the biochemical characteristics of organisms are far less diverse than morphological features. Many physiological adaptations entail not biochemical but behavioral or structural changes ... The basic biochemical pathways and even the kinds of cells that make up an animal are almost invariant throughout the Metazoa; and the evolution of changes in morphology involves changes in the developmental patterning of cellular mechanisms, not of the cellular mechanisms themselves (Futuyma 1986: 409–10).

Although members of mammalian species wear different morphological clothes, underneath those clothes they have a highly similar biochemistry and metabolism. That explains the animal researcher's attraction to a reductionist view of biology. As Caldwell has pointed out, "Zbinden has said that the similarities of structure and function of higher organisms at the molecular level mean that the mechanisms of toxicity, usually, are identical in animals and man" (1992: 652). In short, researchers will be inclined to perceive causal disanalogies between humans and non-human animals as mere differences in wardrobe, not in substance. If they further adopt the classical view of analogical reasoning – as they are wont to do – then they will understandably conclude that any disanalogies between species will not be sufficient to undermine the scientific utility of weak CAMs using judiciously selected animal species. For at the biochemical level of description, the similarities are many and the differences are few.

How, then, will researchers, who embrace both reductionism and the classical view of analogical reasoning, interpret findings that two closely related species react to the same drug or chemical in substantially different ways? They would likely reason that (a) the species must be causally dissimilar in ways we had not noticed, (b) the small number of differences about which we do know are more significant than we thought, or (c) the identified similarities are not as relevant as we thought.

This creates a problem for toxicologists. For they report that members of different mammalian species often react very differently when exposed to the same chemical. How could this be given (a) that there are broad biochemical and metabolic similarities across species, and (b) the classical view of analogical reasoning? The answer, as you might have predicted, springs from the complex, hierarchically structured nature of evolved biological organisms. This feature of biological systems suggests that the classical view of analogical reasoning is an inappropriate analytical tool for studying intact organisms.

The metabolism of xenobiotics

Xenobiotics are pharmacologically or toxicologically active substances that are foreign to the body. The metabolism of xenobiotics can occur in either or both of two phases. In Phase I metabolism, the xenobiotic is metabolized through oxidation, reduction, or hydrolysis. In Phase II metabolism, the original compound, or one of its metabolites (compounds resulting from Phase I metabolism), is joined (conjugated) with an endogenous molecule. These processes may lead to the excretion of any or all of the following products: (a) unchanged compound, (b) Phase I metabolites, (c) Phase II metabolites, or (d) metabolites arising from a combination of both Phase I and II metabolism (Caldwell 1980: 85–8; Sipes and Gandolfi 1993: 88–9).

Toxicologists report both qualitative and quantitative differences in species' metabolisms. Qualitative differences would include any metabolic reactions that are unique to a species. For instance, we know there are at least seven metabolic reactions unique to primates: (1) aromatization of quinic acid, (2) glutamine conjugation of arylacetic and aryloxyacetic acids, (3) O-Methylation of 4-hydroxy-3,5-diiodobenzoic acid, (4) N^1-Glucuronidation of sulfadimethoxine, (5) C-Glucuronidation of pyrazolones, (6) quaternization by glucuronidation of tertiary amines, and (7) carbamate acyl glucuronidation (Caldwell 1992). Likely there are still more unique reactions of which we are currently unaware.

Other qualitative differences include those cases where members of a given species cannot achieve a particular metabolic reaction

145

widely achieved by members of many other species. For instance, cats are incapable of glucuronidation of many compounds (e.g., phenol, naphthol and other phenolic derivatives). Pigs are incapable of certain conjugations with sulfate (as in the metabolization of phenol), and dogs cannot N-acetylate many aromatic amines (Caldwell 1992: 653; Sipes and Gandolfi 1993: 115).

We also find quantitative differences in metabolism. Indeed, these are the most common differences. These differences arise when members of each of several species use more than one reaction to metabolize a given substrate, but differ with respect to the relative extents of the competing reactions – for instance, the different ratios of glucuronidation to sulfate conjugation used by humans and rats to metabolize phenol. According to Caldwell, quantitative differences can have profound biological effects:

> The possible consequences of such variability can be illustrated by a compound which is converted into three metabolites, one an inactive excretion product, another a pharmacologically active metabolite and a third a reactive electrophile leading to tissue damage. In such circumstances, which are by no means unusual, variations between, or indeed within, species in the relative proportions of the compound converted to each metabolite will lead to corresponding variation in its pharmacological and toxicological profile in various species (Caldwell 1992: 654).

Finally, we also find that some differences have both quantitative and qualitative dimensions – for instance, differences in the cytochrome P-450 enzyme system (the most important enzyme system in Phase I metabolism). We now know that there are several forms of cytochrome P-450. Sipes and Gandolfi comment:

> These differ in both the structure of the polypeptide chain and the specificity of the reactions they catalyze. The cytochrome P-450 composition of liver microsomes is altered by the treatment of animals with different chemicals. In addition, the types and amounts of cytochrome P-450 vary with species, organ, age, health, sex, stress and chemical exposure (1993: 91).

As the preceding quotation indicates, differences in this enzyme system are not merely related to species – and thus are of special interest to the current inquiry – but are also related to other intra-specific differences.

Consequently, we have abundant evidence that there are clear and significant qualitative and quantitative differences in species' metabolisms. However, these differences do not dampen the enthusiasm of researchers for the use of animal models. Many researchers think these species differences can be accommodated.

Scaling again

As we explained in earlier chapters, many toxicologists use scaling formulae (usually body weight$^{2/3}$ in carcinogenicity studies) to adjust for quantitative differences between the test species and humans. They assume that, once adjusted, the laboratory animal data will be applicable to humans. As Feron et al. note: "Implicit in the use of animal models is the assumption that data obtained in animals are relevant to man" (1990: 783). Researchers think scaling formulae will make animal data relevant to humans. For some biological phenomena, this is a reasonable assumption. As noted earlier, doubtless the strength of an animal's supporting structures or the weights of its organs may be accurately estimated using such formulae. Moreover, rates at which organisms achieve some physiological functions (e.g., respiration) may likewise be directly related to body weight or surface area.

However, the different ways that members of distinct species react to xenobiotics are not merely relative to size. There is abundant evidence that scaling does not solve the problem of differences in "adverse effects" between species. Moreover, toxicologists know that these differences are often traceable to differences in metabolism, differences discussed earlier. As one widely used pharmacology text sums it up: "The lack of correlation between toxicity data in animals and adverse effects in humans is well known" (Goth 1981: 37).

There are three problems with relying on scaling formulae. First, if scaling formulae were methodologically sound, then we should not expect to find significant intra-specific *strain* or *gender* differences. Yet there are well-documented strain and gender differences in toxicology, differences that are not normally explained by scaling factors. For example, Sipes and Gandolfi note that we see considerable strain differences within species:

In humans, large individual variations exist in the acetylation of the antituberculosis drug isoniazid. The population is generally considered to be bimodally distributed into rapid and slow acetylators ... The incidence of slow and rapid activators is not the same in all racial groups. Among Caucasians, a slightly higher percentage of slow acetylators predominate (50 to 60 percent). In contrast, in Orientals rapid acetylators predominate (1993: 116).

We also see gender differences within species, although these do not appear to be as marked in humans as they are in rodents and other mammalian species. For example:

Chloroform is converted to a reactive intermediate (phosgene) ten times faster by microsomes obtained from the kidneys of male mice than those from female mice. Male mice are susceptible to chloroform-induced nephrotoxicity, whereas female mice are resistant (Ibid.).

Nevertheless, the differences we do find are not explicable on the basis of scaling by body weight.

Second, since intra-specific variation in adverse effects is amplified by evolutionary processes, then evolved, toxicologically relevant, interspecific differences will be less likely to be explicable by scaling formulae than will simple strain differences. In fact, we know there are frequently such differences in adverse effects. Consider, for example, Manson and Wise's summary of the results of multi-species/multi-strain tests of thalidomide:

An unexpected finding was that the mouse and rat were resistant, the rabbit and hamster variably responsive, and certain strains of primates were sensitive to thalidomide developmental toxicity. Different strains of the same species of animals were also found to have highly variable sensitivity to thalidomide. Factors such as differences in absorption, distribution, biotransformation, and placental transfer have been ruled out as causes of the variability in species and strain sensitivity (1993: 228).

Third, the reader should recall the theoretical arguments from Chapter 5. Even if distinct species achieve similar functions at *rates* related to body size, we still cannot infer that the mechanisms underlying these functions are similar. This was termed the causal/

functional asymmetry. Recall that pigs metabolize phenol through glucuronidation, whereas cats metabolize the same substance through conjugation with sulfate. Moreover, although antibody probes have been used to identify human counterparts to rat liver cytochromes P-450, Sipes and Gandolfi caution:

> It should be emphasized, however, that the function of structurally related cytochromes P-450 is not always conserved across species lines and that the same function may be served by structurally unrelated cytochromes P-450. Therefore, an antibody to a rat liver cytochrome P-450 responsible for a particular reaction in that species may not recognize the cytochrome P-450 responsible for the same reaction in humans (1993: 95).

So notwithstanding conservative evolution, we can see the causal/functional asymmetry even in enzymatic metabolism. In short, researchers who assume, without further supporting evidence, that similar metabolic functions are achieved by similar causal mechanisms, commit the *modeler's functional fallacy*.

Toxicologists are aware of many of these difficulties. As Feron *et al.* explain, they try to find other ways to accommodate species differences.

> Quantitative extrapolation involves two steps: a first step to adjust for differences in body size between laboratory animals and man, and a second step that involves the application of a safety factor to compensate for: (a) uncertainties and observational errors inherent in toxicity data; and (b) inter- and intra-species variation in biological sensitivity (1990: 784).

These safety factors are also thought to accommodate environmental variations (laboratory conditions, including food and bedding, etc.). The aim of adding safety factors is to ensure that any humans exposed to the allowable level of the substances do not suffer adverse effects.

However, as Feron *et al.* point out: "The size of the safety factor may vary widely, for example between 2 and 100 or more. The more relevant the available toxicity data are, the smaller the safety factor can be" (1990: 785). The problem, of course, is that relevance can be established only by correlating human and animal data. To the extent that these correlations are unknown, then the safety factors have to be higher. Feron *et al.* continue:

149

all of these considerations do not alter the fact that the size of the safety factor is arbitrarily set and should be established by experienced toxicologists after having studied all the available data and after having considered all uncertainties. Because establishing a safety factor is a question of "turning the matter over in one's mind", and independent experts acting "à titre personnel" have a social background too, it is imperative to publish the way in which a guideline ... has been deduced from the toxicity data (1990: 786).

Thus, in the absence of human data, the safety factor can at most be an educated guess. Though that is exactly what Feron *et al.* claim we should do – make an educated guess – they are forthright about the problems facing toxicologists. For example, in discussing tests for mutagenicity, they note: "Available methods for estimating the risk to humans of exposure to mutagens are still so full of uncertainties that for the time being no method can be recommended" (1990: 787).

A DIFFERENT MODEL: RECONCEPTUALIZING THE PHENOMENA

The previous analysis shows that the conditions for successful analogical arguments (on the classical model) are satisfied: the general mechanisms of toxicity are nearly identical in humans and non-human animals. Therefore, we should expect to find that humans and non-human animals respond to xenobiotics in roughly similar ways. That, however, is not what we find. Different species often react substantially differently to these chemicals, and these differences cannot be explained by scaling formulae. These experimental results are inexplicable on the model of classical analogical reasoning.

Classical analogical reasoning assumes that biological systems are *simple systems.* What we need is a different way to understand analogical reasoning in the biological sciences. As we mentioned in Chapter 6, where the *complexity* of biological systems was highlighted, the most promising theoretical tools for understanding these phenomena appear to be provided by *dynamical systems theory.* To help elucidate the theory, we shall first begin by explaining the differences between *simple* and *complex* systems.

Simple systems versus complex systems

Casti (1994: 271-2) has suggested that simple systems may be differentiated from complex systems in a number of ways: predictable behavior, few interactions and feedback/feedforward loops, and decomposability.

Predictable behavior

Simple systems behave in ways that can be reliably predicted from knowledge of initial conditions and standard scientific laws. Thus, we can describe the dynamical characteristics of these systems using linear equations. Put differently, simple systems exhibit *stability with respect to initial conditions*; that is, if the initial conditions of two such systems differ only slightly then their further behaviors will likely be similar. Any differences will, at most, be amplified linearly in time. In contrast, two complex systems may behave in radically different ways even when their initial conditions are quite similar.

Few interactions and feedback/feedforward loops

The behavior of simple systems manifests few internal, "self-interactions" among their components (often themselves few in number). As Casti notes:

> simple systems generally consist of very few feedback/feed-forward loops. Loops of this sort enable the system to re-structure, or at least modify, the interaction pattern among its variables, thereby opening up the possibility for a wider range of behaviors (1994: 271).

In contrast, complex systems have internal connections between their component sub-systems. The biochemical synthesis of iso-leucine (an amino acid) illustrates these connections among the components of a complex system. The metabolic conversion of the amino acid threonine, into isoleucine, involves five different reactions. Lehninger *et al.* comment:

> If a cell begins to produce more isoleucine than is needed for protein synthesis, the unused isoleucine accumulates. High concentrations of isoleucine inhibit the catalytic activity of the first enzyme in the pathway, immediately slowing the production of the amino acid. Such feedback keeps the

151

production and utilization of each metabolic intermediate in balance (1993: 13).

This interconnectedness between the components of a dynamical system is best modeled by nonlinear equations. Since systems whose dynamical behavior is described by nonlinear equations are designated nonlinear systems, complex systems are nonlinear systems. As mathematician John Paulos points out:

A nonlinear system is one whose elements ... are not linked in a linear or proportional manner. They are not linked, for example, as they are in a bathroom scale or a thermometer; doubling the magnitude of one part will not double that of another, nor is the output proportional to the input (1995: 23).

Consequently, even small changes at one place in such systems can have significant effects on other parts of the system. Ultimately it can change the behavior of the entire system.

Decomposability

Typically the components of simple systems interact only weakly. Thus, if we eliminate some of these interactions, we will not significantly alter the overall behavior of the system. This explains why we can usually predict the behavior of simple systems if we know a system's initial conditions. For instance, we can predict how a lump of clay will fall once we know its mass, the mass of the Earth, and the distance between them. The internal state of the clay (which we might alter by reshaping it) does not affect the way the clay falls. Moreover, if we remove 50 percent of the clay, thereby eliminating some of the internal molecular bonds, the remaining lump will still fall in a predictable way. Not so for complex systems.

Complex processes, on the other hand, are irreducible. Neglecting any part of the process or severing any of the connections linking its parts usually destroys essential aspects of the system's behavior ... You just can't start slicing up systems of this type into sub-systems without suffering an irretrievable loss of the very information that makes these systems a "system" (Casti 1994: 272).

To state the point dramatically, if we remove an arbitrary 50 percent of a bat, then although it may still fall predictably, its significant behavior as a complex biological system will likely have ceased.

We now see how these differences between simple and complex systems are relevant to both the empirical data and the theoretical expectations. Researchers who predict the biological behavior of humans from findings in laboratory animals, apparently treat biological systems *as if they were simple systems.* That is, they assume when the similarities between systems are many and the differences few, that we can reliably extrapolate the observed behavior of one system to the likely behavior of the other. That is why many toxicologists are not bothered by seeming small violations of condition (3). They assume that if two biological systems are only slightly different, then the systems will react to the same xenobiotics in roughly the same way.

Yet, the evidence suggests that the differences in "adverse effects" between members of different species are common and biomedically significant. The right explanation is that biological systems are not simple systems at all, but are, instead, complex systems with mutually interactive sub-systems. Small changes within complex systems can cause sudden, marked, and unexpected differences in response to stimulation. Hence, even small, seemingly minor, differences *between* complex systems may result in widely divergent reactions to identical stimulation. Thus, for complex systems, where the differences between them are few and the similarities many, there is no expectation, as there was in the context of classical analogical reasoning, that phenomena observed in one such system, will, with a high probability, likely occur in another such system.

The key to understanding this feature of complex systems, as was noted in Chapter 6, is to notice that such systems exhibit dynamical properties that are best described using nonlinear equations. However, it is difficult to explain, with any quantitative precision, the nonlinear nature of the complex, connected, mammalian metabolic system. We do not pretend, in the discussion below, to offer precise nonlinear quantitative analyses of biochemical (metabolic and toxicological) phenomena. Although there is a growing recognition of the nonlinear nature of biological phenomena, theorists can offer only tantalizing hints how such modeling techniques can be applied. As Mayr has pointed out, the biggest gaps in biological knowledge concern complex systems

> with a very high number of interacting components, regulatory mechanisms, and feedbacks. Whenever it is possible to isolate single components and unitary processes from such systems, it is found that they are completely explicable by known chemico-physical laws. What is unknown and unpredictable, however, in most of these cases is the regulation of the interactions of the vast number of components. Nowhere in the inanimate world can one find a system, even a complex system, that has the ordered internal cohesion and coadaptation of even the simplest of biological systems (1986: 57–8).

Nevertheless, an examination of nonlinearity and its dynamical consequences provides a way of *reconceptualizing* the limitations of classical analogical arguments in biology. As should now be apparent, researchers rely on these arguments to justify their claims that findings in one species can be applied, by analogy, to another. Yet we now find that the significance of small (partial) violations of condition (3) is considerably greater if these differences are conceptualized as nonlinear phenomena.

Nonlinearity and dynamical systems theory

Let the set $\{X_i\}$ denote the set of variables characterizing the instantaneous state of a nonlinear dynamical system of interest. Nicolis comments:

> In a physico-chemical system $\{X_i\}$ may denote temperature, hydrodynamic velocity, chemical composition, electric polarization and so forth. In a biological system they may describe the density of cells in a nutrient medium or the electric potential across the membrane of a neuron. One may likewise apply the picture . . . to problems arising outside the domain of strict applicability of the physical sciences. Thus in a human society $\{X_i\}$ may represent populations of workers exerting different kinds of economic activities, the price of goods, and so forth (1989: 330).

We can describe changes in this system over time using an equation of the following general form:

$$[1] \; dX_i/dt = F_i \, (X_1, \ldots, X_n; \lambda_1, \ldots, \lambda_n), \; (i = 1, \ldots, n),$$

in which $\{F_i\}$ is the set of rate laws and the set $\{\lambda_i\}$ is the set of control parameters – representing the state of the system's environment.

Typically functions in the set $\{F_i\}$ characterizing the state of systems are nonlinear functions of the variables $\{X_i\}$. This, according to Nicolis, is rather significant:

> In chemical reactions or in biology it has to do with the ability of certain kinds of molecules to perform autocatalytic or other regulatory functions. And in animal or human populations, nonlinearity may reflect the processes of communication, competition, growth, or information exchange. In short the equations of evolution of all these systems should admit under certain conditions several solutions, since by definition multiplicity of solutions is the most typical feature of a nonlinear equation. Our basic working assumption will be that these solutions represent the various modes of behavior of the underlying system (1989: 330).

Thus, we are likely to find that the complex, connected metabolism in mammals is best described using nonlinear equations. In such metabolic systems, chemical reactions are causally interdependent. And as Lehninger *et al.* point out, biochemical systems are dynamical systems:

> The interplay among the chemical components of a living system is dynamic; changes in one component cause co-ordinating or compensating changes in another, with the result that the whole ensemble displays a character beyond that of the individual constituents (1993: 4).

As Nicolis explains, one interesting feature of nonlinear systems is that dynamical equations can have multiple solutions. This means that one dynamical system may behave differently as the variables representing the environment with which it interacts – its context – are changed: "The mechanism which is at the origin of this diversification is the *instability* of a "reference" state and the subsequent *bifurcation* of new branches of states as the parameters $\lambda_1, \ldots, \lambda_n$ built in the system are varied" (1989: 333). In chemical systems, the existence of multiple solutions is evidenced in different patterns of chemical activity, shown by the same chemical system, when inputs, outputs and other contextual factors are varied (e.g., the different patterns of chemical activity seen in the Belousov–Zhabotinski reaction discussed in Chapter 6).

On this account, two similar, indeed identical, dynamical chemical systems can behave differently if the parameters constraining the dynamics of the systems differ. Or, directly related to the current concerns, two similar metabolic systems may behave differently if the parameters fixing the context of chemical reactions differ. In mammals we observe differing patterns of chemical activity in what are essentially similar biochemical systems. As Caldwell points out:

> Most xenobiotics which undergo metabolism do so by more than one pathway, either involving the same functional group or different regions of the molecule ... it is generally true that all mammalian species have the potential to carry out all of the metabolic options open to a given molecule. However, interspecies variations commonly exist in the relative extents of the various reactions which a compound may undergo (1980: 93).

What is the source of these differences in chemical reactions? What corresponds, biologically, to changes in the parameters governing metabolic systems? Part of the answer is suggested by Lehninger *et al.* in their discussion of the unity of biochemistry:

> Although there is a fundamental unity to life, it is important to recognize at the outset that very few generalizations about living organisms are absolutely correct for every organism under every condition. The range of habitats in which organisms live, from hot springs to arctic tundra, from animal intestines to college dormitories, is matched by a correspondingly wide range of specific biochemical adaptations. These adaptations are integrated within the fundamental chemical framework shared by all organisms (1993: 5).

The intact organism, as shaped by its evolutionary history (including genetic and environmental factors), and its current environmental conditions (including the actions of parasites and pathogens), is the "context" within which biochemical reactions occur. This context will thus reflect factors such as species, strain, nutrition, sex, age, time of day, and disease states, to name but a few.

In short, these will be the parameters governing metabolic

interactions. These will be set not only by the organism's chemical inputs and outputs, but also by its internal structure that determines where a given reaction occurs, and relative extents of competing reactions. As Caldwell notes:

in order to be metabolized *in vivo*, compounds must pass several membranes to reach the metabolizing enzymes, and in only a few cases are only one set of enzymes involved. Although the oxidation of foreign compounds occurs principally (but not exclusively) in the microsomes, as does the hydration of epoxides and glucuronic acid conjugation, many reductases are present in the cytosol, as are the sulfate conjugating enzymes ... Additionally in the whole animal many organs other than the liver can contribute to metabolism, sometimes catalyzing reactions that cannot occur in the liver, e.g., dog kidney can conjugate benzoic acid with glycine while the liver cannot and the gut flora can perform several reactions not carried out by the tissues (1980: 109).

As you may recall, researchers claim that biological phenomena are generally best studied in whole, intact animals. Nowhere is their point better taken than in the study of metabolism. If the evolved biological context is disrupted, as when reactions among purified biochemicals are studied *in vitro*, this will lead to further changes in the parameters governing the reactions, so that the resulting reactions may not reflect biological reality at all. As pointed out by Lehninger *et al.* in a discussion of *in vitro* studies:

Although this approach has been remarkably revealing, it must always be remembered that the inside of a cell is quite different from the inside of a test tube. The "interfering" components eliminated by purification may be critical to the biological function or regulation of the molecule purified. In vitro studies of pure enzymes are commonly done at very low enzyme concentrations in thoroughly stirred aqueous solutions. In the cell, an enzyme is dissolved or suspended in a gel-like cytosol with thousands of other proteins, some of which bind to that enzyme and influence its activity. Within cells some enzymes are parts of multienzyme complexes in which reactants are channeled from one enzyme to another without ever entering the bulk solvent ... In short, a given molecule may function somewhat differently within the cell than it does *in vitro* (1993: 48).

This point is illustrated by enzyme studies, which are often done *in vitro*. Caldwell notes that in such studies researchers found only minor differences in microsomal metabolism of rhesus monkeys, squirrel monkeys, tree shrews, pigs, and rats when applied to model substrates (such as phenol or amphetamine). However, in *in vivo* studies of the same species, we find considerable differences in xenobiotic metabolism:

> Since it is clear from the data quoted previously that enormous differences exist in the fate of foreign compounds in these species *in vivo*, it is important to consider the difficulties in extrapolation from *in vivo* to *in vitro* studies (1980: 109).

In short, the biological context in which biochemical reactions take place is all-important. Organisms are not mere passive vessels in which reactions occur, rather they, along with their evolutionary histories and current environmental circumstances, constrain these reactions in ways that are biomedically significant.

Since species differences in the metabolism of xenobiotics reflect an organism's evolutionary history, then, as we might expect, one particular source of these differences will be the process of phylogenetic compromise. Evolved changes and adaptations in a subsystem of an organism typically require changes and compromises in the sub-systems with which it interacts. However, there are typically many ways (within the limits imposed by developmental constraints) to achieve these compromises. Organisms facing different selection pressures will not necessarily reach the same metabolic compromises. Hence, the process of phylogenetic compromise is likely an important source of difference in evolved species' metabolisms.

Our hypothesis – that metabolic species differences are best described and conceptualized using nonlinear complex systems theory – seems to best accommodate the empirical facts and the theoretical expectations. It better explains these phenomena than does the classical view of analogical reasoning. It suggests that biological systems of different strains or species may respond differently to similar stimuli simply because their metabolic dynamics are different. In fact, what is most relevant are the evolved, nonlinear metabolic dynamics.

Hence, this analysis suggests we should make more efforts to study biological systems using nonlinear, dynamical systems theory. Doing so will provide a powerful way to understand the effects of evolutionary processes. Specifically, viewing biological systems as complex systems explains why we cannot extrapolate findings in laboratory animals to humans. Neubert notes of tests to screen for adverse toxicological effects:

> In a case like this it is of considerable advantage to have a system available as complex as possible, not too distant in biological complexity from the human organism. This, at our present level of scientific knowledge, will certainly be an intact mammalian organism (1990: 193).

In short, Neubert recognizes that complexity is a causally relevant factor in biomedical research using non-human animals.

However, to the extent that mammalian systems are complex nonlinear systems – and the previous arguments suggest they are – then even small internal dynamical differences between such systems undermine the legitimacy of extrapolations from one to the other. Put differently, if these arguments are plausible, then we have good reason to think that the classical model of analogical reasoning is inappropriate in biology. It is not enough for model systems to be complex, they must be similarly complex – not just quantitatively but also qualitatively (i.e., they must have the same kind of complexity). Evolutionary theory predicts, and the evidence appears to support, that there are significant causally relevant disanalogies between species, disanalogies explained by differences in the quantity and quality of complexity of the respective systems.

Consequently, the hope that animal models will be useful CAMs of human biomedical phenomena, in predictive contexts, appears ill-founded. Evidence shows that animal models are not strong CAMs, and further suggests they are not predictively useful when construed as weak models. Nonetheless, some researchers claim animal experimentation is still immensely valuable.

10

EVADING CAUSAL DISANALOGY
It just works

The arguments so far have shown that animal models are often not good CAMs of human biomedical phenomena. Since the proffered rationale for doing biomedical experiments on animals is that they uncover significant causal information about humans, this is a surprising and unfortunate conclusion.

However, as we noted earlier, there is a gap between the stated and the real rationale for animal experimentation. Any number of researchers think animal models need not be either strong or weak CAMs to be scientifically valuable. In fact, some would claim that questions about causal isomorphism, causal disanalogy, etc., are just red herrings, ways of diverting attention from the demonstrated success of animal experimentation. On this view we "just know" animal experimentation works.

"IT JUST WORKS"

Some researchers contend that we know by experience that animals are good models of human biomedical phenomena – even if we don't understand why. All we need know is that the model serves some particular scientific purpose. That, researchers say, we can and often do know.

Katz (1981) suggests a taxonomy based on the purpose or use of the model rather than the degree of isomorphism between the animal model and the human situation. They are used because they are useful – they work! He offers two model types. The *empirical/utilitarian* model (e.g., drug screening) is useful when a theoretical rationale may be offered, but is not needed. *Theoretical* models are used to test specific hypotheses about etiology, mechanism, and so forth. Most models are not pure representatives of either type but have elements of both (Nonneman and Woodruff 1994: 9).

Some defenders of animal research straightforwardly acknowledge that there are clear differences between humans and animal test subjects, but claim the differences in no way undermine the value of animal experiments. For instance, when discussing tests to determine the carcinogenicity of saccharin, Giere says:

> The relevance of animal studies was questioned for two reasons. First, humans are different from rats . . . Second, the amount of saccharin used (5 percent of the rats' diet) was quite large. Some critics calculated the 5 percent of the human diet corresponds to the amount of saccharin in 800 bottles of diet soda. Who drinks 800 bottles of diet soda a day? There is something to these criticisms, but not nearly as much as many critics thought . . .
>
> As for the statement that humans are not rats, that is obviously true. But of the approximately thirty agents known definitely to cause cancer in humans, all of them cause cancer in laboratory rats – in high doses. From this fact it does not necessarily follow that anything causing cancer in rats will also do so in humans. Again, it is difficult to justify basing practical decisions on the assumption that saccharin is an exception. And taking account of differences in dose and body weight, those fourteen cancers in ninety-four rats translate into about 1200 cases of bladder cancer in a population of 200 million people drinking less than one can of diet soda a day (1991: 232–3).

In other words, *we just know* that experiments on rodents work. That is, given our experience with rodent assays, and given that we have no particular reason to think that saccharin is a carcinogen only for rodents, then we can legitimately conclude that the current test results are relevant to humans. As it turns out, Giere's claim is misleading.

According to the International Agency for Research on Cancer (IARC) there are twenty-six (of 60,000) chemicals shown to be carcinogenic in humans. (The list of probable human carcinogens is somewhat longer.) Giere's claim suggests rodent bioassays are a good way of determining cancer risk in humans. However, his claim is misleading because a test's *usefulness* is a function not just of its *sensitivity* (the proportion of human carcinogens that is carcinogenic in rats), but also its *specificity* (the proportion of human non-carcinogens that is non-carcinogenic in rats). Such tests, however, are likely inadequately specific. For instance, in the standard bioassay for carcinogenesis, researchers expose groups of rats and mice (usually about fifty) to maximum tolerated doses (MTDs) of suspect substances for their entire lives. They then examine pathological manifestations in necropsied animals and compare them with control populations. The National Cancer Institute/National Toxicology Program has used this assay to test hundreds of substances. Private corporations have also used these assays to test an unknown number of substances to satisfy FDA or EPA requirements (Salsburg 1983: 63). According to many researchers giving lab animals the maximum tolerated dose skews test results because the source of carcinogenesis at such high doses is simply that the chemicals kill healthy cells, a mechanism which is not operative for humans facing low exposures to these same chemicals (e.g., Ames and Gold 1990a and 1990b). More generally, other researchers have noted that this standard carcinogenesis assay was never validated before use. As Salsburg notes:

> Common scientific prudence would suggest that this assay be tried on a group of known human carcinogens and on a group of supposedly innocuous substances ... before we either (1) believe that it provides some protection for society (sensitivity) or (2) believe it identifies mainly harmful substances (specificity). There is no substitute for such proper validation on any new bioassay. However lacking proper validation prior to its use, we might be able to examine the validity of the assay using the results of 200 or more compounds subjected so far to the bioassay (1983: 63).

The results are not encouraging – even for the list of twenty-six known human carcinogens.

Of the twenty-six known carcinogens, humans are exposed to seven of them by inhalation. Salsburg comments on the sensitivity of these rodent bioassays as follows:

> Most of these compounds have been shown to cause cancer in some animal model. However, many of the successful animal models involve the production of injection site sar-

comas or the use of species other than mice or rats. If we restrict attention to long-term feeding studies with mice or rats, only seven of the 19 human non-inhalation carcinogens (36.8%) have been shown to cause cancer. If we consider long term feeding or inhalation studies and examine all 26, only 12 (46.2%) have been shown to cause cancer in rats or mice after chronic exposure by feeding or inhalation. Thus the lifetime feeding study in mice and rats appears to have less than a 50% probability of finding known human carcinogens. On the basis of probability theory, we would have been better off to toss a coin (1983: 64).

Tossing a coin might be a good idea, since the direct cost of a rodent bioassay is $1 million per chemical tested (Lave *et al.* 1988: 631).

If rodent studies are not particularly sensitive, are they at least specific? As we noted in the previous chapter, specificity may be as low as 0.05 (Lave *et al.* 1988: 631) – rodents have shown carcinogenic responses to nineteen out of twenty probable human non-carcinogens. Evidence proving the limitations of animal tests for carcinogenicity has become so overwhelming that even governmental agencies are beginning to rely more on non-animal-based research methodologies (Brinkley 1993; Vainio *et al.* 1992: 27–39). More than a decade ago Salsburg concluded:

Presently the lifetime feeding study preempts the field. As long as it is considered to be useful in detecting human carcinogens this very expensive and time-consuming procedure will continue to drain the toxicological resources of society. This report questions its usefulness and suggests that it is time to consider alternatives (1983: 66).

However, this procedure is currently part of the governing scientific paradigm. As such, researchers tend to use it without question and often without attempts at further validation. In such circumstances, and when there are relatively few disasters from introducing new chemicals, people get the impression that the procedure "just works." Then, when there are failures, like FIAU discussed earlier, such failures are treated as aberrations.

Are there other ways of cashing out the claim that animal experimentation "just works"? Are there ways of discerning the adequacy of animal experimentation without worrying whether the model is causally analogous to the subject being modeled? Explaining what this could mean is no easy matter. However, some researchers have claimed that purely correlational models would "work" even if the models were not causally analogous with the system they supposedly model.

Parametric relations and correlational models

According to Woodruff and Baisden, animal models will be biomedically useful if they are appropriately correlated with the object they model. Thus, even when these models are causally dissimilar from the human condition they supposedly model, they may be useful, for example, when assessing drugs as candidates for human clinical trials. They note:

> [A] particular behavior, such as activity in an open field, may be changed in a dose-related fashion by drugs that have a recognized clinical effect in psychiatric patients, but the rat behavior may not have any clear relationship to the human psychopathology. This model is not necessarily useful for the study of the cause and progression of the disease or of its pathophysiology. Rather, its validity relates to a consistent parametric relationship between the effect of a drug on this behavioral measure and the clinical efficacy of the same drug (1994: 319).

The following example helps illuminate exactly what this means:

> Because of the known correlation between the clinical effectiveness of commonly used anxiolytics and their ability to inhibit seizures in rats, the dose–response curve for inhibition of pentylenetetrazol seizures in rats is a fairly good predictor of the ability of a newly proposed anxiolytic compound, and this test is widely used as a preclinical screen by pharmaceutical companies (Ibid.: 320).

All that matters scientifically is observed behavior. The investigator is not "forced to make assumptions about the cognitive structure of the rat and to construct intervening variables so as to explain the observed behavior in human clinical terms" (Ibid.: 320). Moreover, the substances do not have to be chemically related: Valium and pentobarbital both inhibit seizures in rats and are both anxiolytics, but they are not chemically related.

164

Woodruff and Baisden introduce four possible criteria for validating animal models in psychopathology (1994: 320):

1 Similarity of inducing conditions.
2 Similarity of behavioral states.
3 Common underlying mechanisms.
4 The dependent variable measured in the model should react to therapeutic intervention in a way that is predictable from the effects of the same intervention when applied to humans.

Models satisfying all four conditions would be similar to CAMs as we have described them. Correlational models, however, are valid if they satisfy condition 4. That is why we think it is best not to see correlational models even as weak models, but rather as models exemplifying the "It Just Works Argument." Researchers using correlational models do not claim that they reveal underlying causal mechanisms. Such models are simply instrumental tools that presumably reveal biologically significant information, even if we know not how. As Woodruff and Baisden explain:

> The symptoms of interest presented in the model do not have to be analogous to those of the human disease. Therefore this type of model may be created without much knowledge concerning the pathology of the endogenous disease being modeled. As suggested above ... the most frequent use of correlative models is as screening devices for new therapeutic treatments (1994: 321).

Drug companies use these models as screening devices to identify drugs with the desired pharmacological properties:

> Newly designed drugs that produce greater effects on the animal model without significant detrimental side effects would then be likely candidates for clinical trials (Ibid.: 319).

In summary, Woodruff and Baisden claim animal models may be valuable even if the model and the object modeled are causally disanalogous. Are they correct? It seems unlikely. Admittedly, researchers may sometimes find a dose-related correlation between the reactions of animal subjects and humans to the same drug. However, from that we should not conclude that drugs that are relatively safe in the animal model will be likewise safe in humans, especially when the drug is not chemically related to previously discovered anxiolytics that also inhibit seizures in rodents. The causal details are all-important.

Correlations and carcinogens

Correlational models are also used to validate rodent carcinogenicity bioassays. Salsburg describes this procedure:

> it is standard practice, when setting up a bioassay, to determine the operating characteristics of the assay. To do this, the bioassay is applied to some compounds that are known to be positive and to others that are known to be negative with respect to the property sought. Error rates are then determined that describe the sensitivity and the specificity of the assay (1983: 63).

Is this, however, a plausible expectation? Suppose scientists knew that rats and humans responded in the same ways to previously tested chemicals 80 percent of the time. Could we then safely infer that if some new chemical were carcinogenic in rats, then there would be an 80 percent likelihood that the same chemical would be carcinogenic in humans? Such an inference would be plausible only if we had reason to think that the sample class tested represented all carcinogens. Under what conditions would that be a reasonable assumption?

Suppose, for the sake of argument, that twenty-four of the thirty chemicals (mentioned by Giere 1991), that are both human and rodent carcinogens, are members of a given chemical class – perhaps they are aromatic amines, for example. Under these circumstances, the most these previous tests could establish is that rats and humans react similarly to this class of chemicals. That is, those findings might suggest that if a previously untested chemical of the same class was discovered to be carcinogenic in rats, then it would likely also be carcinogenic in humans. Perhaps, though, these findings wouldn't even show that. Suppose the new chemical was a member of a class of chemicals several of which had been previously tested in rats and humans, and had been found carcinogenic in both species. The inference from rats to humans would be of predictive value (though hardly a 100 percent guarantee) only if the metabolic (causal) features of both rats and humans that led them to react similarly to other members of this class of chemicals are the same features involved in the metabolism of the new chemical. Otherwise the *questions of relevance* (both ontological and epistemological) raised in Chapter 2 again rear their ugly heads.

In fact, we needn't rely on this theoretical argument. We have overwhelming empirical evidence that even if the drug tested were of the same class, we could not assume that it would react in the same way as other members of that class. First, we know that rodents do not respond similarly to all members of a given chemical class. In tests of sixty-five distinct aromatic amines, rats developed tumors in response to only thirty-five of those chemicals. In tests of thirty-four nitro aromatics and heterocycles, rats developed tumors in response to seventeen. For eighteen Azo compounds, they developed tumors in response to ten of them (Gold *et al.* 1989: 214). In short, even if we know that rats develop tumors when exposed to some members of a chemical class, we do not know that they will respond similarly to all members of that class.

We cannot even assume that animals of a given species will respond similarly to substances with virtually identical chemical structures. For example, benzopyrene-(a) causes cancer at several distinct target sites of several species; whereas benzopyrene-(e) is not carcinogenic at all, although the only difference between the chemicals is the arrangement of their respective benzene rings. Phenobarbital and sodium barbital are liver carcinogens in rats and mice, while closely related amobarbital and barbituric acid are not. The phorbol ester, TPA, turns out to be a mouse skin carcinogen, whereas its analog, phorbol, is not carcinogenic anywhere. Finally, one by-product of the manufacture of TNT, 2,4 dinitrotoluene, is a liver carcinogen in rats and mice, whereas 2,6 dinitrotoluene is not. (We are indebted to Dr Lynn Willis of the Department of Pharmacology and Toxicology at the Indiana University Medical School for these examples.)

We find a similar phenomenon in developmental toxins such as thalidomide. Thalidomide is teratogenic in several species of primate, and certain strains of rabbit. Yet as Schardein notes:

> Several other thalidomide analogues, including WU-334, WU-338, and WU-420 had no teratogenic activity in primates, while a number of substituted isoindolines, quinazolines, and benzisothiazolines were not teratogenic in the rabbit (1985: 233).

In short, some chemicals that are structurally related to thalidomide do not induce the same effects.

Of course, were the chemical not a member of the class in question, we would have no reason to assume that the same causal mechanisms were involved in metabolism (e.g., the same cytochromes P-450); so we would have no reason to think we could legitimately extrapolate the test findings from rats to humans. Findings in test animals will be relevant to humans only if they share relevant metabolic mechanisms, and there are no significant causal disanalogies. If we do not know their mechanisms are similar, then we cannot rationally extrapolate findings in past cases to future cases.

Of course, we have not identified the carcinogenic potential of many chemicals, nor do we know many mechanisms that produce cancer. What we need to know, if general predictive inferences from rats to humans are to be strong, is that the previously tested chemicals are representative of all chemicals to be tested. But think for a moment about what it means to say that the sample class of carcinogens represents all carcinogens. It is to say that the chemicals *cause* similar *effects* in rats and humans. In short, there is no way to avoid it: researchers cannot do without causal knowledge of these biological systems.

Yet, according to Lave *et al.*, the standard rodent carcinogenesis bioassay does not uncover causal mechanisms:

> For almost all of the chemicals tested to date, rodent bioassays have not been cost effective. They give limited and uncertain information on carcinogenicity, generally give no indication of mechanism of action, and require years to complete (1988: 633).

Hence, mere correlational knowledge will not suffice. We have no reason to think that the mechanisms of action in the animal model are causally similar to the mechanisms in humans simply because we find some mathematical correlation between the behavior of these two systems.

Finally, some commentators have claimed that in rodent bioassays for carcinogenicity, the relevant correlations are the results of regulators' fiat and not empirical evidence. As Lave *et al.* argue:

> attributes of carcinogenicity such as potency, route of administration, site of tumour, histopathology, strength of evidence, pharmokinetics and extent of malignancy are ignored in our analysis. This positive-negative simplification and the assump-

tion that any chemical carcinogenic in mammals is carcinogenic in humans, do not reflect the growing sophistication of current mechanistic research in health assessments. But neither the regulatory agencies in the United States nor the IARC use such data in their decisions (1988: 631).

Moreover, according to Lin *et al.* (1996) the "discovered" correlations are often more the results of experimental bias rather than biological fact. Because of this bias "the observed concordance can seriously overestimate true concordance" (p.1).

To relate this discussion to the epistemological problem of relevance, we are justified in thinking the systems are causally similar only to the extent that we have detailed knowledge of the conditions and mechanisms of metabolism *both* in humans and in animal models. Yet toxicologists rarely have this knowledge. In fact, the very purpose of toxicological screening programs is to determine safety without this detailed knowledge.

This problem of relevance creates another dilemma for animal researchers. If we did know (or were reasonably confident) that non-human animals were causally similar to humans, and thus that inferences from one to the other had a high likelihood of truth, then we would already have to know a great deal about the mechanisms of human disease – the very mechanisms the non-human CAM are designed to reveal. That is, the very evidence that would justify the belief that animal models are strong CAMs of human systems would be the very evidence that would diminish their usefulness.

History shows "it works": evidence of historical benefits

A somewhat different, albeit related, instrumentalist argument goes like this: surely we just know, from (a) surveys of primary research literature; and from (b) histories of medicine, that the general practice of animal research is a powerful source of biomedically significant information about humans. Often this justification of animal experimentation lurks in the background of all justifications of the practice. Consider, for example, the prima-facie case for research summarized in Chapter 1. That case, as exemplified in the AMA White Paper and the Sigma Xi "Statement of the Use of Animals in Research," rests on claims about the specific historical benefits of animal research. Similar claims can be found elsewhere in the research literature (Smith and Boyd 1991: 25–9; Leader and Stark 1987: 470–4).

The first thing to notice is that this response, even if defensible, does not show that animal models are good CAMs of human conditions. Even if merely reciting historical episodes did show that animal research had been valuable, it would not show that animal models were good CAMs. That is, even if the primary literature did reveal that animal experiments were a vital source of information about humans, the advocates' recounting of them in public policy documents would not enable us to extract the historical role that animal CAMs played from the roles that other uses of animals might have played.

Moreover, surveys of primary research literature are not an effective way of determining the success of animal experimentation. For although it is likely that such sources of information will report some failures of research, they will likely seriously under-report manifest dissimilarities between animals and humans. Some scientists intentionally underreport failures or negative findings. There is mounting evidence that even some "giants" of biomedical science have misreported data that conflicted with their anticipated finding. Louis Pasteur, often identified as *the* paradigm of what a scientist should be, manipulated, suppressed, and even fabricated data to ensure that the "evidence" supported his preconceived notions (Geison 1995).

However, we do not want to suggest that scientists are dishonest. Indeed, we needn't make such an assumption to explain why failures of science are underreported. If a researcher is trying to discover the nature of human hypertension, and conducts a series of experiments on a hamster only to discover that the animal cannot develop hypertension, then the investigator will likely not report the findings – not because he wants to suppress relevant information, but because many other scientists just won't be interested in that information. Even when scientists do report negative findings, other scientists are less likely to read and discuss them – especially if the results do not help explain the negative results. These facts are recognized by researchers:

One of the reasons that many contributors have missed the point is that they have drawn conclusions from published data, which represent only a small sample of the many screening tests performed. Moreover, these represent a biased sample because of the generally greater interest in positive results and the tendency of editors, whether of a sensational newspaper or an erudite journal, to cater to the tastes of their readers. Consequently, lessons gained from the high proportion of negative results and borderline cases that occur in practice are lost, as are also the occasional positive responses which regrettably never see the light of day, for commercial or political reasons (Palmer 1978: 216).

It is true that there is no such thing as a failed experiment, in the sense that we can always learn from good experiments even if the results are negative. Nonetheless, scientists are more likely to publish their positive results, while negative results may be interpreted as experimental failures. That is why positive results, which are consonant with the current paradigm, are more likely to be read and discussed. Therefore, it is misleading to assess the fecundity of the practice of animal experimentation simply by tallying successes – or even ratios of positive results with reported negative results – in the extant research literature.

Documenting the success of animal experimentation by citing standard "histories" of biomedical research is likewise difficult. When historians of medicine discuss the history of some biomedical advance, they typically underreport negative results, even when those experiments appear in the primary research literature. Historians tend to report – or at least highlight – only those events crucial to understanding the current state of the science. Negative experimental results, usually vital to the actual development of science, are often underreported, perhaps, because of their ubiquity.

This is not to question either the accuracy of these historical reports by, or the integrity of, medical historians. Careful studies of the history of medicine can be extremely instructive. The question here is not the accuracy of the facts, but how those facts are interpreted in discussions of the effectiveness and societal benefits of biomedical research. Given the human tendency to rewrite even our personal histories in light of our present beliefs (Ross 1989: 342–4), it would be surprising if medical historians did not write the history in a way that articulates their current understanding of that science. Since the use of non-human animals as CAMs is integral to the current paradigm in the biomedical sciences, we should not be surprised to find that these histories often emphasize the apparent "successes" of the paradigm. This does not show that animal experiments have been useless, but it gives us a further reason to think that it is no simple matter to substantiate their successes. More is required than counting "successes" reported in the literature.

After all, scientists themselves often caution lay people for depending unduly on anecdotes. Most of us will, in less cautious moments, leap to conclusions based on simple anecdotal evidence – either our own or that offered by others. We may hear about someone who reports being cured of liver cancer after taking a regimen of particular vitamins and herbs. Such a report might, in some circumstances, warrant further study. However, this sort of anecdote can never prove that this medicinal mixture cured anything, let alone cancer. The belief that this anecdote constitutes evidence of the curative powers of these herbs would be, in the scientists' eyes, a modern form of alchemy that they would properly deride as decidedly unscientific.

This is not just armchair speculation. Defenders of research used just this argument when trying to justify legislation requiring proper regulation of food and drugs. Eventually what that meant was that all new drugs must be tested on animals before being tried on humans. In a treatise which inspired passage of the bill establishing the Food and Drug Administration in the US, Samuel H. Adams identified the problems of anecdotal evidence:

> The ignorant drug-taker, returning to health from some disease which he has overcome by the natural resistant powers of his body, dips his pen in gratitude and writes his testimonial. The man who dies in spite of the patent medicine – or perhaps because of it – doesn't bear witness to what it did for him. We see recorded only the favorable results: the unfavorable lie silent ... while many of the printed testimonials are geuine enough, they represent not the average evidence, but the most glowing opinions which the nostrum vender can obtain (1906: 4).

Yet when it serves their purposes, the defenders of animal experimentation often resort to just this type of anecdotal evidence to defend the biomedical *status quo*. They act as if anecdotal evidence was a scientifically respectable measure of the success of animal experimentation. However, the recitation of examples and anecdotes can never be a *measure* of success. As the quotation from

Adams suggests, those who try to justify the practice through a simple reading of the historical literature often succumb to two pitfalls. They may be duped by the *shotgun effect* and may also unintentionally commit the *fallacy of selective perception*. Researchers may succumb to the shotgun effect when they cite their past successes as a rationale for the continuance of the practice. The practice of animal experimentation is a multi-billion dollar enterprise. Researchers conduct thousands of experiments annually. Thus, we should not be surprised to find some substantial successes when we survey the practice over several decades. If you fire a shotgun (with thousands of pellets) in the general direction of a target, there is a good chance that several pellets will hit the target.

The researcher then commits the fallacy of selective perception if he counts the hits and ignores the misses. This fallacy is one we all are prone to commit. If there is some view to which we are antecedently committed, we often focus on evidence that supports our view and downplay evidence that conflicts with it. These tendencies are further complicated by two factors. In the *"hard-to-measure-benefits" defense* of animal research, researchers claim it is difficult to judge when a pellet has missed the target, while in the *numbers game*, they offer artificially low estimates of the numbers of animals used in experiments, and thus skew the estimates of the ratio of hits to misses.

The "hard-to-measure-benefits" defense

Researchers do not try to justify their practice in just one way. They deftly move back and forth between a series of defenses of their practice. If objectors challenge, for instance, the "it just works" argument and the argument from "evidence of historical benefits," then defenders of animal research may resort to the "hard-to-measure-benefits" argument. According to this argument, we should not ask for evidence that the practice is efficacious since in all scientific research such evidence is generally not forthcoming. However, this overstates the case. The success of a scientific practice may be difficult to measure, but that does not mean that we should not strive to ascertain its success scientifically. To the extent that researchers cannot measure the benefits of a practice, to that extent, at least, they should not claim to know that the practice is beneficial.

For example, the authors of the Sigma Xi "Statement" caution against hastily estimating the scientific importance and significance of any *particular* experiment involving animals:

> [T]he body of scientific data generally increases by pains-taking research that advances knowledge in small, incremental steps. Many such advances are usually needed to produce significant breakthroughs, and the value and importance of individual experiments are difficult to assess until the entire process has been completed. Therefore, it often is impossible to estimate the value of such experiments soon after they are finished, and thus to consider their worth in relation to any animals that may be used in the work (1992: 76).

At least in the short term, they claim, demanding incontrovertible evidence of the significance and utility of research is inappropriate. Moreover:

> [N]ot only is it difficult to predict the value of results before an experiment is performed, or even immediately afterward, but the ultimate value may be unrecognized for some time. In advance of contributions to a line of research or other applications, we cannot determine with certainty which results will have applications, what these applications may be, or when that application will arise (1992: 76).

The researchers are correct: assessing the value of research in the short term is often difficult. Demanding that every experiment be a success would be silly. After all, by their very nature most scientific experiments fail. However, how can defenders of experimentation square their caution about judging the value of animal experi-mentation with their strong claims about the substantial contribu-tions of such research to human health? Thus, we accept that we must be cautious in evaluating the success – or the failure – of the practice. That helps explain why we think that these public policy advocates should not make exaggerated claims about the benefits of the practice.

In summary, it is one thing to contend that scientific research slowly and incrementally contributes, in unpredictable ways, to human health. It is quite another to mislead the public with empirically unsubstantiated claims of immediate and direct bene-fits to humans.

The numbers game

We can determine the success of animal research only by measuring its benefits relative to its costs. In the previous section we explained why we often have difficulty precisely determining the benefits of animal experimentation. We likewise have difficulty judging at least one of its costs – namely, the number of animals used in those experiments. Animal experimentation is not just science performed for its own sake. It consumes scarce health care resources. Resources spent on animal research are resources that cannot be spent on other forms of research. Thus, although some consumption of experimental subjects may be worth the benefits, a much larger use of animals may not be "worth it."

For instance, we determine the value of a gold mine not only by how much gold we retrieve, but by the ratio of gold to tons of ore mined. If we had boundless resources and wanted gold at any cost, then we may not be especially concerned if this ratio is quite large. If, however, we have scarce resources, we would be immensely concerned if the ratio of gold to waste was large, if we had to mine immense amounts of ore for a minor payoff. So it is crucial to determine, with some precision, the number of animals used in research.

Both sides of the debate recognize the importance of the "numbers" issue. Researchers, for example, go to some effort to explain that they don't "waste" any of these resources. As the AMA explains it:

> Research today involves intense competition for funding; for example, less than 25% of studies proposed to, and approved by, federal agencies each year are actually funded. Therefore, scientists on research evaluation committees are not likely to approve redundant or unnecessary experiments. Also, given the competition for funds, scientists are unlikely to waste valuable time and resources conducting unnecessary or duplicative experiments (1992: 15).

This claim only shows, however, that researchers do not conduct (many) needless experiments. However, it still does not show that the benefits of experiments are worth the costs. We can determine that only after we know the number of animals used in experimentation. About the numbers of animals used, there is considerable disagreement. Those opposed to the practice offer high estimates, while those in favor offer lower estimates. For reasons that will emerge below, there may be no straightforward way to settle the matter.

The AMA estimates that fewer animals are used:

> The number of animals being used in biomedical research is not known. Animal activists place the figure as high as 150 million, but such estimates have no basis in any known data. An authoritative estimate was made by the Office of Technology Assessment (OTA) ... The OTA examined data from both public and private sources and estimated that, for 1982 and 1983, the number of animals used in laboratory experiments in the United States was between 17 and 22 million (1992: 15).

Notice that even the OTA is itself uncertain about the number of animals consumed. The AMA continues:

> Surveys conducted by the Institute of Laboratory Animal Resources of the National Research Council indicate that the number of animals being used may be decreasing. In its 1978 survey, the Institute estimated the total was 20 million, a 40% reduction from the number noted in its 1968 survey (1992: 15).

However, it is difficult to accurately determine the total number of experimental animals used. Rowan *et al.* state that "The statistics on laboratory animal numbers in the United States are crude and relatively unreliable" (1995: i). Why cannot we know exactly how many animals are used in research each year? Surely we could go to the library or some appropriate database and find an answer. However, matters are not so simple. For instance, in 1984, Andrew Rowan estimated that the total number of animals used in research in the US was about 70 million. Yet the Institute for Laboratory Animal Resources (ILAR), quoted by the AMA, claimed only 20 million animals were used. Why the discrepancy? Rowan offers the following suggestions:

> It is not clear why the ILAR survey should produce figures so much lower than other estimates, but one clue comes from the identification of the proportionate value of the research covered by the survey returns, namely $2.2 billion. This is only 25% of the total annual expenditures for biomedical research

programs in the United States. Multiplying the ILAR 1978 survey figures by four gives a total of 80 million animals (1984: 67).

In short, estimating the actual numbers of animals consumed is tough. As Rowan notes, "Probably the best source of information on laboratory animal demand is the major commercial breeder. However, for various reasons, representatives of such companies are not particularly forthcoming on precise numbers" (1984: 69). This is not to say that evidence cannot be gathered. However, it is not a simple observational matter; we must make inferences from the evidence we do have. For instance, Rowan explains how, using information from the Charles River Laboratories – a large breeding facility – we might estimate the number of animals used each year.

> Probably the best information on Charles River's production is found in a stock market analysis (Brown & Sons 1981). The report notes that Charles Rivers produces 22 million animals annually, more than 5 million of which are produced overseas. This would indicate that domestic (i.e., US) output is approximately 16 million animals. The report indicates that that Charles River holds 20% of the total domestic market. Thus, extrapolation would indicate that about 70 million rodents are produced each year for the American market. This would not include rabbits, dogs, cats, frogs, and birds. The first three of these species probably account for about 1 million animals while the last two account for 5 to 10 million animals annually (1984: 70).

Rowan now contends that his original figures are probably off by as many as 20 million animals a year:

> I now believe that my 70 million estimate may have been high (the actual total may have been around 50 million produced and 35–40 million actually used). I am also reasonably certain that animal use has declined ... My estimate is that the decline is around 40% although it may be more (or less) (Private correspondence, quoted with permission).

Minimally the best evidence suggests that the actual number of animals used is empirically underdetermined. Moreover, the best estimates are, in fact, somewhere between the estimates of the AMA and estimates by animal activists. As Rowan explains:

I think the AMA estimate may be low (it may be double that) but it is almost impossible to come up with accurate estimates of total use across the USA. The USDA reports and the ILAR stats only have time-series data on six species (primates, dogs, cats, rabbits, hamsters and guinea pigs) leaving out mice, rats and birds which account for 85% or more of total use in other countries. So we are still reduced to inferences and wild guesses (Private correspondence, quoted with permission).

Since we cannot determine the numbers of animals used with any certainty, that makes it more difficult to judge the scientific success of the practice. As we will explain in Chapter 15, the numbers debate will be especially relevant to an assessment of utilitarian defenses of animal experimentation.

Alternative hypotheses

Some leading biologists are skeptical of the claims that modern medicine has single-handedly caused massive increases in longevity. It is true that average life expectancies have risen dramatically over the last hundred years. Nevertheless, is this – as researchers suggest – the result of modern medicine prolonging the lives of the elderly and sick, or is this – as objectors suggest – largely the result of a massive reduction in infant mortality?

R.C. Lewontin notes that in the last century respiratory diseases were major causes of death.

They died of tuberculosis, of diphtheria, of bronchitis, of pneumonia, and particularly among children they died of measles and the perennial killer, smallpox. As the nineteenth century progressed, the death rate from all these diseases decreased continuously. Smallpox was dealt with by a medical advance, but one that could hardly be claimed by modern scientific medicine, since the smallpox vaccine was discovered in the eighteenth century . . . By the time chemical therapy was introduced for tuberculosis in the earlier part of this century, more than 90 percent of the decrease in the death rate from that disease had already occurred (1991: 43–4).

But what is the cause of falling rates of mortality? As we mentioned in the prima-facie case against animal experimentation, some theorists have hypothesized that improvements in sanitation have played a major role. However, there is some dispute about this. Lewontin continues:

> The progressive reductions in the death rate were not a consequence, for example of modern sanitation, because the diseases that were major killers in the nineteenth century were respiratory and not waterborne. It is unclear whether simple crowding had much to do with the process, since some parts of our cities are quite as crowded as they were in the 1850s. As far as we can tell, the decrease in death rates from the infectious killers of the nineteenth century is a consequence of the general improvement in nutrition and is related to an increase in the real wage. In countries like Brazil today, infant mortality rises and falls with decreases and increases in the minimum wage (1991: 45).

There is certainly some reason to think Lewontin might be correct. Tuberculosis (often drug-resistant strains) has reappeared primarily in our inner cities, among the urban poor – a population notoriously malnourished, and perhaps further weakened by the consequences of drug abuse.

Our best guess is that both sanitation measures *and* improved nutrition and economic well-being have been jointly responsible for the increase in lifespan. For instance, the upswing in government support for biomedical research – especially research using animals – did not begin until after the Second World War. The largest increases occurred after 1970. Yet the overwhelming majority of the increase in lifespan occurred before even the modest increase in expenditures in the early 1950s. For instance, in 1900 an individual had less than a 66 percent chance of reaching the age of 40. By the 1950s, when the increase in biomedical research was just beginning, an individual had a 91 percent chance of reaching the age of 40 – a 60 percent increase in the probability that a person would reach that age. By 1991, the probability had increased to 95 percent – less than a 6 percent increase in the probability that a person would reach the age of 40 (NCHS 1995: 13).

In short, only a relatively small increase in lifespan occurred after the big increase in biomedical research. So, whatever the cause of the decline in mortality, the cause of the decline was not solely or even primarily interventionistic medicine, although medicine has doubtless made some contribution to this decline. Moreover, no doubt some of this contribution from scientific medicine is derived from research on animals. But it would be a gross mistake to claim that scientific medicine (especially that derived from animal research) was a major causal factor in this decline. The decline in death rates is a complex phenomenon with a complex cause, a cause that includes contributions from scientific medicine, to be sure, but also includes social factors.

Overall evaluation of applied research

Researchers claim that non-human animals can be used as CAMs to uncover underlying causal mechanisms of human disease. We disagree. We have argued that animal tests are unreliable as tests to determine the causes and properties of human disease. Available evidence and the theory of evolution lead us to expect that evolved creatures will have different causal mechanisms undergirding similar functional roles. Or, more precisely, we can never know in advance if there are no causal disanalogies. Therefore, we can never be confident that condition (3) is satisfied and direct inferences from animal test subjects to humans will be questionable.

Some researchers will concede our point. However, they will say, the real benefits of animal experimentation come from the use of animals in basic research. Before we can discuss basic research in any detail, however, we must turn to discuss a new development in animal research which has both applied and basic elements: transgenic animals.

11

AVOIDING CAUSAL DISANALOGY
Transgenic animals

Researchers have recently devised methods of designing new test subjects – either by introducing foreign genetic material into natural animals, or by otherwise interfering with their genetic constitution. Most researchers recognize naturally occurring animals are *weak models* of human biomedical conditions. Thus, they have attempted to design animals that will more closely resemble the human subjects they model. To use the language from earlier in the book, models using such animals aim to reduce the extent to which condition (3) is violated. Since strong CAMs do not exist in nature, perhaps they can be created in the laboratory. At the very least, the hope is that humans may improve what nature has provided.

There is some reason to think transgenic animal models, like other modeling techniques, might be useful in basic research. Researchers have expressed the further hope that transgenic animals will also be valuable in applied research as Causal Analogical Models. Because many researchers see transgenic animals as causal substitutes for the elusive panacea species, we may even postulate a *transgenic Krogh principle* underlying such research: for each problem of interest it ought to be possible to create an animal on which the problem can be most conveniently studied. This branch of biotechnology is comparatively new, and, as such, biomedical researchers do not yet know exactly what will come of it. Nonetheless, many researchers think it holds great promise, and is thus worthy of careful consideration. Garattini notes:

> Animal research should actually gain fresh impetus from the new technologies available in the area of genetic engineering. The development of transgenic animals is a powerful tool for

181

reproducing human diseases with more accuracy, allowing the expression or the suppression of enzymes, proteins and hormones characteristic of certain human diseases (1990: 1).

Liggitt and Reddington add:

Twelve years ago the idea that exogenous genetic material could be injected into a pronucleus of an embryo, integrated, retained and expressed in a newborn animal was so novel that it lacked a name. Since then the proof of concept of what has become known as transgenic animals has been fulfilled and the technology has erupted into an extremely active area of investigation with significant and broad potential. As with any new technology, initial investigatory efforts have been predominantly directed toward exploration of the varied techniques, breadth and tolerances of the system rather than applications. Hence, currently there is more promise than proof available that transgenic mice and other species will prove to be useful particularly in the area of drug development/evaluation (1992: 1043).

There is no doubt that transgenic animals give researchers new tools. However, the question is: how relevant are these tools for studying human biomedical phenomena? Many researchers think such tools are highly relevant. They think that by genetically designing research subjects they can avoid the causal disanalogies they acknowledge to exist in natural animals. Whether this is a reasonable expectation can, in the end, only be determined empirically. Nevertheless, it is possible to extend our previous arguments to evaluate the use of transgenic animals as CAMs. Given the evidence to hand, in most contexts (the possible exception is discussed later) transgenic animals will be subject to the same limitations that beset models using natural animals. That is, we have no reason to think such CAMs will be less likely to be susceptible to the causal disanalogies that render natural animal CAMs weak.

USES FOR TRANSGENIC ANIMALS

There are at least three methods for generating transgenic animals: (a) foreign DNA can be directly micro-injected into a pronucleus, (b) retroviruses can be used to infect the host, shuttling in the foreign DNA, or (c) foreign DNA can be introduced into embryonic stem cells, which can then be introduced into blastocysts from foster mothers. These methods are designed (i) to obtain phenotypic manifestations of the foreign DNA, or (ii) to result in the mutation or ablation of genetic material in the host (Liggitt and Reddington 1992: 1046–7).

There are currently several kinds of biological phenomena that transgenic animals might be used to study: (1) the role of genetic factors in the susceptibility to and development of disease; (2) the mechanisms of genotoxicity; (3) the toxic effects of xenobiotics; (4) the mechanisms of evolution; (5) "gene therapies" to replace defective genes; (6) enhancing agricultural output (improved milk production, etc.). They may also be used as (7) "bioreactors" for the production of designer biochemicals or cells (Caldwell 1992; Liggitt and Reddington 1992; Cavener 1992). Since we are primarily interested in the use of transgenic animals as models of human biomedical phenomena, we will focus our attention on issues arising from (1), (2), (3), and (5).

Transgenic models of cystic fibrosis and diabetes

The most promising use of transgenic animals has been as models of diseases caused by single gene defects. One widely discussed case, a case that has established a paradigm for research on transgenic animals, is the development of a transgenic model of cystic fibrosis (CF). CF is an often fatal disease that affects about 1 in 2,500 children of European descent (and about 1 in 100,000 Asians). A specific genetic mutation at a single locus is responsible for the disease. If a child receives two mutant alleles, one from each parent, then that child will develop CF.

To generate a mouse model of CF, researchers do not inject foreign DNA into the mouse genome; rather, researchers "create" a mouse with a defective, nonfunctional, cystic fibrosis transmembrane conductance regulator (CFTR) gene. The result, according to Singleton *et al.*, is an excellent model of human CF.

This experiment is significant because mice that are homozygous for the mutant CFTR gene exhibit many cystic fibrosis symptoms found in humans. These symptoms include a general failure to thrive, glandular alterations, and obstructions of glandular secretion ability . . . The inescapable con-

183

clusion of the experiment is that CFTR (-/-) mice are an excellent model system to mimic cystic fibrosis in humans (1994: S6).

Since there are similarities in the condition in humans and mice, researchers rightly contend that by tests on mice, they can form hypotheses about the causes and course of the disease in humans. Thus, the CF mouse model may be promising in basic research.

Since CF is a monogenic disease (a disease caused by one gene), it appears this model may also avoid the problems of causal disanalogy which compromise natural animal CAMs. However, even if the CF-mouse model turns out to be a superb way of studying this genetic disease, the model may be successful simply because CF is a monogenic disease. Many genetic illnesses result from epistatic interactions between a multiplicity of genes. Therefore, the success of this model does not show we could successfully use transgenic animals to study polygenic diseases.

Is the model, in fact, helpful in developing therapies for this disease? Merely knowing the genetic origins of a disease does not determine which therapeutic strategies we should try. It does not even show that there is a therapy. Knowing the genetic basis of the disease is necessary, but not sufficient, for the development of therapies.

However, some researchers have tried to use this information to develop *gene therapies*. The idea is this: find the gene responsible for the disease, insert "healthy" versions of that gene into the organism, and hope that these new genes will undo the damage caused by the defective genes. Unfortunately, the therapies developed to date have been less than successful in humans. As Eliot Marshall explained in a Special News Report in *Science*:

> Already, researchers have transferred a working gene (known as CFTR) into the surface airway cells of lab animals. This success has inspired 11 human trials. But any expectation that these tests would quickly demonstrate therapeutic benefits has dwindled as researchers have run into problems in transferring sufficient quantities of the CFTR gene into patients' cells. In addition, the virus vector they are using as the transfer agent has provoked an immune reaction in some patients (1995: 1052).

It does not follow from this current state of affairs that new transference techniques cannot be developed, or that other therapeutic strategies cannot be devised. However, the CF case reminds us that simply knowing the genetic causes of CF does not mean we can straightforwardly cure the disease. If this information leads to a cure, it will likely be in a much more circuitous way than some researchers, and the media, have led the public to believe.

Moreover, researchers using transgenic mice will face the same obstacles developing and testing drugs for CF patients as they faced using natural mice. Since we have no good reason to think that the causal disanalogies between natural mice and men will miraculously disappear once we use transgenic mice, then we cannot be confident, prior to tests on humans, that humans and designer animals will respond similarly to the same drugs. The nature of the developed organism, and not merely its genes, is what is biologically important. Since developmental factors (including which genes are activated, and when) are typically different in humans and animal models, they will likely be a source of causal disanalogies. Transgenic mice are not men writ small. Thus, while the disease in mice may be functionally similar to the disease in humans, we cannot conclude that mice and humans will have similar causal and systemic properties, so that drug therapies that are efficacious in mice will also be efficacious in humans.

Consider, for example, the search for transgenic models of human insulin-dependent diabetes mellitus (IDDM). The disease in humans has both genetic and epigenetic causes. Some researchers have hypothesized that genetic defects in the major histocompatibility complex (MHC) predispose human subjects to develop IDDM. Specifically, researchers hypothesized that faulty expression of class II antigens contributes to the development of diabetes.

They used two types of transgenic mice. The first type of mouse expressed the antigens directly using an MHC class II structural gene; the second type expressed the antigens indirectly using an interferon-gamma structural gene (Liggitt and Reddington 1992: 1048; Rossini et al. 1990: 217). However, as Rossini et al. note:

> In all cases IDDM developed as a result of depletion of pancreatic beta cells. In the case of IFN-γ, cell depletion was associated with an inflammatory process. None of these models created a pathology phenocopy of what is thought to be the general progression of the disease in human diabetes, although each recapitulated part of the damage noted. No

185

lymphocytic infiltration was observed in histological sections of the pancreas from transgenic mice, indicating that islet destruction was not immuno-mediated and therefore that aberrant MHC expression does not directly induce auto-immunity, even though it is sufficient *per se* to cause beta cell destruction (1990: 217).

Here the models fail as CAMs: they do not mimic the causal mechanisms of IDDM in humans. Nonetheless, they may well serve as tools in basic research to provoke new ways of thinking about human conditions of interest. This possibility will be pursued in the next chapter.

Transgenic tumors

Generally, researchers studying carcinogenicity prefer to study spontaneously occurring tumors:

> because, among other reasons, their growth, behavior, location, tissue context and histological diversity are more akin to the clinical situation. Unfortunately, spontaneously occurring tumors, even in susceptible laboratory strains, are of low numbers, of poorly-predictable occurrence and site ... (Liggitt and Reddington 1992: 1047).

Researchers want to find tumor models that are causally similar to tumors in humans. In short, they seek strong CAMS of human tumors.

However, the empirical evidence shows standard carcinogenicity studies, based on natural rodent models, have been less than satisfactory (see Chapter 9). So researchers seeking models not beset by causal disanalogies that plague natural animal models might reasonably assume transgenic animals will do the trick. A common research strategy involves placing oncogenes (cancer-causing genes) in transgenic animals to try to simulate spontaneously occurring tumors.

There is even some reason to think that researchers can produce site-specific tumors, thus avoiding one common criticism of using natural animals (Rossini *et al.* 1990: 215). Yet some researchers urge caution:

> Investigators obviously should exercise caution in unconditionally accepting tumors in transgenic mice as strict

analogues of naturally-occurring tumors ... For instance pancreatic tumors derived from elastase-ras constructs lack features typically associated with malignancy including aneuploidy, invasiveness and metastasis. It is also obvious that factors in addition to oncogene expression are necessary for tumor development (Liggitt and Reddington 1992: 1047).

In short, the hope for transgenic tumor CAMs may be thwarted, since it appears the tumors in these animal models are not causally similar to naturally occurring tumors. In basic research, however, these may be fruitful models despite these causal disanalogies.

Transgenic mice in toxicology

Notwithstanding the previous arguments, some toxicologists think transgenic mice will be a powerful new tool for chemical screening. Scientists can easily create transgenic mice that are very sensitive to specific carcinogens. Here is the description of one such mouse:

These mice are predisposed to develop lymphosarcoma but the spontaneous occurrence of this tumor is only about 10% by 240 days of age. If these mice, on the other hand, are exposed to a single low dose of a chemical carcinogen (ethylnitrosurea; ENU) nearly 100% of the pim-1 transgenics develop tumors *versus* 15% of ENU treated nontransgenics). An obvious implication is that this system, once further characterized and validated, may be useful for the screening of carcinogens in industrial or environmental settings (Liggitt and Reddington 1992: 1047).

It is difficult to see, however, how this will aid the predictive toxicologist. After all, we normally test new chemicals to determine the risk humans might face if exposed to a substance, not to study substances antecedently known to be human carcinogens. It is not enough that these mice be sensitive to xenobiotics; they must also be sensitive to *the same* substances that are carcinogenic in humans. That is, we must know that (a) the transgenic mice are sensitive to the same sorts of chemicals that are harmful to humans; and (b) that they do not elicit positive responses to chemicals that are safe in humans. In fact, one primary concern about standard carcinogenicity tests is that they are already too sensitive. Rats develop cancers when exposed to nineteen out of twenty probable human non-carcinogens (Lave *et al.* 1988: 631). Therefore, developing super-sensitive mice may only exacerbate an already serious problem.

More generally, some toxicologists already realize the difficulties of using transgenic animals predisposed to develop various cancers:

> At this stage of our knowledge, it is difficult to describe a specific strategy, since no one proto-oncogene is probably appropriate for the variety of tissue interactions of most chemicals. Also, proto-oncogenes provide only one component of what appears to be a multi-genic phenomenon. The allelic differences between the mouse strains on which the transgene is carried undoubtedly influence responses to specific chemicals (Griesemer and Tennant 1992: 435).

To make reliable predictions, we would ideally need a mouse with a human metabolism writ small. Merely inserting single genes into mice will not produce a human metabolism dressed up differently. Again it appears that transgenic mice will manifest the same causal differences that compromise studies on natural mice. As Caldwell points out:

> Unfortunately, in applying this technology to toxicology, we are faced with the complexity of metabolic pathways of toxic chemicals and of the toxic responses themselves which means that the current single gene approaches are excessively simplistic for our purposes (1992: 658).

Transgenic AIDS research

Many people are concerned about AIDS. This has prompted massive efforts to identify the causes of and treatments for AIDS. Given the current paradigm, this research must be on animals. So there is a pressing need to find many affordable research subjects. Until now, most models of AIDS have been primate models. However, primates are expensive to maintain, genetically heterogeneous, and in many cases close to extinction. So some researchers have developed transgenic mice that might serve as models of human AIDS. Can these be strong CAMs? As we might expect, researchers find that although these models are, in certain respects, functionally analogous to human AIDS, they are also causally disanalogous in ways that undermine their use as CAMs of human AIDS. As Bentvelzen explains:

Another approach is the production of transgenic mice, which carry HIV provirus in their germ line. Such mice are highly interesting with regard to pathogenesis, but do not provide such a realistic model. Spread of virus is not a prerequisite for the development of an immunodeficiency in such mice. Drugs interfering with "reverse transcriptase" will not work in such mice and vaccination against HIV does not seem possible in transgenic mice (1990: 158).

In short, researchers are already well aware of the causal disanalogies between this model and the human condition. Indeed, they acknowledge that these differences will undermine the usefulness of the model to develop preventive and therapeutic measures. Perhaps researchers can develop other models that can surmount these limitations. However, we see no reason to think that by using transgenic animals researchers can avoid the causal disanalogies that afflict natural animal models.

PROBLEMS WITH USING TRANSGENIC ANIMALS

All the researchers we have discussed are enthusiastic about the prospects of using transgenic animals. Yet we do not know enough about the biology (especially the molecular biology) of transgenic animals, or even of the humans they are supposed to model, to warrant this enthusiasm. We can know that transgenic animals reveal significant information about human biomedical conditions only if we know more details about human and animal-model genetics. However, R.C. Lewontin claims our knowledge of genetics is still slim:

we do not know even in principle all of the functions of the different nucleotides in a gene, or how the specific context in which a nucleotide appears may affect the way in which the cell machinery interprets the DNA; nor do we have any but the most rudimentary understanding of how a whole functioning organism is put together from its protein bits and pieces. Third because there is no single, standard, "normal" DNA sequence that we all share, observed differences between sick and well people cannot, in themselves, reveal the genetic cause of a disorder (1991: 69).

Genetic determinism

The use of transgenic animals is founded on the doctrine of *genetic determinism*. Yet we know enough about genetics to know that genetic determinism is false. According to this doctrine, the nature of an organism (including anatomy, physiology and behavior) is determined or fixed by its genetic constitution. It is not difficult to see how the concept of genetic determinism undergirds transgenic modeling. For example, modelers assume that if they want to study some human biomedical phenomenon, X, they should isolate the relevant gene(s) for X in humans, transplant the gene(s) into a non-human host so that it manifests phenomenon X, which they then study.

Not all transgenic models incorporate fragments of human DNA. In some transgenic models, researchers insert some genetic material (perhaps an oncogene), to "create" an animal with a specific biomedical property; for example, a strong predisposition to develop certain forms of cancer. Nonetheless, these models still reflect the researchers' belief that biomedically significant properties are genetically determined.

However, this view of the role of genes in biomedical disease is simply wrong. As Lewontin argues:

> Unfortunately, it takes more than DNA to make a living organism ... Even the organism does not compute itself from its DNA. A living organism at any moment in its life is the unique consequence of a developmental history that results from the interaction of and determination by internal and external forces. The external forces, what we usually think of as "environment," are themselves partly a consequence of the activities of the organism itself as it produces and consumes the conditions of its own existence. Organisms do not find the world in which they develop. They make it. Reciprocally, the internal forces are not autonomous, but act in response to the external (1991: 63).

The "internal" forces to which Lewontin refers are not simply genetic. Non-genetic, developmental factors also produce individual variation within a species (this explains why even identical twins have different fingerprints). As we noted earlier in the book, these developmental factors will lead to more substantial differences between species. External, environmental factors, including complex evolved relationships with other organisms, including microorganisms, are likewise relevant. Although we know they influence the development of the organism, we cannot determine that influence with any precision. Yet we know all these factors vary from species to species.

Once we understand the complex ways that genes, developmental factors, and the environment interact, we see why genetic determinism is implausible. The organism is not simply an unfolding of a genetic plan. It results, rather, from dialectical "negotiations" between a host of factors, only some of which are genetic. Thus, even if transgenic models mimic some features of human diseases (especially where there is a strong monogenetic determinant), it may miss other epigenetic or environmental features of that disease. New tools are not necessarily relevant tools. As Liggitt and Reddington note:

> However, past "knowing" the structure of the fusion gene that is transferred, the investigator remains at the mercy of the host genome and controlling genetic and epigenetic elements for integration and expression of the novel gene (1992: 1052).

In other words, it is one thing to insert foreign DNA into an organism but another matter altogether to expect that the inserted material will be expressed in the same way as it is in the natural organism from which it was originally extracted.

All this bodes ill for the use of transgenic animals as CAMs. Researchers have assumed transgenic animals would be more genetically similar to humans in relevant respects, and, in virtue of this, that they would also be more causally similar. However, the theoretical arguments offered above and also in Chapter 7 give us reason to doubt that transgenic animals could avoid the causal disanalogies that haunt natural animal models. Transgenic animals, no less than natural animals, are intact biological systems. If the natural animal's intact system differs from human systems, it will still differ after researchers have inserted a fragment of new genetic material. These differences will be especially relevant when the phenomena researchers are studying are systemic phenomena, generated by mutual interactions of interconnected biological subsystems. As Liggitt and Reddington explain it: "Transfer of novel genetic material from one species to another must be undertaken with the understanding that this is happening 'out of context'" (1992: 1052). Nonetheless, perhaps, transgenic animals will serve researchers better in basic research.

12

BASIC RESEARCH

We should distinguish between basic and applied research even though the distinction is not always clear. Although there is a range of cases for which it might be difficult to decide whether the research is primarily applied or basic, there are clear cases of basic research and there are clear cases of applied research. Until now we have focused our attention on clear instances of the latter – where the findings in laboratory animals are thought to be directly relevant to human biomedical phenomena. Now we will discuss basic animal research – where the findings in laboratory animals do not even pretend to be directly applicable to humans, but where those findings are thought to expand our knowledge of biological organisms in ways that may be indirectly applicable to humans, usually in unexpected ways.

THE NATURE OF BASIC RESEARCH

Do our previous criticisms of strong and weak animal models show that basic animal research is not valuable? Not in any straight-forward way. For the existence of causal disanalogies between species in no way affects basic animal research designed to discover the biology of non-human animals. Those engaged in such research do not aim or claim to tell us anything at all about human biomedical phenomena. In fact, in comparing the biology of humans and non-human animals, researchers have often un-covered evidence of causal disanalogies between species.

However, comparative anatomy and physiology is merely one form of basic research. Much basic animal research is intended to be relevant to humans, even if not in the *same way* that applied

193

animal research is. Basic research is thought to be *indirectly* relevant to human biomedical phenomena. That is, in basic animal research, animals do not serve as CAMs – they are not causal test beds to confirm or falsify hypotheses about human biomedical conditions. Animal test subjects are not assumed to be causally similar to humans, and thus experiments on them do not *prove* or *establish* anything about human conditions. Instead, experiments on animals prompt the formation of hypotheses about biomedical phenomena in humans. We call such animal models *hypothetical analog models* (HAMs). This form of basic animal research is sometimes thought to be a primary engine for the advance of human medicine.

> It may seem impractical even to scientists to solve an urgent problem, such as developing treatment for a disease, by pursuing apparently unrelated questions in basic biology or chemistry. Yet it is a fact that throughout the history of medical science the pursuit of basic research has been the most practical and cost-effective route to the development of successful drugs and devices (Kornberg 1995: 1799).

On this view, what is good for basic research generally is likewise good for basic animal research. Animal research may be exceedingly beneficial for humans even if it is not aimed at serving any specific instrumentalist purpose. To understand this role better, we must explore the nature and role of hypothetical analog models.

The role of hypothetical analog models

Hypothetical analog models are exceedingly valuable scientific devices, especially in the context of discovery. As Hempel remarks:

> More important, well-chosen analogues or models may prove useful "in the context of discovery," i.e., they may provide effective heuristic guidance in the search for new explanatory principles. Thus, while an analogical model itself explains nothing, it may suggest extensions of the analogy on which it was originally based (1965: 441).

Hypothetical analog models play a significant role in science, especially in the early stages of a science. HAMs were instrumental in the early inquiries into the structure of DNA. As Giere notes:

> In *The Double Helix*, Watson talks about noticing spiral staircases, and of thinking that the structure of DNA might be like

a spiral staircase. He also had the example of Pauling's α-helix. Here we would say that Watson was using the spiral staircase and the α-helix as analog models for the DNA molecule ... One might also say he was modeling the structure of DNA on that of the α-helix or a spiral staircase (1991: 23).

HAMs likewise played a role in the development of immunological theory. Elie Metchnikoff developed his cellular theory of immunity after observing digestion in the "mobile cells of a transparent starfish larvae." Although the larva cells' causal mechanisms are not at all akin to the causal mechanisms of phagocytic cells (the first line of defense against invading organisms), Metchnikoff exploited their functional analogies to understand the human immune system better (Silverstein 1989: 44).

What makes a scientifically useful HAM?

Scientifically useful HAMs are not merely psychological causes that serendipitously prompt a scientist to make a discovery. For instance, a scientist might form an important hypothesis about the metabolism of phenol after jogging a mile, listening to Beethoven's "Fifth," or drinking a cup of coffee. However, that does not mean jogging, listening to music, or drinking coffee is the same as studying a HAM. There is no particular reason why these activities prompted the scientific insight; nor do we have any reason to think they would prompt important insights by other scientists. These are merely unique psychological causes, not scientific devices. Drinking coffee and studying HAMs are very different types of activity.

HAMs are important scientific devices that help spur fertile hypotheses about biomedical phenomena. A HAM is likely to be valuable if there are demonstrable functional similarities between the model and item modeled. Since there are such similarities between humans and our close biological "relatives," biomedical scientists using HAMs infer that the results of tests in animals will likely prompt *ideas and hypotheses* about how to think about and understand functionally analogous human phenomena.

For example, scientists might observe that pigs metabolize phenol primarily through glucuronidation conjugation reactions, and subsequently hypothesize that humans do likewise. This plausible hypothesis, however, turns out to be false. We discover that humans metabolize only 12 percent of phenol in this way. Other scientists observe that rodents metabolize 45 percent of phenol though conjugation with sulfate and subsequently hypothesize that humans do likewise. When we test this alternative hypothesis in humans, we discover it is closer to the truth: humans metabolize 80 percent of phenol by conjugation with sulfate.

Although only the second hypothesis is (partially) confirmed by the data, both are reasonable predictions from the evidence to hand. For not only do we observe functional similarities between humans and other mammals, the theory of evolution suggests that phylogenetic kin will share many functional properties. That is why mammals, our phylogenetic cousins, are usually the HAMs of choice.

Many researchers think that animal HAMs will provide simpler systems, which, while not intended as causal analogs, nevertheless enable them to get a handle on the problem they are studying. For instance, Forni *et al.* have argued that researchers can profitably study rats with immunogenic tumors:

> In many cases, the data have been obtained using very immunogenic tumors which are, however, rare in nature. These models do not present a realistic picture of human tumors, nor do they seek to do so. Rather, they serve to provide basic information. This is made possible by reducing the complex problem to simpler models in which some features of the situation they reflect are deliberately ignored. The use of highly immunogenic tumors in these studies is fully justified by the fact that currently we still have only a vague idea of the cell mechanisms involved in immune resistance to tumors (1990: 128).

Forni *et al.* rightly argue that these sorts of models, useful as they are in basic research, should not be confused with, or treated as, causal analog models:

> Of course the use of models can be dangerous. Some biological functions that appear to be crucial to a simplified system may lose their importance or take on a different meaning in more complex systems. The fact that it is a model, not the real situation, that is being studied may be forgotten (1990: 128).

In fact, researchers using animals as HAMs may even seek species that are demonstrably different (different in ways that could undermine the use of the models as CAMs). They seek to exploit these differences. In so doing, their choice of an animal is guided by the Krogh principle, which states that while there is no species on which all problems of interest can be studied, for each problem there is a species upon which it can be most conveniently studied. To illustrate this principle, Krebs comments:

> Mammals reabsorb sodium from the glomerular filtrate in the distal renal tubules and the collecting ducts by a complex mechanism which involves the hormone aldosterone. In frogs and toads this function of the mammalian kidney is separated from the kidney and is located in the bladder. Thus sodium transport can be studied separately from other kidney functions by using a sheet of toad bladder separating two compartments ... Crabbe discovered ... that aldosterone acts in the toad bladder in the same way as in the mammalian kidney, promoting sodium reabsorption. Once the characteristics of sodium reabsorption had been established in the toad bladder, and it was known what to look for, the key findings were confirmed for the mammalian kidney (1975: 223–4).

Researchers may further exploit species differences when developing hypotheses about therapeutic strategies. According to Gaetano et al. species differences promote significant basic research into the treatment of thrombosis:

> A few examples will show that species' differences are often more useful than similarities ... It is known for example, that the rat is fairly resistant to atherosclerosis induced by a cholesterol diet while the rabbit develops atherosclerotic lesions in the same experimental conditions. The mechanisms by which rats are protected against atheromatous plaque formation are probably more interesting than those mimicking the human vascular lesion. It is of interest to note that human and rabbit veins produce larger amounts of prostacyclin than the respective arteries, while rat vessels behave in the opposite way. As already mentioned, prostacyclin is a natural powerful antiplatelet and vasodilatory compound. Whether vascular prostacyclin generation is a mechanism protecting individuals against atherosclerosis remains to be

established, but this hypothesis has already stimulated intensive experimental and clinical research (1990: 105).

However, it does no good to develop hypotheses about human biomedical phenomena if the hypotheses cannot be rigorously tested.

Testing the hypothesis

The most direct way to test hypotheses about human biomedical phenomena is to conduct tests *on* humans. That is what clinicians and epidemiologists do. However, as we explained in Chapters 2 and 4, animal researchers are suspicious of human research methods. Such methods, being relatively uncontrolled, are deemed to be of questionable scientific value. For example, Palmer notes the limitations of human studies in teratology:

> Even if ethical considerations were waived and new drugs were tested on pregnant human females, there would be difficulties due to uncertain pedigree, and racial and dietary variations; and as Woollam . . . has mentioned, the human female takes up to 20 years to mature and then produces only one or two young per year (1978: 219).

Since human studies are thought to be of limited experimental value, researchers must use non-human animals, with all their evolved species differences, as CAMs to evaluate hypotheses about human biomedical phenomena. However, as we have argued in previous chapters, we cannot directly extrapolate findings in non-human animal CAMs to humans. After all, there are evolved biomedically significant differences between species. When discussing the implications of evolved uniqueness, Mayr comments:

> It explains the almost incomprehensible diversity of the living world. It explains why in the course of evolution so often different organisms adopt different pathways to achieve the same adaptation. It explains why the response to a selection pressure is only probabilistic. Indeed, it is one of the reasons why predictions in biology are so often impossible (1986: 56).

The main point here is that animal CAMs are not reliable devices for testing hypotheses about human phenomena. And, if the researchers are correct, human clinical and epidemiological studies are also inadequate tests of these hypotheses. In short, both available methods for testing hypotheses derived from animal HAMs appear to be scientifically flawed. Consequently, if hypotheses derived from animal HAMs are relevant to humans, they will be only indirectly relevant.

The role of basic research

Although public policy advocates often speak as if animal models were CAMs, when we carefully examine the history of those cases standardly offered as proving the enormous benefits of animal experimentation (polio research, diabetes research, etc.), we see that most often, animals were used as HAMs not CAMs. That is to say, any benefits associated with these experiments arise indirectly from their having prompted insights and hypotheses that ultimately led to new understanding of, or treatments for, human disease. Nevertheless, there is a big difference between an animal model being a good source of hypotheses and its being a good means to test hypotheses. The case of the war against polio illustrates this point.

In Chapter 8, we explained some ways in which animal CAMs had misled polio researchers. However, animal HAMs may have played a more positive role. Experiments on chimpanzees prompted new ways of looking at the pathogenesis of poliomyelitis. Specifically, this research supported the earlier clinical data by properly focusing attention on the alimentary tract (Paul 1971: 451). By prompting a different account of the pathogenesis of polio, these findings helped clinicians who were becoming increasingly disenchanted with the paradigm-guiding rhesus monkey CAM. To this extent, animal HAMs helped correct some errors derived from animal CAMs.

It appears other animal HAMs also played a contributory role in understanding polio. In 1934, Theiler isolated a virus (TO) which caused paralysis in mice. This virus was not pathogenic for rhesus monkeys, nor did it have any immunological relationship to human polio. Nevertheless, some experimenters claimed that findings in mice infected with TO inspired new ways of thinking about human polio. Other researchers claimed to gain new insights when, in 1948, Dalldorf and Sickles isolated a new member of the Coxsackie family of viruses, a virus that induced paralysis in mice. However, as Paul comments:

Indeed one of the most extraordinary things about the new agent was that the damage responsible for paralysis of the limbs turned out to consist of widespread lesions in the skeletal muscles rather than in the central nervous system. The abnormality was primarily a myositis instead of an encephalomyelitis (1971: 400).

These experiments did not uncover causal information that could be directly extended to humans. Perhaps, though, they did encourage researchers to think about polio in new ways. If so, they were valuable HAMs.

Consequently, while some animal experimentation likely led to a better understanding of polio, the blind faith of leading experimentalists in the "Nasal Hypothesis," supported by the rhesus monkey CAM, substantially hindered that understanding. In short, some types of animal model (HAMs) may be scientifically valuable, while other types of model (CAMs) can be highly misleading. Is there some way to reconceptualize the role of animal experimentation so it can contribute to biomedical discovery without leading researchers to ignore significant clinical findings? We think so.

Many polio researchers failed because they had adopted a Bernardian view of the biomedical sciences. They thought results of animal experiments could be directly applied to human beings. Those holding this view were inclined to ignore or "explain away" conflicting (and relatively uncontrolled) clinical data. For instance, Flexner and his followers rejected the clinical findings that suggested the disease began in the alimentary track. This decision led Flexner astray. As Paul comments:

The experimental path he had elected to follow in later years only led him further and further away from the human disease and deeper into the woods. He had convinced himself that the virus was a strictly neurotropic one that entered the body via the nasal route and proceeded directly to the central nervous system . . . He steadfastly held out against the alimentary tract as the portal of entry. Remarkably enough he was resistant to the idea that polioviruses are actually a family composed of several types with different antigenicity. But more than that he held out doggedly against methods of clinical investigation which included clinical virology – approaches that eventually made possible the unraveling of the whole story (1971: 117–18).

For all of the complaints about the deficiencies of clinical studies, they remain essential to biomedical advancement.

Suppose that researchers had seen animal experiments, not as causal models revealing truths directly applicable to humans, but as HAMs, heuristic devices prompting further lines of inquiry? The nasal hypothesis would have been one among many hypotheses – a hypothesis that could have been abandoned in favor of more powerful, more convincing, clinically generated hypotheses. If researchers saw animal experimentation as merely one avenue to biomedical *discovery*, rather than as the experimentalists' "gold standard," providing models which reveal human biomedical *causality*, then they would be less inclined to ignore human clinical data.

We now have a powerful pragmatic reason for distinguishing between HAMs and CAMs. As heuristic devices to generate suggestions about human disease, animal HAMs may be fruitful tools of basic research. HAMs may be useful devices despite causal disanalogies, including differences in complexity. They may even exploit such differences. Thus, animal HAMs may be useful in precisely those circumstances where animal CAMs are undermined.

EVALUATING BASIC RESEARCH

What exactly is the contribution of basic animal research to human health and well-being? This is a complicated issue. We do know this: any benefit will be largely *indirect*. But how indirect? Perhaps it may be very indirect. For example, Lewontin comments:

> Most cures for cancer involve either removing the growing tumor or destroying it with powerful radiation or chemicals. Virtually none of this progress in cancer therapy has occurred because of a deep understanding of the elementary processes of cell growth and development, although nearly all cancer research, above the purely clinical level, is devoted precisely to understanding the most intimate details of cell biology. Medicine remains, despite all the talk of scientific medicine, essentially an empirical process in which one does what works (1991: 5).

One thing is certain, basic animal research, including research in cell biology, gives us detailed biological knowledge of the animal species under study. About these benefits of animal research there is no doubt. Researchers may also use non-human animals as HAMs of human medical conditions. That is, they can use species-specific knowledge of animal systems to pose hypotheses about human biomedical phenomena. So, to assess the biomedical payoff of basic research using non-human animals, we must decide whether the knowledge derived from this species-specific research – and the hypotheses about human biomedical phenomena derived from it – will help us better understand and treat human disease. In determining the contributions of basic animal research to human health and well-being, we must be careful that we do not demand too much – or too little.

We must not demand too much by expecting every individual experiment or even every individual line of inquiry to be fecund. Every successful research program includes failed experiments and failed lines of inquiry. As we pointed out in Chapter 2, that is the nature of science. Therefore, it would be silly to expect every particular line of inquiry to be successful. Rather, we must assess the benefits flowing from the *institutional* practice of basic research using animals.

Neither must we demand too little. It is not enough to establish that a line of inquiry or even an institutional practice is *associated* with beneficial scientific results. For, as we pointed out in the prima-facie case against experimentation, the law now requires certain sorts of animal tests before the release of a new drug or the use of a new surgical technique. Therefore, advocates of animal research can always point to some experiment or other which preceded a given biomedical development.

However, such correlations do not establish that the animal experiments are either directly or indirectly responsible for the advance in human biomedicine. If all we need do to judge that the practice of basic animal research is successful is to find some animal experiments that preceded biomedical advancement, then we would naturally find that the practice is successful. However, that makes the justification of the practice empty. To establish the fecundity of animal experimentation, we must show that the animal experiments caused, and were not merely correlated with, the developments in question. But, as the arguments in Chapter 10 showed, it is not easy to measure the success of the current research paradigm from the primary literature, from reading of the history of biomedicine, or from claims made by advocates of animal research. Moreover, since basic research is not targeted to any particular end, it would be even *more* difficult to assess its historical benefits than it would be to assess applied animal research.

For those who claim that basic animal research is the *best* route to biomedical advancement, even this will not be enough. For them the question is not whether, in fact, animal experimentation caused advances, but whether basic research using animals yields results that are better, all things considered, than the alternatives (cell and tissue studies, computer simulations, human clinical and epidemiological methods, etc.). That question is difficult to answer, since we cannot test the claim until we develop alternative research methods enough to judge their potentials as sources of biomedical discovery. Only then could we meaningfully compare the benefits of these methodologies.

Since basic animal research is not aimed at solving any particular practical problem – although it may ultimately result in hypotheses relevant to such problems – it is hard to know even how we could begin to measure the success of the practice. To avoid this measurement problem, it is often said that such research is of *intrinsic value* (which is a convenient way of avoiding the "payoff" issue). As Arthur Kornberg argued in an editorial in the journal *Science*:

> I think back to 1943 when I was studying rat nutrition at NIH and decided that research was more attractive than the clinical medicine I had chosen as a career. There were no grants then, laboratory resources were meager, and academic jobs were almost nonexistent. Those were not the good old days. But rich or poor, science is great! To frame a question and arrive at an answer that opens a window to yet another question, and to do this in the company of like-minded people with whom one can share the thrill of unanticipated and extended vistas, is what science is all about. That is what will sustain us in the days and years ahead (1995: 1799).

Anyone who has been engaged in genuine scientific research will doubtless share Kornberg's enthusiasm. When one has tasted fruit from the tree of basic research, it is tempting to regard the demand for evidence of success or payoffs as inappropriate, perhaps as manifesting the small-mindedness of accountants and bean counters.

However, that response is dangerous. For many who question the value of basic research using animals do not question the value of basic research in and of itself. Nonetheless, they do wonder if there are other ways of conducting basic research that might be equally fruitful, but without the moral costs associated with animal experimentation. A failure to understand this distinction has often led advocates of basic animal research to accuse their critics of being anti-scientific Luddites. However, the issue is not science versus anti-science. Instead, the question concerns the best way to conduct basic research: should we use intact animal methods, or should we focus more effort and resources on non-animal research methods?

However, although researchers may object to the requirement that they must establish the success of the practice they typically do try to justify basic research by citing examples. These examples are not designed to illustrate points of theory (a legitimate use of examples); they are offered instead as measures of success. Having given several examples of such "successes," Arthur Kornberg comments:

> As scientists we lack the skills to make our case effectively. Universities, research foundations, professional societies, and pharmaceutical companies should band together to organize their resources and employ media professionals to convey to citizens and legislators the essential message that basic research is the lifeline of medicine. If the National Rifle Association can be so effective in delivering its message, why can't we do at least as well with a far better one? (1995: 1799).

As we have seen at various points in this book, attempts to justify the practice of applied or basic animal research ultimately rest on the presentation of a rich bouquet of carefully picked examples. In effect the public, along with their political representatives, are invited to commit the *fallacy of selective perception* (counting successes and ignoring failures) – an invitation also extended to the public, and their political representatives, by the NRA, when they publish anecdotal reports of people who saved their lives or their livelihood because they owned a gun.

Thus we have returned full circle to the relevance of examples, first discussed in Chapter 2. We should not discount the examples offered by either side of this debate. However, bare examples will not establish the effectiveness of the practice of animal experimentation. We must interpret these examples in light of our best biological theory. That theory tells us that we should not expect functional similarity to indicate causal similarity. Moreover, dynamical systems theory tells us that in non-linear systems, of which biological organisms are clear exemplars, even small differences between such systems may have enormous and unpredictable consequences: in these cases, effects of considerable biological significance. However, it is not merely that these are the theoretical expectations. These expectations are compatible with the empirical findings. Indeed, they are *more* compatible with the empirical findings than is the old Bernardian theoretical paradigm.

Therefore, we have strong reason to say that *bare* extrapolations from animals to humans (i.e., extrapolations to humans without concrete information about the human phenomenon) are *always* questionable. Thus, basic research on animals may yield new hypotheses and new ways of conceptualizing some phenomena that might then lead to a better understanding of a human phenomenon of interest. However, if it does so, it will not do so because extrapolating findings in animals to humans is generally reasonable, but because the human and the animal systems are analogous in ways that we had no specific reason to anticipate, or because, although the hypothesis derived from the animal HAM was not confirmed, it nevertheless suggests a better way to conceive the human phenomenon.

Other forms of basic research

If animal models are HAMs that can spur research, then clinical investigations, cell cultures, computer simulations, or epidemiological studies might be equally effective HAMs. After all, HAMs may be useful even if they are causally disanalogous to the human systems they model and even if they are not targeted at any specific practical problem. The glory of basic research is that it may be useful in unexpected ways. As Kornberg notes, some advances in biomedicine have come from these non-animal methodologies:

> Investigations that seemed irrelevant to the attainment of any practical objective have yielded most of the major discoveries in medicine. For example, x-rays were discovered by a physicist observing discharges in vacuum tubes; penicillin was isolated during enzyme studies of bacterial lysis; and genetic engineering and recombinant DNA were developed from the study of reagents used to explore DNA biochemistry (1995: 1799).

Of course these examples do not establish the success of non-animal research methods. However, they do suggest that these methods may be an important source of biomedical discovery. At the very least, these other methods need no longer be construed as poor cousins to basic animal research. Some defenders of animal research might claim that we just know, *a priori*, that these methodologies will now be fecund since they are not intact biological systems. However, the inadequacy of that response should not be apparent. The issue of alternative research methods will be visited again in Chapter 15.

The moral costs of basic research

One matter we should not forget in deciding if basic animal research is better, all things considered, than the alternatives, is the moral cost of the institution of animal experimentation. As we have argued from the beginning of the book, everyone involved in this debate, whether opponents or proponents, biomedical researchers or philosophers, acknowledges that animal experiments exact a moral cost. All sides acknowledge that animals have at least some moral status. We cannot legitimately experiment on them unless the benefits are greater than that cost. As fecund as basic animal research may be, there are important questions and challenges that remain. As Balls notes:

> [B]asic research presents one of the biggest challenges to moderate reformers, since it is at present too easy for biomedical research scientists to use historical record and vague promises of benefit to justify their projects. Often, they are also able to give scant recognition to the concept of replacement alternatives, before stating that none are available for their own work. This is an area where the benefit/science/suffering analysis should be most vigorously applied (1990: 232).

Thus, a crucial question in finally evaluating basic animal research requires that we ascertain the precise moral status of non-human animals. In Part III we explore these questions, before finally returning, in the conclusion, to an overall evaluation of the practice of animal experimentation.

Part III

EVALUATING ANIMAL EXPERIMENTATION: THE MORAL ISSUES

13

THE MORAL DEBATE IN HISTORICAL CONTEXT

Are there limits on how human beings can legitimately treat non-human animals? Or can we treat them just any way we please? As we have seen, researchers talk as if animals had some moral status, as if we cannot treat non-human animals just any way we please. In this, researchers agree with most people that animals are due some moral respect.

How much respect, though, is a matter of considerable debate. If there are limits – as most people suppose – what are they? In particular, how does the moral status of animals morally constrain experimentation on them? Should humans seriously curtail, if not eliminate, their use of non-human animals in experiments designed to benefit us? Before we can answer the questions about the precise nature of the moral respect due animals, we will first try to articulate the rationale for saying non-human animals are due some moral regard.

We begin by asking: are there limits on how we can legitimately treat non-human animals? To appreciate this question fully, contrast it with two different ones: (1) are there limits on how we can legitimately treat inanimate objects? And: (2) are there limits on how we can legitimately treat other human beings? In answering the question about inanimate objects we see that there are some limits. If Paula has a pet rock, then Susan can't justifiably take it away or smash it with a sledge hammer. After all, it is Paula's rock.

Or if there is a rock of unusual beauty or special human interest – say the Old Man of Hoy or Mt Rushmore – it would be at least crude, and probably immoral, for someone to blow it up, to deface it with spray paint, or to chisel out a section for use in a slingshot. These limits though, arise not from any direct concern for the rocks; rather, they are imposed because of the interests and rights of other humans. Susan can't take Paula's rock for the same reason she can't take Paula's Ford: it is Paula's, and Paula has a right to those things that are hers. Moreover, we assume people cannot legitimately destroy or deface items of special natural beauty, because by doing so they are indirectly harming the interests of other humans. So there are limits on what we can legitimately do to inanimate objects, but these limits arise from some human concern. (Actually the situation is more complex than we have suggested. A number of philosophers have argued that there are limits on what humans can legitimately do to inanimate objects, and that those limits are not exhausted by human's interests in them (Taylor 1986). But that position is admittedly controversial, and is largely irrelevant to the present concerns.)

Matters are rather different, though, when we consider the moral constraints on our treatment of other humans. It is inappropriate, from the standpoint of law and morality, to treat a human being in just any way we wish. Susan cannot legitimately steal another human; that would be kidnapping. Nor can she permissibly smash another human's head with a sledgehammer; that would be, depending on the outcome, assault, attempted murder, or murder. The reason Susan cannot do these things has nothing to do with what third parties do or do not want. It concerns the interests and desires of the person she assaults or kills, or from whom she steals. It is wrong for Susan to hit Paula, not because other people like Paula or because other people would be offended, but because Paula is a *person*.

Thus, there is a fundamental contrast between those objects we can treat as we please (unless limited by the interests of other humans), and those we cannot. Ordinary rocks fall into the first camp; humans into the latter. Now the question facing us is: what about ducks and pigs and chimpanzees and rats?

There are reasons to believe that many animals, and certainly other mammals, are more like humans than they are like rocks – after all they are our phylogenetic cousins. They are biologically similar to us in some respects, and thus, perhaps, morally similar as well. To the extent that they are relevantly similar to us, then we have reason to think there are constraints on how we can legitimately treat them, whatever our particular wishes and desires. Of course that, in fact, is what most people already do believe. That is, most of us assume that treating animals just any way we wish is morally illegitimate. For example, most of us believe it is wrong to wantonly kill or torture mammals, merely for entertainment.

To illustrate this presumption, suppose we discovered that some member of our community, say Jones, has a habit of picking up stray dogs or cats and decapitating them with his homemade guillotine; or we learn he has invented a machine that slowly draws and quarters them. He uses these machines because he revels in the animals' pain, because he relishes the sight of their blood. Here we rightly surmise that Jones is immoral. We wouldn't want him to be our president, our friend, our next door neighbor, or our son-in-law.

Our response to this case graphically reveals our sense that there are limits on how we can properly treat non-human animals, and that these limits arise because of the nature of the animals. That is, acts like Jones's are wrong, not merely because other humans are bothered by them: we would think them equally wrong if they were done in secret. We think these acts are wrong because of what they do to the animal. Thus, there is a strong element of contemporary thought that suggests that non-human animals have moral worth, and their worth constrains how we can legitimately treat them.

On the other hand, we are also part of a culture that rather cavalierly uses animals for food, for clothes, for biomedical research, and to determine the safety of household products. Many of these uses inflict considerable pain on animals. Of special interest here is the use of animals in biomedical research. There we use animals in ways in which decent people would never contemplate using humans. How, precisely, can we square our intuitions about the fictional Jones and our widespread use of animals in biomedical experiments?

Although there is an increasing awareness of, and sensitivity to, the cognitive abilities and cognitive complexity of non-human animal life, most people apparently believe that our mental prowess gives us the moral right to use non-human animals as we see fit. Most people think we need grant the animals only some minimal respect. Thus, most people think we can use animals for biomedical research, but would be appalled at someone who neglects their dog, even if the neglected dog receives better treatment than many laboratory animals. To this extent, the contemporary view of animals is arguably schizophrenic.

The contemporary view that sees humans as vastly superior to non-human animals, and as having dominion over them, has its roots in ancient and modern thought. The belief that animals are here for our use is often rooted in theological beliefs about the preeminent place of humans in the world order. The secular expression of the superiority of humans stems from the Greek view that only humans are rational animals. We shall briefly identify some crucial players in that history. This will set the stage for the contemporary moral debate. It will help isolate both the elements of moral thought that have relegated non-human animals to a lower moral status and those elements of morality that are now being used to challenge our current treatment of animals.

A BRIEF LOOK AT THE HISTORY OF THE DEBATE

The ancients

According to the ancient philosophers, both humans and many lower creatures often have similar appetites. We all crave food, water, shelter, sex, and perhaps dominance. However, although humans and animals alike may be "spirited," only human beings are intelligent or rational. That is what distinguishes us from the lower beasts. (Of course these same thinkers also believed many human beings – especially women and slaves – lacked these intellectual abilities. For the Greeks, rationality was not so much the distinguishing characteristic of all humans, but the distinguishing characteristic of free men.)

However, it is not merely that humans are different from non-human animals, these differences have profound moral significance. Just as the appetitive and spirited elements of humans should be ruled by their rational elements, the appetitive and spirited non-human animals should be ruled by their rational superiors, the humans. "When there is such a difference as that between soul and body, or between men and animals . . . the lower sort are by nature slaves, and it is better for them as for all inferiors that they should be under the rule of a master" (Aristotle: *Politics*, ch. 5).

The intellectual offspring of Greek and Christian thought, embodied in Aquinas, merges the Greek emphasis on rationality with the Judeo-Christian view of the spiritual superiority of humans. The result: the belief that humans have "dominion" over animals. According to Aquinas, "by divine providence they ('dumb animals') are intended for man's use in the natural order" (*Summa Contra Gentiles*: ch. CXII).

The moderns

Descartes

Descartes likewise claimed that non-human animals were not rational. But he took the argument a step further: he claimed that higher animals' seemingly complex behavior was nothing more than the outward signs of an inward physical mechanism. Animals, in Descartes' view, lack the vital element that animates humans. After all, he said, "art copies nature." Since humans are capable of making automata which move without thought, "it seems reasonable ... that nature should produce its own automata, much more splendid than artificial ones" (1970: 244).

As mere automata, animals are not merely without thought and volitional movement, they are without feeling as well. All movement in animals "originate[s] from the corporate and mechanical principle ... [This is evidenced in] convulsive movements [as] when the machine of the body moves despite the soul, and sometimes more violently and in a more varied manner than when it is moved by the will" (Ibid.: 243). Thus, what we interpret as pain in an animal is no more than movements and noises generated by nature's machine.

Not surprisingly, Descartes thought those who use animals need not worry about depriving animals of their lives. Nor need they morally consider the animal's pain; after all, animals don't feel pain. There is no way to harm animals; they have no interests that can be harmed. Therefore, we can use animals however we see fit, without any moral qualms whatever.

Early vivisectionists were clearly guided by Cartesian views of animals: they nailed fully conscious dogs to boards and then cut them open so people could see their inner workings. The animals' yelps and cries were interpreted as squeaks in the animal machine. These views of animals, although once taken as gospel, are no longer acceptable to most people, not even to most of those who use animals in biomedical research. Nonetheless, elements of Cartesianism are still embodied in our contemporary view of animals. That is, many people think that although animals have interests, their interests clearly count less than those of humans.

The explanation for why human interests are morally more weighty often stems from the ideas of Immanuel Kant.

Kant

Kant, representing the spirit of the Enlightenment in the eighteenth century, echoed the voice of the ancients: non-human animals are non-rational, and hence demonstrably inferior to humans. However, he added a philosophical twist that helps ground one very common argument used to morally justify our treatment of animals. Most philosophers before Kant thought morality and rationality were closely related. Still, none wedded them in quite the way that Kant did. For Kant, rationality was not merely a tool for discerning morality. In his view, morality only made sense as the dictates of a rational and autonomous agent. Moral rules are those maxims that each autonomous agent could rationally will to be a universal law – those rules that all rational agents would be willing to follow, and expect all others to follow.

Kant's claim is not that people are psychologically disposed to follow rationally determined maxims, but that the very nature of rationality reveals these maxims and demands that we follow them absolutely. These maxims – which exhausted the content of morality – were binding on all and only rational agents. Non-rational creatures could not understand or follow maxims. Such creatures cannot be expected to live according to those maxims. That is why moral maxims, according to Kant, do not and could not concern non-rational creatures. Put simply, non-human animals are just not part of the game of morality. They needn't follow its dictates; consequently, rational agents do not, and could not, have any obligations to them. To use the contemporary language, non-human animals are not members of the moral community.

Nonetheless, Kant did not think we should mistreat animals. This belief, however, had nothing whatever to do with the effect of such treatment on the animals themselves. To use the distinctions from the beginning of this chapter, non-human animals were more like rocks than like humans. Just as we have no direct duties to rocks, we have no direct duties to animals either. Any moral limitations on how we can treat rocks and non-human animals stems from the effects that such treatment might have on humans.

There is, in Kant's view, one important difference between rocks and non-human animals. What we do to rocks has no effect whatever on how we treat humans. However, how we treat non-human animals does affect how we treat humans. "Animal nature has analogies to human nature, and by doing our duties to animals in respect of manifestations of human nature, we indirectly do our duty towards humanity" (1963: 240). That is, we should be kind to animals because if we are, we will more likely be kind to humans; if we are mean to animals, we will more likely be mean to humans.

In short, within Kant we see the two linchpins of current moral thought about animals: (1) the belief that humans are superior to animals because of our intelligence, and (2) the belief that we have some minimal duties toward animals – that we ought, when possible, to promote their welfare. These undergird the contemporary belief that, although we should not be cruel to animals, we can use them for our purposes. Or, to use language that Kant would not especially like: non-human animals have some moral worth; but not very much.

Bentham: a challenge to the orthodoxy

The initial philosophical challenge to the modern view of animals is directly traceable to Jeremy Bentham's eighteenth century defense of utilitarianism. Central to utilitarianism is the principle of equality. That principle states that creatures should be treated similarly unless there is some general and relevant difference between the creatures that morally justifies a difference in treatment. Moreover, in deciding how to act, we should count each creature as one and no more than one.

This formal principle of equality, however, can do little philosophical work until we determine what are morally relevant similarities and differences. For the ancients and the moderns, rationality was the single (or at least the most important) morally relevant feature. They thought that since animals were non-rational, then we could treat them differently than we treat other humans. Many went so far as to say we could use animals however we saw fit.

Bentham challenged the moral orthodoxy. He not only challenged the reigning view of moral principles, but, perhaps more important, he challenged the emphasis moralists had put on a creature's mental abilities. To determine a creature's moral worth, Bentham argues, we should not ask "Can they *reason?* nor Can they *talk?* but Can they *suffer?*" (1989: 26; emphasis his). Having done so, "It may come one day to be recognized, that the number of legs, the villosity of the skin, or the termination of the *os sacrum,* are reasons equally bad for abandoning a sensitive being to the same fate [the caprice of a tormentor]" (Ibid.).

THE CONTEMPORARY DEBATE

Most contemporary philosophers reject the Cartesian and Kantian views of animals. That is, they acknowledge what the opening argument in this chapter tried to establish: that animals have non-negligible moral worth. Nonetheless, many continue to believe that humans can use non-human animals for human ends, e.g., in biomedical experiments. Thus, most would be loathe talking about animals having rights, or perhaps of humans having strong obligations to animals. Nonetheless, almost everyone, including most researchers, will say we have a duty to be concerned for the *welfare* of animals.

Welfarists

On this view, although non-human animals do have moral worth, they do not have rights. As superior creatures, humans must look after animals' interests and try, when possible, to promote their welfare. However, this does not mean we cannot use them for human purposes, particularly if we do our best to ensure that their suffering is kept to a minimum.

Recent laws specifying cage size, procedures for alleviating pain and distress, regulations requiring oversight of laboratory experiments, etc., are not only morally proper, but show the moral sensitivity of most scientists – most scientists desire to promote and protect animal welfare. Once such regulations are in place and in full force, then we will have adequately protected animals' welfare. Once we have protected their welfare, the scientists and apologists conclude, we have done all that is morally required. Thus, most researchers think that if they abide by current guidelines and expectations, they (and we) can use animals for our purposes.

To this extent, the modern researchers' views are relatively in line with the contemporary view of non-human animals. Both views continue to embody important elements of the ancient and Kantian views of animals. In particular, the current view still holds that humans are morally superior because they are mentally superior.

This view gets elaborated in a variety of ways. We will carefully examine two of them.

Fox has formulated a sophisticated philosophical defense of animal experimentation, a defense that displays facility of philosophical argument and familiarity with the relevant scientific literature. The central element of his argument, the idea of a moral community, is clearly Kantian in character and is clearly reflected in the ordinary understanding of our responsibility to animals.

> [The moral community] . . . is a group of beings that shares certain characteristics and whose members are or consider themselves to be bound to observe certain rules of conduct in relation to one another because of their mutual likeness. These rules create what we call obligations and derive in some intimate way from the characteristics which the beings comprising the moral community have in common . . . [T]he beings in question possess certain salient characteristics, are capable of recognizing these in other, similar beings, and acknowledge possession by other beings of the characteristics in question as grounds for following certain rules of conduct toward them (1986: 49).

In this view, morality is reciprocal: only beings capable of *acting morally* can expect other creatures to act morally toward them. Or to use common lingo: liberties imply responsibilities. Since most people think animals are not capable of moral action toward us, then they are not, in this view, properly the beneficiaries of moral action by those who are members of the moral community – namely, human beings. That is, creatures *incapable* of respecting the rights of others cannot be the bearers of rights themselves. Nonetheless, it remains true that we should not treat animals cruelly – to that extent we have duties toward them. However, these are duties of beneficence, not duties that arise because of common membership in a moral community.

A more recent attempt to undermine the claim that animals have significant moral standing is offered by Peter Carruthers in *The Animals Issue*. Carruthers argues, much like Fox and Cohen before him, that animals are not members of the moral community because they cannot choose how to act or be moral. However, he takes this argument a step further and argues, much as Frey does in his early works, that animal experience is not sufficiently like ours for us to give it moral credence:

The fact that a creature has sense organs, and can be observed to display in its behavior sensitivity to the salient features of its surrounding environment, is insufficient to establish that it feels like anything to be that thing. It may be that the experiences of animals are wholly of the non-conscious variety ... If consciousness is like the turning on of a light, then it may be that their lives are nothing but darkness (1992: 171).

It is not only, says Carruthers, that their lives *may* be nothing but darkness, that is likely the case. After all, non-human animals lack a language. Since they do not have a language, then they cannot have second-order beliefs. And,

[I]f it is implausible to ascribe second-order beliefs to birds, mice, or dogs, it is even more unlikely that such creatures might be thinking things unconsciously to themselves ... I assume no one would seriously maintain that dogs, cats, sheep, cattle, pigs, or chickens consciously think things to themselves (let alone that fish and reptiles do). In which case ... the experiences of all these creatures will be of the non-conscious variety (1992: 184).

Since their experience is non-conscious, presumably we cannot harm them in any straightforward way. They will not feel pain as we do; certainly they will not have a sense of themselves as continually existing creatures. Therefore, killing them for our purposes will not deprive them of a life they want to keep.

Liberationists

In *Animal Liberation*, Peter Singer picks up the Benthamite mantle and develops what has become the most widely read, widely cited defense of the moral status of animals. Singer argues that any creature capable of suffering has moral worth. "If a being suffers, there can be no moral justification for refusing to take their suffering into consideration" (1990: 8). Once their suffering is placed on the moral scales, then, says Singer, their suffering counts as much as the suffering of any other creatures, including humans. Since many animals, and certainly mammals that are the preferred test subjects of most biomedical experiments, can suffer, then their interests must be counted right alongside the interests of humans. That is what the principle of equality demands. Singer approvingly echoes the words of an earlier utilitarian, Henry Sidgwick: "The good of any one individual is of no more importance, from the point of view (if I may say so) of the Universe, than the good of any other" (Ibid.: 5).

Admittedly, we may feel some special kinship to our own kind. However, that feeling carries no moral weight. "It is an implication of this principle of equality that our concern for others and our readiness to consider their interests ought not to depend on what they are like or what their abilities might be" (Ibid.). To act otherwise – to treat humans better than non-human animals merely because they are members of our species – is to engage in *speciesism*. And speciesism is every bit as morally objectionable as racism and sexism. Racism, sexism and speciesism all treat certain creatures differently because of some morally irrelevant trait.

Yet our standard treatment of non-human animals, Singer argues, clashes with the principle of equality. That is vividly shown by "the problem of marginal cases." Apologists for the use of animals in research (e.g., Cohen, Fox, and Carruthers) morally distinguish humans from non-human animals by emphasizing that humans are rational, autonomous agents, while animals are not. However, there are marginal humans who are neither rational nor autonomous. How can we square treating them better than non-human animals? As Singer argues:

> [T]here will surely be some non-human animals whose lives, by any standard, are more valuable than the lives of some humans. A chimpanzee, dog, or pig, for instance, will have a higher degree of self-awareness and a greater capacity for meaningful relations with others than a severely retarded infant or someone in a state of advanced senility. So if we base the right to life on these characteristics we must grant to animals a right to life as good as, or better than, such retarded or senile persons (Ibid.: 19).

Defenders of research have offered a variety of responses to the problem of marginal cases. Some claim that even if Singer is right that some animals have mental lives richer than those of marginal humans, that these particular similarities are morally irrelevant. For what is at issue are not the abilities of particular creatures, but the nature of the species of which they are members. As Carl Cohen explains it:

This objection [the problem of marginal cases] . . . mistakenly treats an essential feature of humanity as though it were a screen for sorting humans. The capacity for moral judgment that distinguishes humans from animals is not a test to be administered to humans one by one. Persons who are unable, because of some disability, to perform the full moral functions natural to human beings are certainly not for that reason ejected from the moral community. The issue is one of kind (1986: 866).

Cohen here embraces what might be called *bare speciesism*, the brand of speciesism that Singer attacks. This view holds that the bare difference in species justifies a moral difference in treatment. Other thinkers embrace what we call *indirect speciesism*. This view encapsulates the Greek and Kantian view of animals. That is, what morally distinguishes humans and non-human animals is not species membership *per se*, but the abilities typically associated with members of species. Both forms of speciesist do not think "the problem of marginal cases" is really a problem. For in their views, there are genuine moral differences between humans and non-human animals.

Animal rights

In the public debate, most of those who believe our obligations toward animals are sufficiently strong to seriously restrict how we can treat them are said to believe in animal rights. However, the idea of animal *rights* is, in fact, a recent addition to the philosophical debate. Although Singer occasionally uses the phrase "animal rights," he has made it abundantly clear that, as a consistent utilitarian, he prefers not to speak of animal rights – or of human rights, for that matter. Speaking of *rights* introduces what appears to be a strong anti-utilitarian consideration into moral reasoning: that is, when people normally say that humans have rights, they are claiming that there are some things they cannot do to the right holder even if the action would maximize the greatest happiness for the greatest number.

That is *exactly* what Tom Regan has in mind in *The Case for Animal Rights* (1987). Regan claims non-human animals have sufficiently strong moral standing to have rights. As holders of rights, their interests cannot be sacrificed, even to benefit human beings. In this way, someone who speaks of animals having rights attempts to short-circuit some justifications of our uses of animals, namely, that their use benefits us.

What is Regan's argument? Why does he claim that animals have rights? Regan begins with what virtually all ethical theorists take to be a fundamental moral principle: creatures should be treated the same unless there is some *general* and *relevant* reason that justifies a difference in treatment. This formal principle is universal: it applies to all creatures equally. It thereby rules out discrimination based on irrelevant reasons. Regan then argues that both moral agents (those who are obliged to act morally) and moral patients (those whose interests can be advanced or hindered by the actions of others) can be harmed in similar ways. Therefore they should be treated similarly – at least in those respects in which they are similar. Thus, if cutting off two fingers hurts me, and cutting off two digits of a guinea pig hurts it, then no one should cut off our digits. Or, to use the language of rights, each of us has a right that our digits not be excised to promote someone else's interests. (Obviously this argument parallels Singer's argument for the principle of equality.)

What about other rights, like the right to vote? Most adult human beings have the capacity to vote. In a democracy, the right to vote should be guaranteed by law. A severely retarded adult does not have the mental wherewithal to vote, and thus has no right to vote. Nevertheless, the absence of his/her right to vote does not imply that we can use a retarded human in experiments (because, being retarded, such a person cannot consent), even if such experiments would be exceedingly beneficial to normal humans. Also, a guinea pig does not have the mental capacity to vote; so the guinea pig should not vote. However, as a creature capable of feeling pain, neither should the guinea pig be used in an experiment designed to benefit humans, since the guinea pig cannot consent.

However, the issue is not merely whether animals feel pain. If that were the only issue, then uses of animals that did not cause them pain would be morally legitimate. For Regan all creatures who are subjects of a life have inherent worth. Many non-human animals, as well as humans, are subjects of a life. That is, they have aims, desires, wishes, and beliefs, just as do humans. As such, they have inherent worth and should be afforded the same rights as humans.

Regan distinguishes between the value *of* creatures and the values attainable *by* creatures. Pleasure and the avoidance of pain, for

221

instance, are said to be intrinsically valuable. However, they are not valuable in the abstract. They are valuable only *to* creatures capable of valuing; in particular, to creatures capable of thought, pain, and pleasure. Put differently, creatures capable of having intrinsically valuable experiences are themselves inherently valuable. When seen in this way, the seat of value is in creatures who have the capacity to value. What they value, even if valued in and for itself, is derivative from their being creatures who value it.

Regan argues that any creature capable of *valuing* is inherently valuable. A creature either can or cannot value. If they can value, then they have the same inherent value as any other creature who can value. Doubtless there are myriad differences between creatures who can value: some creatures have greater abilities than others; some use their equal abilities uniquely. Such differences, as important as they might be for some purposes, are morally irrelevant for determining the inherent value of creatures.

For instance, whether one is a "subject of a life" is, like the notion of life itself, all or nothing. That is not to say there are no gray areas, no things about which we are unsure whether they really are alive (are subjects of a life). But it is to say that if we decide they are alive (are subjects of a life), then they are as much alive (as much subjects of a life) as any other living creature (subject of a life). Put differently, simply because creature X has the ability to experience fewer and less varied experiences, we should not infer that creature X has less of an ability. We do not make that assumption for humans. Why should we make it for non-human animals? The problem of marginal cases raises its ugly head again.

No doubt (most) humans have more cognitive abilities than most other animals. However, it is likewise true that not all humans have the same abilities, nor do they use those abilities that are equal, equally. Yet we do not (we hope) think smarter or more artistically inclined humans have more moral worth than their less intelligent and artistically blander brethren. For instance, although Albert Einstein was smarter, and Mother Theresa kinder, than most of us, they have no greater inherent value than do we. *That* is just what we mean when we assert that we are equally deserving of moral respect. Nor do we have greater inherent worth than a retarded person or an uneducated homeless urchin. Inherent value, in this view, is morally all or nothing, we have it or we do not. We do not have it in degrees. It is a function of the kind of creatures we are. In particular, we have it if we are subjects of a life.

Regan thus contends that since humans have powerful rights that limit how others can treat them, even if the treatment would have substantial benefits for those others, then non-human animals have similar rights.

Animals have standing, but less than humans: R.G. Frey

As mentioned above, Frey's early works staked out a position not unlike that later adopted by Carruthers. However, in the past decade, perhaps in response to the liberationists and animal rights advocates, his position has evolved. He continues to maintain that humans can legitimately use non-human animals in research. Yet he does not see this as a categorical right to use animals in any way we wish; nor does he think we can categorically rule out the possibility that we might, in at least some cases, use humans for similar research.

For instance, Frey, unlike Cohen, states explicitly that animals are members of the moral community, and thus, that the claims of apologists that "'anything goes' . . . is too extreme" (1994: 1068).

> Once one allows that animals are part of the moral community, . . . then one's act of inflicting pain and suffering upon them or killing them must be justified . . . In my view pain is pain, as much an evil for an animal as for a human, and I agree with animal liberationists that it is a form of speciesism or discrimination to pretend otherwise (1994: 1068–9).

In short, Frey takes "the charge of speciesism – the attempt to justify different treatment or the attribution of a different value of life, by appeal to species' membership – very seriously" (1987: 196). Nonetheless, Frey is no liberationist. He thinks the use of animals must be justified; he just happens to think some, perhaps most, experiments on animals can, in fact, be justified. For, although morality requires that we consider both the suffering of animals and the deprivation of an animal's life, it is also true that most humans' lives have more value than the lives of non-human animals, and that is what justifies our using animals in research. What gives the human's life more value? The quality of life.

> [T]he value of a life is a function of its quality, its quality of its richness, and its richness of its capacities or scope for

enrichment. A rat has ... a life of some quality or other and is thus of some value. Nonetheless, science and observation tell us that the richness of its life is not comparable to ours precisely because its capacities for enrichment are severely truncated when compared to ours (Frey 1994: 1072).

However, although most humans have a higher quality of life than most rats, we must not assume all humans have a higher quality of life.

[B]ecause some humans lives are drastically below the quality of life of normal (adult) human life, we must face the prospect that the lives of some perfectly healthy animals have a higher quality and greater value than the lives of some humans. And we must face this prospect, with all its implications it may have for the use of these unfortunate humans by others, at least if we continue to justify the use of animals in medical/scientific research by appeal to the lower quality and value of their lives (Ibid.).

Consequently, although Frey thinks there are reasons why we should generally use animals instead of marginal humans, these do not show that experimentation on non-human animals can be categorically distinguished from similar experiments on "marginal" humans. Many supporters of vivisection would find that a most unwelcomed conclusion. As it turns out, that response is what many supporters of animal liberation/animal rights count on. Most believe, as does Frey, that there is no good way to morally distinguish *all* humans from *all* non-human animals. Since they further assume most people will categorically reject non-consensual experiments on all humans (even marginal humans), we should likewise reject the use of all animals in experiments.

THE CENTRAL ISSUES

In order to come to grips with the moral issues there are several empirical and conceptual questions which must be answered. First, we must have some understanding of the nature of animal experience. In particular, we must know if animals feel pain; we must also have some understanding of the nature or character of that pain. That they feel pain of some kind seems uncontroversial, although there are some philosophers who question whether they suffer.

It is perhaps more difficult, though, to discover the cognitive abilities of animals. Do they think? Can they reason? Do they have desires? Can they make choices? Are they capable of following a moral code? Do they have a sense of themselves as an ongoing entity? These issues are more difficult to answer, and are more contentious.

To answer questions about cognition (and perhaps even the sentience) of non-human animals, requires that we answer some conceptual questions about the significance of language. As we mentioned earlier, Frey argues that only creatures with a language can properly be said to have beliefs, and only creatures with beliefs can properly be said to have interests. Carruthers has argued that only creatures with a language can suffer. Since the evidence on the linguistic abilities of non-human animals is limited, and almost exclusively applicable to primates, then we should investigate the precise relevance of language for making plausible ascriptions of sentience and sapience.

Having answered these empirical and conceptual questions, we will also need to have a better sense of the meaning and role of the principle of equality. That will inevitably engage us in debates about the nature and significance of species differences. Discussing species differences will then force us to discuss more carefully the moral significance of marginal cases.

Finally, we must recognize the differences between a utilitarian and rights-based account of the worth of animals. Then we must argue for one or the other view, or we must show how, at least on certain minimal assumptions, their views give similar directives about the moral status of non-human animals. However, we need not answer all these questions to morally evaluate experimentation.

A SNAPSHOT OF OUR VIEW

Virtually everyone now recognizes that many animals, and certainly all mammals, feel pain – even if there is some disagreement about the severity or nature of that pain, Moreover, virtually everyone agrees that we cannot morally ignore that pain: we cannot do just whatever we want to animals, at least if it causes the animal pain.

For instance, everyone understands the locution "Jones tortured his dog." However, such a claim would not just be false but nonsense if dogs did not feel pain. It would make no sense, for example, to say that Jones tortured a rock – not even Paula's pet rock. For rocks have no sense of pain; hence they cannot be tortured. However, many forms of non-human animals can experience pain, and therefore can be tortured. Furthermore, most people assume that the death of non-human animals (at least mammals) is a loss, even if not a particularly weighty moral loss. That is, most people assume that killing a mammal just for fun would be wrong, even if the death were painless. In short, most people assume there are limits on what we can do to animals, and that these are traceable to the effects of our actions on the animal.

This shows that most people, researchers included, believe that non-human animals have some non-negligible moral status. Thus, the use of animals in research has to be morally justified; it cannot merely be assumed. That is, researchers must be able to justify experiments that kill animals; moreover, they must have especially potent justifications for experiments that cause test animals pain.

This is a minimal assumption. But minimal as it is, it is potent. For if experiments on animals are questionable even on these minimal assumptions, then they will be especially vulnerable if some critics of experimentation, like Singer and Regan, are correct. For instance, as we noted earlier, a crucial element of the animal rights/animal liberation view is the emphasis on marginal cases. We happen to think this is a serious problem that cannot be blithely dismissed as so many apologists for research are wont to do. However, as it turns out, the arguments in this book require only the meagerest appeal to the *problem of marginal cases*: we briefly mention the problem to help explain why bare speciesism is indefensible. We do not emphasize that argument because we want our claims to depend only on weak assumptions.

A full resolution of the moral status of animals also seems to depend on whether one is a utilitarian or a deontologist. Although we would not wish to belittle the differences between these ethical perspectives, we intend to show that, given only the minimal assumptions mentioned earlier, there are serious moral objections to animal experimentation on both utilitarian and deontological grounds.

14

SPECIESISM
The deontological defense

Anti-vivisectionists charge that animal experimenters are speciesists: people who unjustly discriminate against members of other species. Until recently, most defenders of experimentation denied the charge. After the publication of "The Case for the Use of Animals in Biomedical Research" in the *New England Journal of Medicine*, experimenters had a more aggressive reply: "I am a speciesist. Speciesism is not merely plausible, it is essential for right conduct" (Cohen 1986: 867). Many researchers now embrace Cohen's response as part of their defense of animal experimentation.

Cohen asserts that both rights and utilitarian arguments against the use of animals in research fail because they "refuse to recognize the moral differences among species" (Ibid.: 868). If we appreciate the profound differences between humans and non-human animals, he says, we would understand why animals do not and could not have rights *and* why animal pain does not have as much moral weight as human pain. Animal liberationists think speciesism is immoral because they mistakenly equate it with racism and sexism. Cohen claims this equation is "unsound," "atrocious," "utterly specious," and "morally offensive." Doubtless Cohen is right that the charge of speciesism is founded on an analogy with racism and sexism. He is mistaken, however, in asserting that the comparison is categorically illicit.

Animal liberationists compare speciesism with racism to focus our attention on the human tendency to unreflectively accept contemporary moral standards. We are fallible. Even our deeply held views may be wrong. Our ancestors forgot (or never knew) this important lesson: many held blacks as slaves, apparently without the slightest moral qualms. Although most of them were not evil

227

people, they indisputably did evil things. We must be leery unless we err in our treatment of animals. Of course, these historical observations do not entail that our treatment of animals is morally unacceptable. It does, however, suggest we should critically examine our treatment of animals, especially when liberationists have offered arguments that are plausible, even if, in the end, people do not find them conclusive.

This is especially sage advice given the close historical connection between speciesism and racism. Historically the two are inextricably intertwined, the former being used to bolster, explain, and justify the latter. According to nineteenth century Harvard biologist Louis Agassiz, the biblical Adam was the Adam only of the Caucasians. Different ancestors explained racial differences (equated with species differences), differences that Agassiz thought indisputable. Additionally, prominent atheist David Hume similarly equated racial differences with species differences, although he justified it in different ways (Gould 1986: 40–1). Of course, it does not follow that contemporary speciesists are racists – or that all forms of speciesism are indefensible. It does show, however, that speciesism and racism are sufficiently similar so that analogies between them cannot be blithely dismissed as category mistakes.

Of course experimenters could argue that there are differences between speciesism and racism – differences that make speciesism morally justified and racism morally objectionable. But that must be shown. To show that the comparison between racism and speciesism is specious, apologists must argue that although we cannot justify treating blacks and whites differently simply because they are members of different races, we *can* justify treating humans and non-human animals differently simply because we are members of different species.

How, though, can that be shown? Humans and non-human animals are biologically distinct. However, the issue is not whether they are different but whether they are different in *morally relevant respects*. Morality requires that we treat like cases alike. A teacher should give equal grades to students who perform equally; the teacher should give unequal grades only if there is some general and relevant reason that justifies the difference in treatment. For instance, it is legitimate to give a better grade to a student who does superior work; it is illegitimate to give her a better grade because she is pretty, wears pink, or is named "Molly."

Hence, to decide if speciesism is morally defensible, we must first determine if species differences are morally relevant. Speciesism, though, comes in either of two forms. The *bare* speciesist claims that the *bare* difference in species is morally relevant. The *indirect* speciesist claims that although bare species differences are not morally relevant, there are morally relevant differences typically associated with differences in species. We can illuminate that distinction by analogy: a *bare* sexist might claim that we should give men certain jobs *because they are men*, while an indirect sexist might contend men should be given certain jobs *because they have certain traits* that distinguish them from women – traits that make them better able to do the job.

BARE SPECIESISM

Are bare biological differences morally relevant? We don't see how. To say we are humans (rather than dogs or ducks) is *just* to say that we are members of a "group or population of animals potentially capable of interbreeding." However, a bare biological divide cannot be morally relevant. That is exactly why racism and sexism are morally indefensible: they assume that a mere biological divide marks an important moral divide. Of course there are differences between the races and the sexes, but so what? The differences are merely biological. Of course, there are differences between the species, but so what?

However, Cohen and other speciesists think species differences are more fundamental than racial and sexual differences. But exactly what this means – and why they think species differences are morally relevant – is not obvious. Why should our "primary" classification (whatever that means) be our species rather than biological class (mammals), biological order (primates), sub-species distinctions (race), or cross-species distinctions (gender)? For some purposes (identifying units of evolutionary selection) species may be considered biologically primary; for other purposes (identifying creatures susceptible to sickle cell anemia) sub-species distinctions may be primary; and for still other purposes (identifying creatures capable of giving birth) cross-species distinctions would be best. Finally, even if we could decide that one and only one of these classifications was *biologically* primary, how would that make this biological divide morally relevant?

Stephen Post offers one answer. He claims speciesism is grounded in "species loyalty" (1993: 294). Species loyalty is "the outgrowth

of millennia of human evolution shaped by natural selection ...
[This] 'kin selection' or 'kin altruism' is deeply ingrained in the
human 'biogram'" (Ibid.: 295). In short, speciesism is morally
justified because favoring one's kin is biologically natural.

To say that such loyalty is natural, however, suggests it is un-
avoidable; something we do instinctively, something we cannot
avoid. However, since some people are non-speciesists, speciesism
cannot be natural in this strong nomological sense. Therefore,
when Post claims favoritism toward kin is "natural," he must mean
something weaker; namely, that biological creatures have a *tendency*
to favor their own species. Finally, he must believe this biological
tendency should be encouraged by morality and law.

Why should we assume, however, that such a tendency (if it
exists) is morally permitted, let alone required? There are other
biological tendencies we think morality should constrain. For
instance, we probably have a tendency to prefer those who look like
us – those who have the same tint of skin and slant of eye. (Perhaps
we think of them as kin?) We also have biological tendencies toward
aggression. Moreover, our hormones sometimes move us to have
sex at inappropriate times. However, we do not encourage, praise,
or morally sanctify these tendencies. Morality should tame these
impulses, not lionize them. Therefore, if some "natural" tendencies are morally permitted while others are prohibited, then the
bare tendency cannot be what is moral (or immoral). In short, we
are not convinced speciesism *is* natural; but even if it were, we see
no reason to believe morality should promote or even permit it.

The deficiencies of bare speciesism can be vividly shown by a bit
of science fiction. Suppose aliens arrive on earth. They are phylogenetically discontinuous with humans. They are not even carbon-
based life-forms. We find them aesthetically repulsive. They look
like giant slugs – and we call them Slugantots. We have no natural
sympathies for them. However, we find their behavior reveals that
they are intelligent, purposive, sentient creatures – although the
exact contours of their abilities elude us because of their peculiar
embodiment.

Post, Cohen, and other speciesists claim that species loyalty gives
us the right to favor humans over them – all other things being
equal. If this is *not* their view, then they are not bare speciesists but
indirect speciesists. That is, they assume that the mere biological
difference does not make a moral difference. We assume, however,
they are bare speciesists. If not, talk of "species loyalty" is not only

out of place, it is unnecessary. (Notice, too, bare speciesism would likewise gives the aliens the right to favor themselves over us. Perhaps experiments on us would help them find a cure for their most dread diseases.) We do not see, however, how our aesthetic dislike for them justifies our favoring a human over a similarly situated Slugantot, just as an affinity for people of like tint does not give Caucasians the moral right to mistreat people of color.

This should not be surprising. After all, moral properties and biological properties are categories from different domains. We cannot merely assume a particular biological property is morally relevant; we must show it is relevant. Even if it were shown, its relevance would be established by referring to moral principles, not brute biological facts. Bare speciesism, like racism and sexism, is simply indefensible. Bare speciesism cannot morally justify either applied or basic research. That is something even defenders of research recognize (Frey 1987, 1994). Of course, there are differences between humans and non-human animals, and these differences may be morally relevant. If they are, then treating humans and non-human animals differently would not be morally wrong. But, neither would it be speciesism. The difference in treatment would be justified not by differences between species, but by citing the morally relevant characteristics of a species' members.

Since bare speciesism is indefensible, defenders of animal experimentation should cease calling themselves speciesists. Yet since some defenders of research insist on calling themselves speciesists we must be charitable and interpret them as advocating indirect speciesism – the view that there are morally relevant differences which accompany species differences. Before we can decide if differences between humans and non-human animals are morally relevant, we must first explore the relationship between moral properties and biological properties. That requires a detour into biological theory.

CAUSAL PROPERTIES, FUNCTIONAL PROPERTIES, AND MORAL PROPERTIES

As we saw in Chapter 6, the biological world exhibits hierarchical, organizational complexity. Emergent biological properties arise from this evolved hierarchical organization. The organization of biological entities and properties at lower levels in the hierarchy produces biological entities and properties at higher levels (macromolecules to cells, cells to tissues, tissues to organs, organs to organisms). The biological properties at each level cannot be inferred by knowing the biological actions at the other, lower levels. As Mayr notes:

> The belief that wholes may be more than the sum of their parts has also been designated *holism*. When first proposed, this had a vitalistic flavor, but the modern emergentist accepts constitutive reduction without reservation, and this fully excludes vitalism. Nor does belief in emergence mean that the organism can be studied only as a whole. On the contrary, every effort must be made to carry the analysis of its components, and of their components, as far as this is possible, always realizing, however, that this will not necessarily explain the emergent qualities of such systems at higher hierarchical levels (1986: 58).

So accepting the existence of emergent properties does not mean that levels in the biological hierarchy are entirely independent. Emergent properties arise only when the lower levels exhibit sufficient complexity. Properties at each level can generally be described in both causal mechanistic terms and in functional terms. Usually we describe and understand action at the lowest biological levels (e.g., the chaining of simple proteins or the shape of antibodies) in causal mechanistic terms, although even here it is possible to talk about evolved functional properties. On the other hand, we typically describe and understand the whole organism in functional terms: in terms of what the creature does and how it responds to external stimuli. We often describe intermediate level biological phenomena in either causal or functional terms, depending on our purposes. For instance, a physiologist might describe the operations of the liver in causal terms (e.g., the precise mechanism by which it removes bilirubin from the albumin) or in functional terms (as purifying the blood). Although these middle level phenomena may be described in either functional or causal mechanistic terms, biomedical scientists are primarily interested in an organism's causal mechanisms – even when these mechanisms could be described, for other purposes, in functional terms. Thus, they are more interested in the liver's mechanisms for purifying blood than in the simple fact that it purifies blood. Only by knowing these causal mechanisms can researchers hope to prevent or cure the disease or condition they are studying. Only then can they tell physicians how to intervene medically.

Of course scientists must identify an organism's functional properties before they can explore underlying mechanisms. For instance, the scientist cannot determine how a fish oxygenates the blood unless it is first known that it can oxygenate the blood. Nor can the scientist understand how the liver purifies the blood until it is known that it does purify the blood. In short, biomedical investigators typically note functional properties and then seek causal mechanisms underlying these biological functions. Indeed, this likely explains why the researchers were prone to commit the modeler's functional fallacy.

Researchers first noted that humans and non-human mammals often achieved similar biological functions. As investigators working under the classical deterministic paradigm, as incorporated into physiology by Claude Bernard, they assumed that similarity of biological function implied similarity of causal mechanism. Consequently, they understandably thought they could safely generalize experimental results in animals to human beings. As we argued in some detail in Chapter 6, this assumption overlooks the inferential gap between an organism's underlying causal mechanisms and its emergent, functional properties.

As we stated it there, there are three major consequences of evolutionary processes for the relationship between structure and function:

Consequence 1: from similarity of biological function we cannot infer similarity of causal mechanism.

Relatedly, we also noted:

Consequence 2: from differences in causal mechanisms we cannot infer differences in functional properties.

However it is also true that two creatures with identical properties at all levels of complexity, subject to identical environmental stimulation, would exhibit identical functional properties. Thus:

Consequence 3: from similar causal mechanisms (and values of causally relevant parameters) we can infer similar functional properties.

These three facts, taken together, yield what we called the *causal/ functional* asymmetry:

233

C/F asymmetry: although we cannot infer similarity of causal properties from similarity of functional properties, we can infer differences in causal properties from differences in functional properties.

This causal/functional asymmetry undergirds our argument that experiments on animals cannot be straightforwardly extrapolated from non-human animals to humans. It helps explain why animal CAMs cannot be strong, and even weak animal CAMs are not directly relevant to human biomedical phenomena. It also helps explain why any benefits of basic research must be indirect benefits which can be judged only by showing that the practice is successful, more successful than alternative methodologies.

The asymmetry likewise gives shape to a moral dilemma for researchers, especially once we understand how moral properties are related to functional and causal properties. What, precisely, is the relationship between biological properties – either causal or functional – and moral properties? Certainly the relationship is not one of direct determination: moral properties cannot be straightforwardly reduced to biological properties. That was the error of bare speciesism.

The relationship is perhaps best viewed as one of supervenience. Properties of type A (moral properties) supervene on properties of type B (biological properties) if any difference in A-properties implies a difference in B-properties, but not necessarily vice versa. For example, consciousness supervenes on the properties of the neural substrate since changes in conscious states imply changes in neural states, but not every change in neural state implies a change in conscious states.

Supervenience is a ubiquitous relationship in biological systems. Biological properties found at lower levels in the hierarchy may not be found at higher levels. Moreover, since systems have emergent biological properties, properties found at higher levels in the hierarchy may be absent from lower levels. So if moral properties supervene on biological properties, on what sorts of biological property do they supervene?

They do not supervene on lower level causal properties: we do not determine if an organism has moral worth by determining its mechanism for removing bilirubin or by discovering the geometric structure of its antibodies. Nor do moral properties supervene on an organism's lower level functional properties – for example, the fact that it has cells capable of microtubule formation. Rather, moral properties supervene on a proper subset of a creature's organism-level functional properties. Of course not all organism-level functional properties are morally relevant. For instance, it might be biologically significant, but not morally significant, if a creature can run 30 miles per hour.

So what organism-level properties are morally relevant? Many people think that sentience – in particular, the organism's ability to feel pain – is morally relevant. A mammal may feel a pain in a limb, but it is the organism, not the limb (or other body part), that feels the pain. We think humans should not be made to feel needless pain *because they suffer*. The moral property (the right not to be made to feed needless pain) is "connected" to the relevant functional property (the ability to feel pain). The exact causal mechanisms of sentience are morally irrelevant. Likewise sapience is a morally relevant property. We think humans deserve moral consideration *because of their cognitive abilities*, which are organism-level functional properties. The exact causal mechanisms of sapience are morally irrelevant.

In summary, what is morally relevant is what an organism does and experiences, not the stuff of which it is made, nor the organization and interaction of its components. This fact becomes especially significant in light of the causal/functional asymmetry. That asymmetry tells us (a) that from similarity in organism-level functional properties (what a creature does) we cannot infer similarity in causal properties, and (b) that from differences in organism-level functional properties we can infer differences in lower level causal properties.

THE DILEMMA

Biomedical researchers offer scientific justifications of animal experimentation: since humans and non-human animals share significant biological properties, experiments on animals can teach us a great deal about human biomedical phenomena. Researchers have also offered moral justifications for experimentation: humans and non-human animals are substantially different in morally relevant respects. At some level these justifications are at odds. Other writers have noted the tension. Rachels, for example, argues that these justifications conflict, at least for psychological research:

The problem may be expressed in the form of a dilemma that can arise for any psychological research that uses animals for the human case. If the animal subjects are not sufficiently like us to produce a model, then the experiments may be pointless (that is why Harlow and Suomi went to such lengths in stressing the similarities between humans and rhesus monkeys). But if the animals are enough like us to provide a model, it may be impossible to justify treating them in ways we would not treat humans. The researchers are caught in a logical trap: in order to defend the usefulness of research they must emphasize the similarities between the animals and the humans, but in order to defend it ethically, they must emphasize the differences. The problem is that one cannot have it both ways (1990: 220).

As a dilemma for psychological research this has considerable plausibility, even in this unqualified form. However, although the dilemma poses some difficulty for all animal research, it is not entirely convincing as it stands. Since moral properties do not supervene directly on lower-level causal biological properties, it is logically possible that humans and non-human animals have (nearly) identical causal properties, yet substantially different moral properties.

Logically possible, but not biologically plausible. The causal/functional asymmetry shows why. Causally isomorphic biological systems, identically stimulated, will have the same organism-level functional properties, while, in partially isomorphic biological systems, similar functional properties may not be supported by similar causal mechanisms. This asymmetry enables us to spell out the dilemma so that it has moral and scientific bite. The dilemma explains why any experimentation which claims to directly benefit humans will be morally questionable, while experimentation which is morally unobjectionable will not likely have any direct benefits to humans.

To justify experimentation morally, the experimenter must identify substantial and significant organism-level *functional differences* between humans and experimental animals, differences that morally justify a difference in treatment. To justify experimentation scientifically the investigator must identify substantial and pervasive *causal similarities* between humans and non-human animals, similarities that justify inductions from animals to humans. But how can the investigator identify enough relevant *functional differences* to morally justify the experiments without finding sufficient *causal dissimilarities* to undercut their direct applicability to humans? Conversely, how can the investigator identify enough relevant *causal similarities* to scientifically justify experiments without finding sufficient *functional similarities* to undercut their moral acceptability? Given the causal/functional asymmetry, it is unlikely that this can be done.

To see more clearly why this is so, let us ask: what are the functional properties that morally justify experiments on non-human animals but not experiments on humans, not even marginal humans? Many lay-people might answer that humans have a soul which non-human animals lack. Yet no sober-minded researcher would be willing to settle important questions of science and public policy by appealing to religious beliefs that many people deny and none can establish scientifically. Perhaps some scientists do think soul is the relevant difference. Nevertheless, they think that the presence (or absence) of a soul can be explained and identified in scientifically respectable terms. Such a view likely collapses into the view that identifies cognitive and emotional abilities as the functional properties morally distinguishing humans from non-human animals. People who hold this view claim that language, the abilities to distinguish truth from falsity and to act morally or enter contracts are traits unique to *Homo sapiens*. As Cohen put it:

> Animals ... lack this capacity for free moral judgement. They are not beings of a kind capable of exercising or responding to moral claims. Animals therefore have no rights, and they can have none (1986: 866).

How, though, do we scientifically explain the presence of these higher moral traits in humans and their absence in animals? The only plausible scientific answer is that humans have an advanced cerebral cortex which non-human animals lack. Fox, for instance, claims human mental superiority is reflected in the "encephalization quotient" (EQ), the ratio of the "brain weight of a species with the brain weight of an average animal of the same approximate body weight ... According to this formula, the actual brain size of humans comes out to six times what should be expected of a typical comparable mammal" (Fox 1986: 38). And, as Jacquette points out:

human intelligence evolved through improvements in brain functioning, by a substantial increase in the number, complexity, and interconnectedness of neurons in the brain's connectionist neural network. Human brains have an estimated 10^{11} neurons, some of which may have as many as 10^5 synaptic connections. By comparison, chimpanzees, our closest living genetic relatives, have only one fourth as many cortical neurons (1994: 130).

There is compelling evidence that there are genuine differences in the cognitive abilities of humans and most non-human animals. Notice, though, that these are differences in quantity, not differences in kind. That is, it is not that non-human mammals lack intelligence and higher mental functioning; they just have less of it. Moreover, there is mounting evidence that the mental lives of non-human animals – especially mammals and birds – are far richer than most people suppose (Griffin 1992; Hoage and Goldman 1986; Bonner 1980), and that, specifically, the gap between humans and other great apes is far less than many people suppose (Cavalieri and Singer 1993). However, since the current question does not require that we determine whether animals have sophisticated mental lives – after all, the dilemma has bite no matter how we finally settle this question – we will assume, for purposes of argument, that humans and non-human animals have dramatically different mental abilities, mental lives.

Is it plausible to believe that cognitive differences (mental complexity, etc.) evolved without any other changes in the animal's biological systems? Are we to believe that whereas humans and only humans have these higher cognitive functions, that all other biological systems – all livers, hearts, neurons, and enzymes – are the same (or causally similar) in humans and non-human animals? Of course not. No plausible evolutionary story makes such an outcome possible or likely. These putative higher-order cognitive differences must both reflect and lead to causal differences in other systems and sub-systems of members of the respective species. To deny this evolutionary claim, researchers must embrace *bio-Cartesianism*.

Bio-Cartesianism

Cartesians claim that the mind and the brain are ontologically separate: they are literally different substances. Having separated the mind and the body, the Cartesians now face a serious problem: how can they get the mind and body back together again; how can two ontologically different substances interact with and influence one other? Animal experimenters have adopted, perhaps unconsciously, a biological counterpart – what we call *bio-Cartesianism*. They assume that the brain, although formed from the same ontological substance as the remainder of the body, developed in ways that neither reflected nor caused alterations in the body and its subsystems. But, of course, such a view makes no more sense for the researcher than its counterpart made for the Cartesian. Indeed, it makes less sense. After all, animal experimenters presumably know that biological sub-systems are tightly interconnected. Therefore, they should know that the process of phylogenetic compromise ensures that changes in the structure and functioning of the brain will require and reflect causal changes elsewhere in the organism. That is, behavioral changes that result from changes in the brain will have further, long-term evolutionary consequences for the organism. Paleontologist Erik Jarvik makes the relationship explicit:

The most prominent feature of man is no doubt his large and elaborate brain. However, this big brain would certainly never have arisen – and what purpose would it have served – if our arm and hand had become specialized as strongly as has, for instance, the foreleg of a horse or the wing of a bird. It is the remarkable fact that it is the primitive condition, inherited from our osteolepiform ancestors ... and retained with relatively small changes in our arm and hand, that has paved the way for the emergence of man. We can say, with some justification, that it was when the basic pattern of our five-fingered hand for some unaccountable reason was laid down in the ancestors of the osteolepiforms that the prerequisite for the origin of man and the human culture arose (quoted in Gould 1993: 65).

The connection between an animal's cognitive abilities and its possession of other biological functional properties has frequently been noted in the literature. Scientists often note that higher cognitive abilities are intricately connected to an organism's overall function.

Thinking has conferred on us a priceless adaptive advantage. Evolutionarily speaking, we are successful because our ability to think has enabled us to remain physically unspecialized. We are the supreme generalists. We prove it by our ability to live anywhere and make our living in a hundred different ways. We don't grow thick coats; we get them from other animals. We don't grow long necks; we invent ladders. We don't have teeth as big as apes do, nor are we as strong, pound for pound. We don't see as well as hawks. We don't run as fast as any large quadruped. But by our wits, and more recently by the devices we make, we can outperform all of them in every way (Edey and Johanson 1989: 383–4).

Or, as Jacquette puts it:

Problem-solving intelligence has survival value in securing habitat, food, and reproductive opportunities. It is certain to be exploited by those naturally gifted with its advantages, appearing first randomly, increasing by increments, and then improved by selective pressures over many generations. We humans are animals, and the most sophisticated minds we know are the minds of animals (1994: 130).

In short, these higher cognitive functional properties arose from the process of natural selection. (How else might they have come about?) This implies that these properties are causally efficacious – animals with these traits were more likely to survive and reproduce. More specifically, differences between species are often associated with differences in specialization and lifestyle, including differences in EQ. These differences are apparent even within closely related primates:

Monkeys are well above average, and apes (especially ourselves) even higher. Within monkeys it turns out that some types have higher EQs than others and that, interestingly, there is some connection with how they make their living: insect-eating and fruit-eating monkeys have bigger brains for their size, than leaf-eating monkeys. It makes some sense to argue that an animal needs less computing power to find leaves, which are abundant all around, than to find fruit, which may have to be searched for, or to catch insects, which take active steps to get away (Ibid.: 189–90).

In summary, differences in mental functioning – differences required to justify animal experimentation morally – must, given a proper understanding of evolution, be differences associated with wider biological differences – causal differences that undermine straightforward inferences from rodents to human beings. As one animal research handbook cautions:

> When selecting non-human primates because of their close relationship to humans, choice of species of non-human primate is important. For example, a completely vegetarian species may not be as useful because of differences in micro-flora of the intestine, which may affect drug metabolism (Mitruka *et al.* 1976: 342).

Biological isolationism

Bio-Cartesianism, the failure to recognize that higher mental functioning reflects and causes other physiological differences in organism, is an instance of a more general belief in *biological isolationism*. Biological isolationism, which denies the strong inter-relationship between biological systems and sub-systems, is related to, and perhaps even derived from, the doctrine of *biological reductionism*. Reductionism, as you may recall from earlier discussions, states that wholes must be understood and analyzed in terms of the properties of their parts. Defenders of animal research often act (and speak) as if biological systems were completely isolable.

For instance, when conducting controlled experiments on non-human animals, many researchers (a) isolate one of the animal's sub-systems and mechanisms, (b) apply stimuli, (c) observe results, and then (d) infer that similar stimuli will produce similar results in humans. The researchers' inference is plausible, however, only if the systems are, in fact, isolable. And the systems can be profitably studied in isolation only if the causal differences between animal subjects and humans can be "reduced" – i.e., scientifically eliminated. Yet, as we argued in Chapters 6–10, that is never something we can assume a priori. In fact, both theoretical and empirical evidence suggests it is something we should not expect.

We now see another dilemma for researchers: researchers recognize the strong interdependence of biological systems and sub-systems – that was the whole motive for the intact-systems argument. The defenders of research argue that they can uncover some biomedically significant data only by studying intact biological systems in non-human species. No other options are acceptable, they claim, because of the highly interlocked nature of an intact biological system. Yet experimenters cannot have it both ways. If the isolationists' thesis were true, their rationale for using intact animal systems disappears. Conversely, if the intact systems argument captures an important element of biomedical phenomena, we can no longer safely generalize from animals to humans. Thus, the flaws of bio-Cartesianism are just the flaws of biological isolationism writ small.

We can now precisely state the moral dilemma: if the cognitive abilities of humans and animals are so drastically different as to morally justify experimentation, then those differences will both reflect and promote other biological differences that undercut straightforward extrapolations of findings in animals to humans. On the other hand, if underlying biological mechanisms are sufficiently similar to justify reasonably direct scientific inferences from animals to humans, then the higher-order traits of the test subjects are likely sufficiently similar to human traits to make research morally troublesome.

We can see the force of this dilemma at work in the current public consciousness. Many people, including many researchers, think chimpanzees are the best test species since they are phylogenetically close to humans. Yet many of those same people are morally uncomfortable with experiments on primates, especially chimpanzees. According to historians, even Claude Bernard refused to do experiments on chimpanzees (Schiller 1967: 255). Why? The same feature that apparently makes them good test subjects also makes them too close to humans for moral comfort.

This dilemma is particularly potent against one form of moral argument first mentioned in the previous chapter, a form of argument frequently used by defenders of research: namely, that humans – but not animals – are members of a moral community. Fox claims:

> [The moral community] is a group of beings that shares certain characteristics and whose members are or consider themselves to be bound to observe certain rules of conduct in relation to one another because of their mutual likeness. These rules create what we call obligations and derive in some intimate way from the characteristics which the beings comprising the moral community have in common ... [T]he beings in question possess certain salient characteristics, are

capable of recognizing these in other, similar beings, and acknowledge possession by other beings of the characteristics in question as grounds for following certain rules of conduct toward them (1986: 49).

An interesting argument. Yet it is irrelevant to this dilemma. For creatures are capable of participating in the moral community only if they have the requisite organism-level properties such as sapience. However, as we have already argued, experiments on *any* animals with such traits would be morally questionable, while experiments on animals without such traits would be scientifically suspect – at least if the purpose of such experiments is, as it is usually, to make direct inferences about similar biomedical conditions in human beings.

The power of the dilemma can be specifically illustrated by looking at two closely related species: rats and mice. Available evidence suggests rats have somewhat higher cognitive abilities than mice, but the differences are not profound (Thomas 1986: 50). Consequently, if we decide that rats have sufficiently developed cognitive and emotional abilities to give them some significant moral standing, mice will deserve the same standing. Conversely, if the abilities of mice are sufficiently limited so they do not deserve significant moral standing, then neither do rats.

In short, we have two creatures with similar moral standing – whatever it turns out to be. Moreover, evolutionarily speaking, rats and mice are phylogenetically closer to each other than either is to humans. Yet they often react differently to the same chemicals. For example, as Lave *et al.* point out concerning carcinogenicity studies:

> The US National Toxicology Program's studies find that 50% of 214 chemicals are positive in each species, but rats and mice give concordant results for only 70% of these chemicals (1988: 631).

Moreover, as noted by Gold *et al.* (1991), rats and mice produce cancers at the same site for only 51 percent of the chemicals tested.

This now gives us a way to state the dilemma concretely: if rats are sufficiently different from humans functionally to justify a difference in moral treatment (experiments on rats but not on humans), then we would expect the non-cognitive biological differences between humans and rats to be even greater than the differences between rats and mice. Since these latter differences are themselves biologically significant, they will undermine direct biological inferences from rats to humans. On the other hand, if the non-cognitive biological differences between rats and humans are sufficiently slight to justify these scientific inferences from the former to the latter, then their cognitive abilities may be much closer than we typically think. Thus, the differences between rats and humans, whatever they are, cannot both morally justify experiments on rats and justify direct inferences of test results in rats to humans.

The reductionistic response

Our dilemma, some might claim, is based on a contentious, anti-reductionistic view of biology. So it is. However, much contemporary biological theory is decidedly anti-reductionist in spirit. Nearly all biologists are physicalists of some fashion. They are not vitalists. As we explained in Chapter 6, most think significant biological phenomena emerge from the complexity of biological organisms, phenomena not straightforwardly reducible to simpler chemical or physical phenomena. Most philosophers of science sympathize with these new directions in biological theory. After discussing the high level attempt to reduce all of biology to molecular biology, Phillip Kitcher comments, "the examples I have given seem to support both anti-reductionistic doctrines . . . [D]espite the immense value of the molecular biology that Watson and Crick launched in 1953, molecular studies cannot cannibalize the rest of biology" (1994: 398). And Elliott Sober, who suggests he rejects any strong form of reductivism, notes that "the thesis of reducibility in principle does not seem to have any direct methodological consequences for current scientific practice" (1993: 26). Put simply, contemporary non-reductivist biology is both scientifically and philosophically defensible.

However, even if we were mistaken, researchers committed to a reductionist biology do not escape the jaws of our dilemma. If anything, reductionistic researchers will be even more susceptible to the dilemma's bite. They (and the philosophers who cheer them on) claim higher level biological properties can ultimately be abandoned in favor of lower-level physical and chemical properties. This doctrine is sometimes known as *hierarchical reductionism*. Dawkins explains the idea as follows:

244

The hierarchical reductionist ... explains a complex entity at any particular level in the hierarchy of organization, in terms of entities only one level down the hierarchy; entities which, themselves are likely to be complex enough to need further reducing to their own component parts; and so on ... It goes without saying ... that the kinds of explanations which are suitable at high levels in the hierarchy are quite different from the kinds of explanations which are suitable at lower levels. This was the point of explaining cars in terms of carburetors rather than quarks. But the hierarchical reductionist believes that carburetors are explained in terms of smaller units ... which are ultimately explained in terms of fundamental particles. Reductionism, in this sense, is just another name for an honest desire to understand how things work (1987: 13).

Or, as Hartry Field explains it using a specific example:

We should not rest content with a special biological predicate "has a haemophiliac gene" – rather we should look for nonbiological facts (chemical facts; and ultimately physical facts) that underlie the correct application of this predicate (1980: 92).

On this view of biology, all organism-level functional properties, and thus all morally relevant biological properties, would be ultimately reducible to the lowest level causal properties.

We think we have given abundant evidence why this view is mistaken. Nonetheless, even if it were true, our dilemma would still be morally and scientifically telling. Why? Similarity of causal properties would straightforwardly imply similarity of morally relevant biological properties and differences in morally relevant biological properties would straightforwardly imply differences in causal properties. Thus, if the moral properties of humans and non-human animals were sufficiently different to justify animal experimentation morally, then we would not be scientifically justified in directly extending results in animals to humans, while if their causal properties were sufficiently similar to justify these direct extrapolations, then the moral appropriateness of these experiments would be called into doubt.

The only way for reductionists to avoid the force of the dilemma would be to embrace bio-Cartesianism and biological isolationism. However, the previous adduced arguments against these views will be as telling against reductive biology as against the new biology we originally discussed.

CONCLUSION

Historically there have been two major routes for defending animal experimentation: deontological and utilitarian. Deontological arguments attempt to identify a fundamental difference between humans and non-human animals that morally justifies a difference in treatment. The previous argument does not directly challenge the claim that humans and non-human animals are different in morally relevant respects. However, the dilemma does suggest that animal experimentation is unjustifiable if humans and non-human animals are relevantly different, because the relevant moral differences imply that they have different underlying causal mechanisms. If humans and non-human animals have different causal mechanisms, then claims about the direct applicability of animal experiments will be scientifically questionable. And, if animal experiments are not directly applicable, then they will be morally objectionable since they waste scarce public resources. On the other hand, if humans and non-human animals have causally similar biological systems, then although experiments on animals may be directly applicable to humans, experiments are likely to be morally objectionable because they are conducted on creatures of substantial moral worth.

Thus, we see that the deontological defense of applied research is untenable and that its defense of the use of animals in basic research is likewise flawed, although for a slightly different reason. If the use of animals in basic research is morally justified, then there are sufficiently large causal differences between humans and non-human animals so that the results of that research cannot be straightforwardly extrapolated to humans. Hence, any morally acceptable use of animals – whether in applied or in basic research – can, at most, have indirect benefits to humans.

Nonetheless, there are researchers who claim there are significant indirect benefits of research. In this view, the benefits of experimentation, although indirect, are so overwhelming that they outweigh the cost of experimenting on animals – creatures of some moral worth. For those who wish to take such a tack, their fate will lie with consequentialist defenses of experimentation, which we discuss now.

246

15

INCALCULABLE BENEFITS
The consequentialist defense

Even those biomedical researchers who embrace the deontological defense of animal experimentation often resort to a utilitarian justification of the practice: they claim the practice is justified because of its enormous benefits to human beings. While it is true that animals die and suffer, that is morally insignificant when compared with experimentation's spectacular payoffs. As Cohen explains it:

> When balancing the pleasures and pains resulting from the use of animals in research, we must not fail to place on the scales the terrible pains that would have resulted, would be suffered now, and would long continue had animals not been used. Every disease eliminated, every vaccine developed . . . indeed, virtually every modern medical therapy is due, in part or in whole, to experimentation using animals (1986: 868).

THE MORAL WORTH OF ANIMALS

Researchers would need to prove the success of animal experimentation even if animals had no moral worth. For if animal experimentation were not valuable (or only marginally valuable), it would be a terrible waste of scarce public resources. That is why defenders of research need to provide even more compelling evidence of the success of animal experimentation if non-human animals have non-negligible moral worth. Researchers openly acknowledge the moral worth of animals. For instance, unless animals had moral worth, it would make no sense to say that we must include their deaths and suffering "on the scales." If they are without value, or their value was morally negligible, the impact of

247

experimentation on them would never enter the moral equation. Thus, even defenders of research acknowledge that the interests of non-human animals can outweigh the interests of humans if, in some particular case, the animals' interests are sufficiently greater than the interests of humans. This view is specifically embraced by a working party of scientists and philosophers discussing the evaluation of biomedical research using animals. They argue that the cost to animals must be carefully considered before deciding to conduct any experiment (Smith and Boyd 1991: 138–9).

As we suggested at the end of Chapter 13, we shall simply assume that although non-human animals have non-negligible moral worth, their worth is considerably less than humans. Since they have non-negligible moral worth, then these uses of animals must be morally justified. Without such a justification, the practice would be morally wanting. Then, in Chapter 14, we offered potent arguments against the standard deontological defense of the practice. In the current chapter, we argue that the standard consequentialist defense is likewise flawed. Therefore, there are no compelling moral arguments for biomedical experiments using animals. If these arguments against research are plausible even on this minimalistic assumption, then defenders of research will be wholly vulnerable to any view that holds that the moral worth of animals is similar to, or at least not much less than, the worth of humans.

Exactly what it means for a utilitarian to say that animals have less moral worth than humans is unclear. Historically, utilitarian arguments have been used to evaluate actions involving creatures of the same moral worth. How do we extend these arguments to cases involving creatures of different worth? Like this. Consider, for instance, "cruelty to animal" statutes on the books in most developed countries. Although what counts as "cruelty to animals" varies from government to government, at least this much is true of all such laws: inflicting excruciating pain on an animal merely to bring a human some tinge of pleasure is wrong. For instance, most people think it wrong to kill a gorilla to make an ashtray from its hand, or to kill an elephant to use its tusks for a paperweight.

To state this generally, even if creatures$_A$ have less moral worth than creatures$_H$, as long as creatures$_A$ have non-negligible worth – of the sort specified by "cruelty to animal" statutes – then there must be circumstances under which morality demands that we favor creatures$_A$ over creatures$_H$. For instance, even if creatures$_H$ are more valuable, if the harm to creatures$_A$ is much greater than the harm to creatures$_H$ – or if there are much greater numbers of creatures$_A$ who must suffer that harm – then morality demands that we favor creatures$_A$ over creatures$_H$ in those circumstances. Were that not so, it would make no sense to say that creatures$_A$ had any moral worth.

Thus, a utilitarian would hold that the moral worth of an action would be the product of (a) the moral worth of the creature that suffers (benefits), (b) the seriousness of the wrong it suffers (the significance of its benefit), and (c) the number of such creatures that suffer (benefit). This would give us a straightforward way of characterizing utilitarian judgements involving creatures of different moral worth.

Although this permits us to characterize how we should proceed with a utilitarian calculus, doing the calculus would be exceedingly difficult. For instance, we would have trouble determining the precise moral worth of animals and humans. As we argued in Chapter 10, we would also have difficulty determining the benefits of animal experimentation. Thus, it would be difficult to determine the seriousness of the wrong done to animals. We would have trouble knowing how many animals suffer, and the extent to which they suffer.

We know that the public is quite concerned about the pain and suffering of laboratory animals.

> Public opinion polls and reaction to media stories indicate that when the public becomes concerned, it is primarily concerned with laboratory pain and distress. Even the painless killing of laboratory animals is perceived to carry a cost (particularly by those who work in research laboratories). However, we have very little data on the extent of animal pain and distress in research (Rowan *et al.* 1995: ii).

Yet we are also uncertain about the extent of animal suffering. The USDA requires laboratories to classify their research according to how much pain the animals suffer, and whether that pain is relieved. For instance, research causing pain and distress not relieved by drugs is classified as category E research. According to the USDA, institutions claim that only 5–6 percent of their animals are in category E research. However, Rowan *et al.* note that many institutions are reluctant to classify research in category E – they fear that research will be targeted by animal rights groups.

Moreover, there are no clear guidelines and criteria for classifying research.

In addition, we are also uncertain how many animals are used in research (recall the arguments in Chapter 10); the USDA figures exclude research using rats and mice. Yet 80–90 percent of all animals used are rodents. So how can we sensibly estimate the number of laboratory animals which suffer? One option is to examine the results of surveys in countries that keep better data.

> The only country that has collected systematic data on animal pain and distress is the Netherlands. Their 1990 Annual Report on animal experimentation notes that 53% of the animals experienced minor discomfort, 23% moderate discomfort, and 24% severe discomfort. About one fifth of the animals in this last category were given medication to alleviate pain. Examples of procedures that would place animals in the "severe" category are prolonged deprivation of food or water, some experimental infections, tumor research and LD50 testing (Rowan *et al.* 1995: iii).

Given that rodents are typically the subjects in the forms of research that Rowan *et al.* mention, it seems likely that many rodent subjects in the US – certainly more than 5–6 percent – would suffer severe pain. In short, since we do not know the numbers of animals used or the extent to which they suffer, carrying out this utilitarian calculation will be difficult.

Yet defenders of research often speak as if this utilitarian (cost–benefit) calculation is very easy. The Cohenesque defense of animal experimentation frequently gets cast, at least in the public debate, as if the choice to pursue or forbid animal experimentation were the choice between "your baby or your dog." However, this way of framing the question is grossly misleading. Doubtless there are choices to be made. Perhaps experimentation is justified. Nonetheless, the choice has not been nor will it ever be between "your baby and your dog." It could not be.

Single experiments (and certainly not single experiments on single animals) will never lead to any medical discovery. Only coordinated sequences of experiments can lead to discovery. Animal experiments are part of a pattern of activity – an institutional practice. That practice or *institution* may significantly benefit humans. But no isolated experiment can. Thus, we must reformulate the moral question: should we continue the *practice* of animal experimentation? Apologists of research will say yes: they claim the practice will have enormous benefits for humans.

THREE MORAL ASYMMETRIES

According to Cohen the benefits of research "incalculably outweigh the evils" (1990: 8). Other defenders of research obviously agree. Although this utilitarian claim appears straightforward and uncontroversial, it is neither straightforward nor uncontroversial. As the previous comments showed, apologists must show that the practice of animal experimentation yields greater benefits than any alternative practice. Likely they can show this only by rejecting three widely held moral presumptions.

Acts versus omissions

The researchers' calculation will be implausible unless we reject the widely held belief that there is a significant moral distinction between evil we do and evil we do not prevent. Most people assume that we are more responsible for what we do than for what we do not prevent. For instance, most people assume that killing someone is morally worse than letting them die; it is morally worse to steal than to fail to prevent someone else from stealing; and that telling a lie is morally worse than to fail to correct someone else's lie. Those who say this do not necessarily claim the failure to prevent evil is morally innocent (although some theorists say just that). They do hold, however, that it is not *as* wrong to permit an evil as to perpetrate one (Clark 1977b).

Moreover, most theorists and lay people think that perpetrating an evil is not merely worse than permitting it; they think it is *much* worse. For instance, most people would be aghast if Ralph failed to save a drowning child, particularly if he could have done so with little effort. Nevertheless, aghast as they might be, they would not think Ralph is as bad as his neighbor Bob who held a child's head under water until she drowned. So, although we need not specify what "much worse" means, it means minimally this: the person who drowns the child should be imprisoned for a long time (if not executed) while the person who allowed the child to drown should not be punished at all – although perhaps he should be morally censured for his callousness.

Obviously if the person had some special duties to the child – for instance, if she were a lifeguard at the pond – then she could be held liable for the child's death. But then her obligation would be explained by her special status: she has assumed the responsibility for people swimming in her pond. In the cases in question, however, we are asking about the role this asymmetry plays when the people in question have not assumed any special responsibility for the children. There the situation is quite different. Even in European cultures that have "Good Samaritan" laws, someone who violates such laws (say, by not saving a drowning child) may be punished, but far less severely than someone who killed a child. *That* most assuredly suggests a profound moral difference.

How is this applicable to the experimenters' position? Like this: the experimenter wants to knowingly kill – and often inflict pain and suffering on – creatures with non-negligible moral worth to prevent future harm to humans. That is, they are *doing* an evil act *to prevent* other evil acts. Their actions inevitably run foul of the asymmetry between actions and omissions.

Experimenters, would likely respond that this asymmetry is applicable only if the wrong perpetrated is morally equal to the wrong not prevented. Since animals are not *as* valuable as humans, then the wrong not prevented is morally much more weighty than the wrong perpetrated. For purposes of argument we earlier agreed that humans are more valuable than animals. Even so, this does not free the experimenter from the force of the asymmetry. This asymmetry has moral bite even if the evil not prevented is worse than the evil perpetrated. For instance, it is worse for a child to die than for a child to be spanked for inappropriate reasons (say, because the parent had a bad day at the office). However, this difference in moral weight can be outweighed by the moral asymmetry between what we do and what we do not prevent. For instance, most people think an adult worse for spanking his child (or worse still, a strange child) for inappropriate reasons than for not feeding a hungry child.

A defender of research might then respond that this example is irrelevant since both cases involve children – creatures of the same moral worth. However, for reasons given earlier, this objection fails. That one creature has less moral worth than another enters the moral equation, but it is not the only factor. We must also include the seriousness of the harm (significance of the benefit) and the number of creatures subjected to that harm (recipients of the benefit). This asymmetry is still morally important, even when the creatures subjected to harm have different moral worth.

Suppose Ralph fails to feed a starving child. His next door neighbor, Bob, picks up a stray puppy, takes it home and kills it slowly, causing it great pain – although no more pain than the starving child feels. The law would do nothing at all to Ralph; however, Bob could be arrested and charged with cruelty to animals. Moreover, the community would not condemn Ralph – after all, few of their number would feed the starving child. Yet most people in the community would roundly condemn Bob for his cruelty and callousness. They would not want to live next door to Bob, befriend him, or have him as their son-in-law.

Perhaps some researcher might argue that we have special obligations to people – obligations that override the force of this asymmetry. However, it is not entirely clear why a researcher would say this or what it would mean. Special obligations are just that – special. They are owed to specific individuals. However, to which specific people do researchers owe these obligations? You, me, Aunt Joan? Lifeguards are hired to save people from drowning: they are obligated to save the particular people swimming on their beach, when they are on call. Researchers, though, are hired to prevent disease, not to prevent any specific disease in any specific person. Finally, if we could make sense of the claim that researchers have special obligations to humans who might benefit from their research, we could make still greater sense of the claim that they have special obligations to their lab animals. After all, the law *requires* them to care for their lab animals; it does not require them to benefit specific human beings.

Consequently, if this asymmetry is morally relevant, it is relevant even if humans and non-human animals have different moral worth. The benefits to humans must be much greater than the costs to animals, else the moral benefits will not outweigh the immorality of perpetrating an evil. How much greater we cannot specify numerically. However, unless the defenders of animal research are disingenuous when they assert that animals have some non-negligible moral worth – or repeatedly lower their assignment of worth to ensure vivisection is always justified come what may – then experiments that kill many animals and yield only slight benefits to humans will not cut the moral mustard.

Some theorists do not accept this moral distinction; they think there is no moral difference between what we do and what we permit. For them, this asymmetry provides no objection to animal experimentation. Yet as we argue later, even if we should reject this asymmetry, rejecting it has consequences grossly unacceptable to most researchers. Furthermore, although this first asymmetry may be rejected by a few theorists, the next two are held almost universally.

Definite harms versus possible benefits

The utilitarian defense of experimentation becomes still more problematic once we note that the real trade off is not merely between what we do and what we permit, but what we do – inflicting suffering on animals in the name of biomedicine – is *definite*, while preventing the suffering of humans is *possible*, and the probability of success is likely unknown. For the moment, however, let us assume that we know the probability that a coordinated sequence of animal experiments will benefit humans. We can illustrate the animal experimenter's quandary using game theoretical reasoning for decisions under risk. Giving up some definite benefit B in the hope of obtaining a greater benefit B_i is sometimes legitimate – if B_i is sufficiently greater. For instance, you might give up $10 to obtain a 10 percent chance of gaining $200. Generally speaking, game theoretic reasoning indicates that giving up a definite benefit B for some other benefit is legitimate B_i, if the product of the utility and probability of B_i's occurring is much greater than the utility of B (being definite, its probability is 1). Thus, even if researchers could ignore the first asymmetry, they would still have to *show* – and not merely assume – that the product of the probability and utility of benefits to humans is greater than the product of the certain suffering of laboratory animals (adjusted for the diminished value of the animals) and the number of animals who suffer. That is easier said than done.

In the actual experimental situation, the probability of any sequence of coordinated animal experiments being successful is usually unknown at the time of experimentation. Thus, the experimenter's predicament seems closer to game-theoretic scenarios of decisions under uncertainty, where the various outcomes of actions are (roughly) known, but the probabilities of those outcomes are not. Here, while the harm to animals is definite, the probability that humans will benefit from experiments is unknown. Even this may be too generous – for properly speaking, the various outcomes of a coordinated series of experiments – and not just their probabilities – will also be unknown before experimentation, while the harm to animals is definite.

Consequently, unless researchers can quantify the success of the institution, they will be hard put to justify that institution given the definite evil to animals. Moreover, as we argued in some detail in Chapter 10, assessing the utility of the institution of animal experimentation is difficult, if not practically impossible. There are no agreed measures of the fecundity of a scientific practice. Moreover, as we argued earlier in this chapter, researchers are also uncertain about the numbers of animals used and the extent to which research animals suffer.

Because researchers are uncertain about the benefits and the costs of experimentation, they often find themselves defending animal experimentation by citing examples that presumably illustrate the practice's success. However, as we argued in Chapter 2, merely citing dramatic examples outside a theoretical context (e.g., evolutionary theory) is no substitute for evidence of success. Yet the researchers cannot, in fact, demonstrate the success of the practice. Therefore, since we know that the harm to animals is substantial and definite, it is difficult to know how researchers can provide a utilitarian justification of the practice.

The creatures who suffer versus the creatures who benefit

Researchers sometimes argue that animal research is justified because the research leads to improved veterinary techniques and pharmacological interventions that benefit animals. However, we find this claim questionable and more than a little disingenuous. The experiments are not done to benefit animals. If animals benefit, it is an accidental consequence of experimentation, not its goal.

Moreover, even if true, the creatures that suffer will not be the ones who benefit from that suffering. *Some* dog may benefit, but not the dog who was "sacrificed." Therefore, animal experimentation clashes with the moral presumption against inflicting suffering on one creature of moral value to benefit some other such creature. For instance, although undergoing a painful bone marrow transplant to save the life of a stranger is noble, we think that requiring people to undergo that procedure would be wrong. We assume people should not be required to sacrifice for others. Or, even if we think people should be required to make some sacrifices for other members of their species, most of us think that requiring the ultimate sacrifice would be inappropriate.

Of course the practice of animal experimentation is much worse since, unlike the previous examples, the individuals who pay the costs of experimentation are not even members of the species that reap the benefits. Doubtless, a defender of research might respond that this case is irrelevant since the previous examples involve humans, creatures of the same moral worth, whereas this case involved animals of different moral worth. However, as we argued earlier, for utilitarians the overall moral worth of an action is a product of the moral worth of the creature who suffers (benefits), the seriousness of the wrong it suffers (the importance of the benefit), and the number of creatures that must suffer (benefit). Thus, the third asymmetry is relevant to an assessment of the utilitarian calculation, though we have granted, for purposes of argument, that animals have less moral worth than humans.

For instance, even if we assume that non-human animals have less moral worth than do humans, most people think there are some sacrifices animals should not have to make to benefit us. Most people think it is wrong to kill a chimpanzee to use its eyes for a decoration or to kill an elephant to use its ears to make a bean bag chair. That is, although most people think neither the chimpanzee nor the elephant has the same moral worth as a person, they assume these animals cannot be asked to give up their lives so humans can obtain some relatively insignificant benefits. The defenders of research agree. That is why they claim that the benefits of research are direct and substantial. They want to show that its benefits outweigh the costs to the lab animals.

This cluster of asymmetries drives homes the fact that researchers must identify overwhelming gains if they are to have any hope of morally justifying their practice. Of course they could just reject these widely held moral views. It seems Cohen rejects them, and other respectable ethical theorists have rejected at least one of them (usually the first one). However, the rejection comes at considerable cost. Not only would rejecting these asymmetries clash with widely held moral beliefs, each rejection has consequences that many researchers would find morally most unpalatable.

CONSEQUENCES OF REJECTING THESE ASYMMETRIES

Consider what follows from a rejection of the first asymmetry. If acts and omissions were of equal moral weight, then animal experimenters could not categorically rule out non-consensual experiments on humans – although researchers claim they are so opposed. Here is why. If defenders of animal experimentation deny the act/omission distinction, then they are committed to the claim that we should pursue any activity that yields greater goods than the goods sacrificed by that activity. Consequently, they can never say that any activity is, in principle, morally impermissible: there might always be some greater moral good which is achievable only through that activity.

Therefore, if certain biomedical benefits could only be achieved through non-consensual experiments on humans, then, if the benefits are greater than the costs, such experiments would be morally justified. This is a most unwelcome consequence for animal experimenters, for two reasons. First, most experimenters want to categorically deny the permissibility of non-consensual biomedical experiments on humans (Cohen 1986: 866; AMA 1992: 1). That they cannot do. At most they can say that such experimentation could be justified only if the benefits were substantial, and because such conditions are rarely satisfied, such experimentation on humans is rarely justified.

Second, this line of defense will be difficult to hold. It is implausible to think that experiments on non-consenting humans would never yield substantial biomedical benefits to a far larger number of humans. Certainly some commentators on Nazi war crimes claim that some German experimentation yielded biomedical benefits for other humans. Likewise for human experiments performed by the Japanese during the Second World War. US officials received voluminous data on human responses to infectious agents. Other research protocols involved the vivisection of fully conscious human subjects (Steven Kaufman, private correspondence, cited by permission). Presumably consensual experiments on prisoners have also yielded significant benefits, especially in clinical trials of new drugs. Finally, before being widely used in the human population, all new compounds are eventually tested on small numbers of consenting humans. The reason for all these experiments is clear: humans make good test subjects.

Consequently, if non-consensual experiments on non-humans are justified when the benefits are great enough, it seems likely that experiments on non-consensual humans will sometimes be justified.

On the other hand, if researchers want to rule out such experiments in principle, then it must be that they believe that it is categorically worse to commit an evil than to fail to prevent one. But, as we have already argued, researchers adopting that position will have a difficult time defending animal experimentation. Perhaps this defense would work if the benefits of experimentation are demonstrably overwhelming.

Rejecting the second asymmetry likewise comes at considerable cost. Consider a choice between G_1 and G_2. These Gs will be the product of the value of the creature suffering (benefiting), the nature of the suffering (benefit), the number of creatures suffering (benefiting) – and, the probability that the suffering (benefit) will occur. It would be the height of foolishness to give up any good G_1 for the mere chance of obtaining some other good G_2 if G_2 were not greater than G_1. So, abandoning this asymmetry would be to abandon rationality itself: it would be to license sacrificing any good in the mere hope that some other good will be achieved.

Abandoning the third asymmetry would require abandoning the idea of the moral separateness of creatures, a view central to all Western conceptions of morality. Some theorists interpret this asymmetry absolutely – that we can never, under any circumstances harm one creature of moral worth to benefit another one. This strong interpretation of this asymmetry is at the core of libertarianism (Nozick 1974). Were this interpretation applied to the issue of animal experimentation, animal experiments could never be justified, no matter how great the benefit.

Most theorists, though, interpret this asymmetry more weakly to indicate that one creature of moral worth can never be required to suffer for the benefit of another creature, unless the sacrifice is small and benefits substantial. Even on this weaker version, the benefits of experimentation would have to be overwhelming to justify the practice. For instance, most lay people assume it would be inappropriate to *require* people to undergo a bone marrow transplant to save someone else's life, even though the benefit relative to the pain is considerable. Moreover, virtually everyone would be opposed to *requiring* people to give up one of their good kidneys to save someone else's life. Thus, even if we assume animals have less value than humans, this asymmetry – like the two before – implies that researchers must show staggering benefits of experimentation to morally justify the practice.

WHAT REALLY GOES ON THE SCALES?

Cohen's accounting of what goes on the moral scales is incomplete. For instance, when determining the gains relative to the cost of animal experimentation, we must include not only the costs to animals (which are direct and substantial), but also the costs to humans (and animals) of misleading experiments. As we noted earlier in the book, Flexner's rhesus monkey model of polio (which assumed the nose was portal of entry) seriously misled researchers. For example, Draper, a leading polio researcher, initially had sound clinical insights into the pathogenesis of polio. Yet, as Paul points out:

> Draper had gone over completely to Flexner's views on the nasal portal of entry. The clock had been set back about twenty five years in poliovirus research (1971: 384–5).

How many lives were lost or ruined because of this delay? While no one knows precisely, any losses belong on the scales.

We also know that animal experiments mislead us about the dangers of smoking. By the early 1960s, epidemiologists discerned a strong correlation between lung cancer and smoking (see Brecher and Brecher 1963). Nonetheless, efforts to induce lung cancer in non-human CAMs had failed, leading Northrup to note:

> The failure of many . . . investigators to induce experimental cancers, except in a handful of cases, during fifty years of trying, casts serious doubt on the validity of the cigarette–lung cancer theory (1957: 133).

Furthermore, since we should include *possible benefits* (since no benefits are certain) on the scales, we must also include *possible costs*. For instance, some researchers have speculated that AIDS was transferred to the human population through an inadequately screened oral polio vaccine given to 250,000 Africans in the late 1950s (Elswood and Striker 1993: 175–6). Although the hypothesis is almost certainly false, something like it might be true. We know, for instance, that one simian virus (SV_{40}) entered the human population through inadequately screened vaccine (Hayflick 1972: 813). In fact, several hundred thousand people have been exposed to SV_{40} through vaccines; and in *in vitro* tests the virus causes normal human cells to mutate into cancerous cells. Therefore it is difficult to know how researchers could plausibly claim that there would be no substantial ill-effects of future animal experimentation. These possible ill-effects must be counted.

Finally, and perhaps most important, what is crucial for the moral calculation is not the benefits animal experimentation has produced and will produce, but the benefits that *only* animal research could produce. To determine this utility we must ascertain (a) the role that medical intervention played in lengthening life and improving health, (b) the contribution of animal experimentation to medical intervention, and (c) the benefits of animal experimentation *relative to* those of non-animal research programmes. Since even the AMA recognizes the value of non-animal research programmes, then what goes on the moral scales are not all the purported benefits of animal experimentation but only the *increase* in benefits compared to alternative programmes. Since we do not know what these other programmes *would* have yielded, determining the increase in benefits would be impossible to establish, even if we could easily determine the contributions of animal experimentation. As we argued in Chapter 10, we have no clear way to determine the benefits of animal research. That is something researchers realize: that is why they often resort to the "hard to measure benefits" argument.

CONCLUSION

None of this shows that animal experimentation has been worthless. None of this shows that abandoning animal experimentation will not hinder some biomedical advances. What it does show is that animal experimentation has been less valuable than researchers have led us to believe. In addition, it has shown that researchers will be hard pressed to give a precise accounting of its value. Thus it seems doubtful that researchers can plausibly claim that the benefits of animal experimentation are overwhelming. Yet, given the arguments in this chapter, that is exactly what they need to show to morally justify the practice.

Perhaps researchers might respond that it is we who must demonstrate that research is not valuable, that it is we who must show that the evils of experimentation outweigh it benefits. Not so. For the moral onus always rests on anyone who wishes to perpetrate what is, all things being equal, a moral wrong. Since people on both sides of this debate, researchers included, acknowledge the moral status of non-human animals, then they must provide clear and demonstrable evidence that the value of the institution of research exceeds its moral costs. That they have not done. Given the arguments in this chapter, it is difficult to know how they could.

16

CONCLUSION

The evidence to hand suggests that biomedical research using animals – especially basic biomedical animal research – has benefited humans, albeit indirectly, and might continue to do so. The evidence likewise suggests that biomedical research using animals has been less valuable that most of us have been led to believe; indeed, less valuable than many biomedical researchers themselves believe. How *much* animal research has benefited humans is difficult to say. How *much* the claims for biomedical research have been exaggerated is likewise difficult to say.

That is the rub. If animal test subjects have non-negligible moral worth, even if much less moral worth than humans, then even if such research is valuable to humans, the practice of animal experimentation raises significant moral issues. On the other hand, biomedical research using animals also raises profound political issues – even if animals were without moral worth. We spend vast sums of public and private funds for biomedical research, and much of that money goes toward animal research. Why do we spend these vast sums of money? Presumably because of its immense payoff. If, however, the payoff for human health and well-being is less than overwhelming, then the practice is politically problematic, especially when research funds become scarce.

The arguments through this book demonstrate that the payoff has been less overwhelming than defenders of the practice of animal experimentation claim. How much less is difficult to say. No one – neither defenders nor critics of the practice – have come up with a reliable measure of the efficacy of the current practice. Nor do they have a wholly credible interpretation of the historical record. In short, although we know that claims about the benefits of the practice are exaggerated, we do not know the precise extent of the exaggeration. This is bad news for defenders and critics alike.

Available estimates of the benefits and limitations of animal experimentation are, at best, guesses, and probably bad guesses. As a society, we have been so convinced that animal experimentation is astoundingly beneficial to humans that we have not tried to determine those benefits precisely. Furthermore, human sympathies for other humans are limited. Although we may be distressed by images of human suffering, many of us are not moved to action. Often we become inured to the suffering of others – especially when the others have a different tint of skin or slant of eye. How much more limited must our sympathies be to the suffering of non-human animals? Specifically, how much more limited are our sympathies to the suffering of murid rodents, animals we have been taught to loathe as vermin?

Most animal researchers do not question the practice of animal experimentation. That is not surprising. As we argued in Chapter 2, animal experimentation is part of the current biomedical paradigm. Since a paradigm guides the practice of a science, scientists operating under that paradigm do not typically question it. This is especially true if the scientists are convinced, as we think most animal experimenters are, that the practice "just works." However, the animal research debate is likely to remain stuck in a rhetorical quagmire unless we critically examine the methodology of animal experimentation, and scientifically determine the efficacy of the practice.

There are other non-scientific (i.e., political, socio-economic, and institutional) factors why most animal experimenters do not critically examine their practice. In their attempt to protect public safety, legislators and regulatory agencies insist that pharmaceutical and medical companies test new products on animals, even when they know we cannot reliably extrapolate results from animals to humans. Once these requirements are in place, they have so much political inertia that they are difficult to stop or modify. While we do not propose deregulation, we do think that current regulations need to be evaluated scientifically, rather than simply being a symbol of the government's attempt to protect public safety.

Of course everyone acknowledges we should do our best to protect the public from noxious substances. Still, why should we think this requires animal experimentation? Could we not develop alternative, non-intact animal, research methodologies like cell and tissue cultures? Of course cell cultures will not behave exactly like an intact human animal. But often, neither do non-human intact animals. Given the moral costs of animal experimentation, the search for alternatives is no irrational pipe dream.

The practice of animal experimentation is also sustained and guided by socio-economic factors. Animal experimentation is a multi-billion dollar industry. Animal research laboratories are supported by a vivisectionist version of the military-industrial complex. Laboratories must be built and maintained. Millions of animals must be bred and distributed; these animals must be fed and housed. Companies must build equipment with which to test the animals. Researchers and institutions must obtain grants and other forms of funding; then they must train technicians and support staff. In short, animal experimentation has spawned, and is supported by, a complex web of economic relationships. Many people earn their livelihood, directly or indirectly, from the practice of animal experimentation. These people will be disinclined to criticize or radically alter the practice since so much is at stake economically. Although this does not imply that animal experimentation is simply done for economic reasons, we think that it would be folly to ignore the ways that economic considerations make a candid appraisal of the practice more difficult.

Finally, powerful institutional pressures encourage needless animal experiments. To gain tenure and promotion, a faculty member must conduct research and publish the results. Tenure committees and academic administrators routinely consider not just the quality of research, but its quantity. Consequently, junior faculty wishing to survive professionally must do much research. Since in some fields it may be relatively easy to publish work that replicates (perhaps with minor variations) previous experiments, the faculty in these fields are encouraged to conduct needless experiments. Furthermore, universities and senior faculty are likewise judged by the quantity of their research. Research brings not only prestige, but also grant monies. Together these factors conspire to sustain and even expand experimentation on animals within the biomedical sciences. Again, without sound measures of success, we cannot know exactly how much of this research is inconsequential. However, neither can we decide if this work advances the frontiers of knowledge.

Finally, we find it difficult to assess the worth of animal experimentation since apologists have no agreed-upon defense of that practice. In their public proclamations such as the AMA White Paper and the Sigma XI "Statement on the Use on Animals in Research," defenders make grand claims for research, claims that, in private, many supporters of research acknowledge are exaggerated. Yet we cannot ignore these claims since they are offered to the public as justifying vast public expenditure for biomedical research using animals. Moreover, although exaggerated, they do at least constitute some attempt to articulate a justification for the practice.

Finding a clearly articulated, but less exaggerated defense of the practice is not easy. In both public forums and in private communication we have asked researchers to help us identify a clear, non-exaggerated, and precise defense of the practice. To date no one has provided us with a citation of a single instance. For all its drawbacks, given the current state of biological science, Claude Bernard's *Introduction to the Study of Experimental Medicine* stands alone as a document that defends the practice, *and* which is generally recognized as having provided a defense of that practice. Perhaps the ablest contemporary defender of the practice is Sir William Patton (1993). However, we do not find that researchers generally cite Patton as someone who articulates their view. Perhaps most of them do not see any need to defend the practice.

If we were pressed to identify the most widely held, though not generally articulated, justification for the practice, we would pick out some version of the "it just works" argument, discussed in some detail in Chapter 10. As we argued there, neither we, nor the biomedical scientists, know precisely how to assess the success of biomedical experimentation using animals.

In this book we have explained why we should assess the success of the practice. We have also pointed in the direction of how that can – and cannot – be done. In fact, we think we have taken the first steps toward providing that assessment. However, first steps are not final steps. It would be the height of arrogance to suggest that we have offered the definitive scientific assessment of the worth of animal experimentation.

Perhaps where we have made the most headway is in explaining the role of theory in understanding evidence. As we have argued throughout the book, isolated examples explain or illuminate nothing. They become significant only in the context of well-confirmed scientific theories – theories such as evolutionary biology – which shape the way we conceptualize evidence. Moreover, while examples can illuminate points of biological theory and practice, they do not stand on their own as scientific measures of the *success* of those theories and practices.

In short, we do not take our work to be the final and definitive statement of the issues. We do, however, think we have advanced the debate. We have raised what we take to be crucial questions, questions often overlooked or ignored in the past. If researchers will themselves takes these issues and questions seriously, then perhaps they can help explain the limitations of – and the precise value of – such experimentation. If critics of animal experimentation will likewise take these issues seriously, they, too, may come to see the ways in which animal experimentation may be scientifically legitimate. Finally, we hope both sides will come to realize that the moral questions concerning animal experimentation are much more complex than they have admitted historically.

POLICY RECOMMENDATIONS

Although, as we have said, our arguments in this book do not give a definitive and final account of what we should do, our analysis does help identify what we should know before we decide how to continue. Moreover, although many of our conclusions are tentative, they are sufficiently strong to suggest what we should not do. Finally, our arguments suggest – in a general way – how we might profitably continue. We thus offer the following proposals for the practice of science and for the moral assessment of animal research.

Scientific proposals

We must attempt to assess the scientific value of animal experimentation. Until we do, we will be left with a vague version of the intellectually untenable "it just works" argument. There are certain steps we must follow to ascertain the success of the practice:

1 We must decide exactly what we mean by "success." Certainly the practice would be successful if, as the AMA claims, the practice has been responsible, directly or indirectly, for every biomedical advance of the past half century. However, as we have argued earlier, that claim is simply false, and, moreover, researchers realize it is false. So what, short of these grand claims, would count as success? Most researchers, it seems, are not even certain what they would take as measures of success.

2 Once we decide what would count as success, we must find some relatively precise way of determining whether the practice is successful, given that definition. That will be difficult. Also, success, whatever it is, must always be judged relative to cost.

Thus, before we can judge success, we must know how many animals, and how much money is used in biomedical experimentation. Otherwise, we have no way of judging the cost of the practice. Estimates of the number of animals used vary widely, partly because the most commonly used animals (rats and mice) are not even counted. Therefore, we specifically recommend that all agencies overseeing the use of animals in biomedical research should count rats and mice. Only then can we have a better sense of the cost.

3 Find ways to determine the contribution of animal experimentation to human well-being – especially in comparison to contributions derived and derivable from alternative research methods. This requires, among other things, abandoning animal experimentation as the biomedical "gold standard." Animal experimentation is currently seen as an ineliminable element of the biomedical paradigm. Apologists typically do not prove the success of the practice; rather, they merely assume the practice is successful. Moreover, they assume it should be used to judge the success of other research methodologies. For instance, they decide if cell cultures are a good model by comparing them with animal models – not with the human condition they supposedly model.

Moral Proposals

We should more precisely determine the moral worth of animals. Currently, virtually everyone, including defenders of animal experiments, acknowledge that non-human animals have some non-negligible moral worth – that is, they think it would be wrong to cause pain, suffering, or to kill an animal for no good reason. They think that doing this is wrong because of its effects on the animals themselves. However, this is left unacceptably vague by all sides of the debate. To help find a "solution" we should:

1 Increase our understanding of the nature of non-human animals, especially their intellectual, emotional, and social lives. In Descartes' day, many people doubted that non-human animals

had emotional, intellectual, or genuinely social lives. This view, however, has been abandoned by all but a few. Indeed, there is increasing evidence that animals have far more sophisticated lives than we would have thought possible. However, the evidence is less than definitive. We must conduct more systematic research. Although this will not resolve the moral question, it will inform it. We typically determine the moral worth of a creature, at least in part, by its cognitive sophistication.

2 Think more carefully about how to make moral judgements when comparing creatures of different moral worth. All but a few animal rightists would recognize that humans have greater moral worth than at least most animals (except, perhaps, the great apes; see Cavalieri and Singer 1993). How do we decide how to "weigh" the competing interests of creatures of different worth? In Chapter 15 we suggested some minimal constraints on what that would mean. However, that discussion was purely preliminary. We need to do much more work. In our view, this may be the crucial moral issue for assessing the legitimacy of the practice of animal experiments using animals.

3 We must learn how to measure and evaluate animal pain. We must establish more precise criteria than current USDA standards for classifying research according to the pain experienced by animal subjects. As noted by Rowan *et al.* (1995: iii), some corporations that do toxicity testing report no research in the USDA category E (pain and distress unrelieved by drugs). Such reports are hardly realistic.

Derivative proposals

We need to consider using stronger public health measures to reduce chronic illness caused by environmental factors. For example, research into cures for lung cancer currently involves extensive animal experimentation, yet smoking causes 90 percent of lung cancers. The moral cost of these experiments falls on the backs of researchers and smokers. This moral cost also emphatically falls on the backs of tobacco companies who shamelessly market products known to be lethal in humans. We face similar moral dilemmas about other diet-induced and environmentally induced diseases. There is something morally objectionable about asking non-human animals to pay the costs of human folly.

1 Universities should reconsider the criteria for granting tenure to animal researchers. Likewise animal care committees must scrutinize research proposals and only fund those that have substantial scientific merit. They should refuse to fund projects that are simply a way to obtain funding, tenure, or promotion. We must also undertake basic research to develop sound alternatives to animal research. (Thus, those concerned to reduce the current levels of animal experimentation do not need to think we should decrease the overall level of research. There is plenty of scientific work to be done.)

2 Finally, we must all be open to consider and assess the evidence offered by theorists on all sides of this debate. Only then do we have any hope of reaching an informed and mutually satisfying solution.

BIBLIOGRAPHY

Adams, S.H. (1906) *The Great American Fraud,* New York: P.F. Collier.

Agar, M. and Godwin, I. (1992) "Erythrocyte Metabolism in Two Species of Bats: Common Bent-Wing Bat (Miniopterus Schreibersii) and Red Fruit Bat (Pteropus Scapulatus)," *Comparative Biochemistry and Physiology,* 101B, 9–12.

Amdur, M., Doull, J. and Klaassen, C. (eds) (1993) *Casarett and Doull's Toxicology* (4th edn), New York: McGraw-Hill.

American Medical Association (AMA) (1992) *Statement on the Use of Animals in Biomedical Research: The Challenge and Response* (revised), Chicago: American Medical Association.

Ames, B. and Gold, L. (1990a) "Too Many Rodent Carcinogens: Mitorgenesis Increases Mutagenesis," *Sciences,* 249, 970–1.

—— (1990b) "Chemical Carcinogenesis: Too Many Rodent Carcinogens," *Proceedings of the National Academy of Sciences,* 87, 7772–6.

Anger, W. (1991) "Animal Test Systems to Study Behavioral Dysfunctions of Nuerodegenerative Diseases," *Neurotoxicology,* 12, 403–14.

Bailar, J., III (1979) "The Case for Cancer Prevention," *Journal of the National Cancer Institute,* 62, 727–31.

Bailar, J., III and Smith E. (1986) "Progress against Cancer?," *New England Journal of Medicine,* 314, 1226–31.

Balls, M. (1990) "Recent Progress Toward Reducing the Use of Animal Experimentation in Biomedical Research," in S. Garattini and D.W. van Beekkum (eds) *The Importance of Animal Experimentation for Safety and Biomedical Research,* Dordrecht: Kluwer Academic Publishers, 223–36.

Beardsley, T. (1994) "A War Not Won: Trends in Cancer Epidemiology," *Scientific American* (January), 130–8.

Beeson, P. (1979) "The Growth of Knowledge about a Disease: Hepatitis," *American Journal of Medicine,* 67, 366–70.

Benga, G., Porutiu, D., Hodarnaus, A. and Ferdinand, W. (1992) "Ultrastructural Aspects and Amino Acid Composition of the Purified Inner and Outer Membranes of Human Liver Mitochondria as Compared to

Rat Liver Mitochondria," *Comparative Biochemistry and Physiology*, 102B, 123–8.

Bentham, J. (1989) "The Utilitarian View," in T. Regan and P. Singer (eds) *Animal Rights and Human Obligations*, Englewood Cliffs, N.J.: Prentice-Hall, 25–6.

Bentvelzen, P. (1990) "Animal models for AIDS research," in S. Garattini and D.W. van Bekkum (eds) *The Importance of Animal Experimentation for Safety and Biomedical Research*, Dordrecht: Kluwer Academic Publishers, 153–61.

Bernard, C. [1865] (1949) *An Introduction to the Study of Experimental Medicine*, Paris: Henry Schuman, Inc.

Berra, T.M. (1990) *Evolution and the Myth of Creationism*, Stanford: Stanford University Press.

Bewick, M. (1988) Interview in *The Guardian*, August 1, p. 20.

Bonner, J. (1980) *The Evolution of Culture in Animals*, Princeton: Princeton University Press.

Brecher, E. and Brecher, R. (1963) *The Consumers Union Report on Smoking and the Public Interest*, Mount Vernon, N.Y.: Consumers Union.

Brinkley, J. (1993) "Animal Tests as Risk Clues: The Best Data May Fall Short," *New York Times National* (23 March), C1, C20–1.

British Journal of Medicine (1982) Editorial (August), 459–60.

Brodie B. (1962) "Difficulties in Extrapolating Data on Metabolism of Drugs from Animals to Humans," *Clinical Pharmacology and Therapeutics*, 3, 374–80.

Burggren, W.W. and Bemis, W.E. (1990) "Studying Physiological Evolution: Paradigms and Pitfalls," in M.H. Nitecki (ed.) *Evolutionary Innovations*, Chicago: University of Chicago Press, 191–228.

Cairns-Smith, A.G. (1985) *Seven Clues to the Origin of Life*, Cambridge: Cambridge University Press.

Calabrese, E. (1983) *Principles of Animal Extrapolation*, New York: Wiley.

—— (1984) "Suitability of Animal Models for Predictive Toxicology: Theoretical and Practical Considerations," *Drug Metabolism Review*, 15, 505–23.

Caldecott-Hazard, S., Guze, B., Kling, A. and Baxter, L.R. (1991) "Clinicial and Biochemical Aspects of Depressive Disorders," *Synapse*, 8, 185–211.

Caldwell, J. (1980) "Comparative Aspects of Detoxification in Mammals," in W. Jakoby (ed.) *Basis of Detoxification* (vol. 1), New York: Academic Press, 85–113.

—— (1992) "Species Differences in Metabolism and Their Toxicological Significance," *Toxicology Letters*, 64/65, 651–9.

Carruthers, P. (1992) *The Animals Issue*, Cambridge: Cambridge University Press.

Casti, J. (1994) *Complexification*, New York: Harper Perennial.

Cavalieri, P. and Singer, P. (eds) (1993) *The Great Ape Project*, New York: Random House.

271

Cavener, D. (1992) "Transgenic Animal Studies on the Evolution of Genetic Regulatory Circuitries," *BioEssays*, 14, 237–44.

Chouroulinkov, I. (1990) "The Need for Animal Experimentation in Studying the Carcinogenic Risk of Substances," in S. Garattini and D.W. van Bekkum (eds) *The Importance of Animal Experimentation for Safety and Biomedical Research*, Dordrecht: Kluwer Academic Publishers, 199–210.

Clark, S. (1977a) *The Moral Status of Animals*, Oxford: Oxford University Press.

—— (1977b) "How to Calculate the Greater Good," in D. Patterson and R. Ryder (eds) *Animals' Rights: A Symposium*, London: Centaur Press, 96–105.

Clarke, F. (1973) "Introduction," in F. Clarke, *How Modern Medicines are Discovered*, Mount Kisco, N.Y.: Futura Publishing Company, 2–83.

Cohen, C. (1986) "The Case for the Use of Animals in Biomedical Research," *New England Journal of Medicine*, 315, 865–70.

—— (1990) "Animal Experimentation Defended," in S. Garattini and D.W. van Bekkum (eds) *The Importance of Animal Experimentation for Safety and Biomedical Research*, Dordrecht: Kluwer Academic Publishers, 7–16.

Comroe, J. and Dripps, R. (1974) "Ben Franklin and Open Heart Surgery," *Circulation Research*, 35, 661–9.

Craig, W. (1992) "Experimental Models of Benzene," R. D'Amato, T. Slaga, W. Failand and C. Henry (eds) *Evaluation of Human Cancer Risk*, New York:

Crawley, J., Sutton, M. and Pickar, D. (1985) "Animal Models of Self-Destructive Behavior and Suicide," *Psychiatric Clinical, North American*, 8, 299–310.

Crick, F. (1966) *Of Molecules and Men*, Seattle: University of Washington Press.

Darwin, C. [1859] (1972) *The Origin of Species*, New York: W.W. Norton and Company.

Davis L. (1979) "Species Differences as a Consideration in Drug Therapy," *Journal Of The American Veterinary Associations*, 175, 1014–15.

Dawkins, R. (1987) *The Blind Watchmaker*, New York: W.W. Norton and Company.

—— (1989) *The Selfish Gene*, Oxford: Oxford University Press.

Department of Health and Human Services (DHHS) (1988) *Health United States*, Washington, DC: Department of Health and Human Services, pp. 53, 72.

Depew, D. and Weber, B. (1995) *Darwinism Evolving*, Cambridge, Mass.: MIT Press.

Descartes, R. (1970) *Descartes: Philosophical Letters*, A. Kenney (trans. and ed.), Oxford: Oxford University Press.

Dvořák, I. (1989) "Mathematical Models of Physiological Processes," in Z. Deyl and J. Zicha (eds) *Methods in Animal Physiology*, Boca Raton, Fla.: CRC Press, 90–1.

Edey, M.A. and Johanson, D. (1989) *Blueprints: Solving the Mystery of Evolution*, New York: Penguin.

Ekeland, I. (1988) *Mathematics and the Unexpected*, Chicago: University of Chicago Press.

Elliot, P. (1987) "Vivisection and the Emergence of Experimental Medicine in Nineteenth Century France," in N. Rupke (ed.) *Vivisection in Historical Perspective*, New York: Croom Helm, 48–77.

Elswood, B.F. and Striker, R.B. (1993) "Polio Vaccines and the Origin of AIDS" (letter to the editor), *Research in Virology*, 144, 175–7.

Feron, V., van Bladern, P. and Hermes, R. (1990) "A Viewpoint on the Extrapolation of Toxicological Data from Animals to Man," *Food, Chemistry, and Toxicology*, 28, 783–8.

Field, H. (1980) "Tarski's Theory of Truth," in M. Platts (ed.) *Reference, Truth, and Reality*, London: Routledge, 83–110.

Florkin, M. and Schoffeneils, E. (1970) "Adapted Molecules", in M. Hecht and W. Steere (eds) *Essays in Evolution and Genetics in Honor of Theodosius Dobzhansky*, New York: Appleton-Century-Crofts.

Food and Drug Administration (FDA) (1988) *OPE Study 77*, Washington, DC: Food and Drug Administration.

Forni, G., Caretto, P., Ferraiorni, P., Bosco, M. and Giovarelli, M. (1990) "The Necessity of Animal Experimentation in Tumor Immunology," in S. Garattini and D.W. van Bekkum (eds) *The Importance of Animal Experimentation for Safety and Biomedical Research*, Dordrecht: Kluwer Academic Publishers, 126–32.

Fox, M. (1986) *The Case for Animal Experimentation*, Berkeley: University of California Press.

Freedman, D. and Zeisel, H. (1988) "From Mouse-to-Man: The Quantitative Assessment of Cancer Risks," *Statistical Science*, 3, 3–56.

Frey, R. (1980) *Rights and Interests*, Oxford: Oxford University Press.

—— (1983) *Rights, Killing, and Suffering*, Oxford: Blackwell.

—— (1987) "Moral Standing, The Value of Lives, and Speciesism," *Between the Species*, 3: 191–201.

—— (1994) "The Ethics of the Search for Benefits: Experimentation in Medicine," in R. Gillon (ed.) *Principles of Health Care Ethics*, Chichester: John Wiley, 1067–75.

Friedman L. (1969) "The Role of the Laboratory Animal Study of Intermediate Duration for Evaluation of Safety," *Toxicology and Applied Pharmacology*, 16, 498–506.

Futuyma, D.J. (1986) *Evolutionary Biology*, Sunderland, Mass.: Sinauer Associates.

Gaetano, G., Cerletti, C., Poggi, A. and Donatti, M. (1990) "Animal Research and Recent Progress in Thrombosis Research," in S. Garattini and D.W. van Bekkum (eds) *The Importance of Animal Experimentation for Safety and Biomedical Research*, Dordrecht: Kluwer Academic Publishers, 97–110.

Ganten, D., Lindpaintner, K., Unger, Th. and Mullions, J. (1990) "The Importance of Animal Models for Hypertension Research," in S. Garattini and D.W. van Bekkum (eds) *The Importance of Animal Experimentation for Safety and Biomedical Research*, Dordrecht: Kluwer Academic Publishers, 89–96.

Garattini, S. (1990) "The Necessity of Animal Experimentation," in S. Garattini and D.W. van Bekkum (eds) *The Importance of Animal Experimentation for Safety and Biomedical Research*, Dordrecht: Kluwer Academic Publishers, 1–4,

Garattini, S. and van Bekkum, D.W. (eds) (1990) *The Importance of Animal Experimentation for Safety and Biomedical Research*, Dordrecht: Kluwer Academic Publishers.

Garrett, L. (1994) *The Coming Plague*, New York: Farrar, Strauss and Giroux.

Gartner, D. (1980) "Stress Response of Rats to Handling and Experimental Procedures," *Laboratory Animals*, 14, 267–74.

Geison, G. (1995) *The Private Science of Louis Pasteur*, Princeton: Princeton University Press.

Giere, R. (1991) *Understanding Scientific Reasoning*, New York: Harcourt Brace Jovanovich.

Gold, L., Bernstein, L., Magaw, R. and Slone, T. (1989) "Interspecies Extrapolation in Carcinogenesis: Prediction between Rats and Mice," *Environmental Health Perspectives*, 81, 211–19.

Gold, L., Slone, T., Manley, N., and Bernstein, L. (1991) "Target Organs in Chronic Bioassays of 533 Chemical Carcinogens," *Environmental Health Perspectives*, 96, 233–46.

Good, R. (1968) "Keystones," *Journal of Clinical Investigation*, 47, 1466.

Goodman, M. (1990) "An Hypothesis on Molecular Evolution that Combines Neutralist and Selectionist Views," in E. Dudley (ed.) *The Unity of Evolutionary Biology*, Portland, Oreg.: Dioscorides Press.

Gorbman, A., Dickhoff, W., Vigna, S., Clark, N. and Ralph, C. (1983) *Comparative Endocrinology*, New York: John Wiley & Sons.

Goth, A. (1981) *Medical Pharmacology: Principles and Concepts* (10th edn), St Louis: C.V. Mosby.

Gould, S.J. (1977) *Ontogeny and Phylogeny*, Cambridge, Mass.: Harvard University Press.

—— (1980) "The Panda's Thumb," in *The Panda's Thumb: More Reflections in Natural History*, New York: W.W. Norton and Company.

—— (1982) "Is a New and General Theory of Evolution Emerging?," in J. Maynard Smith (ed.) *Evolution Now*, New York: Freeman.

—— (1986) *The Mismeasure of Man*, New York: W.W. Norton and Company.

—— (1993) *Eight Little Piggies: Reflections in Natural History*, New York: W.W. Norton and Company.

Griesemer, R. and Tennant, R. (1992) "Transgenic Mice in Carcinogenicity Testing," in H. Vainio, P. Magee, D. McGregor and A. McMichael (eds) *Mechanisms of Carcinogenicity in Risk Identification,* Lyons: IARC Press.

Griffin, D. (1992) *Animal Minds,* Chicago: Chicago University Press.

Hardey, A. (1983) "Smallpox in London: Factors in the Decline of the Disease in the Ninteenth Century," *Medical History,* 27, 111–28.

Hart, J. (1990) "Endocrine Pathology of Estrogens: Species Differences," *Pharmacologial Therapy,* 47, 203–18.

Hawkins, D. (1983) *Drugs and Pregnancy – Human Teratogenesis and Related Problems,* Edinburgh: Churchill Livingstone.

Hayflick, L. (1972) "Human Virus Vaccines: Why Monkey Cells?," *Science* (May 19), 813–14.

Hempel, C.G. (1965) *Aspects of Scientific Explanation,* New York: Macmillan.

—— (1966) *Philosophy of Natural Science,* Englewood Cliffs, N.J.: Prentice-Hall.

Hesse, M. (1966) *Models and Analogies in Science,* Notre Dame: Notre Dame University Press.

Hoage, R. and Goldman, L. (eds) (1986) *Animal Intelligence: Insights into the Animal Mind,* Washington, DC: Smithsonian Institution Press.

Hood, R. (1990) "Animal Models of Effects of Prenatal Insult," in R. Hood (ed.) *Developmental Toxicology: Risk Assessment and The Future,* New York: Van Nostrand Reinhold.

Hull, D. (1974) *Philosophy Of Biological Science,* Englewood Cliffs, N.J.: Prentice-Hall.

Institute of Medicine (IOM) (1995) *Review of the Fialuridine (FIAU) Clinical Trials,* Washington, DC: National Academy Press.

International Agency for Research on Cancer (IARC) (1983) *The Miscellaneous Pesticides,* Lyons: IARC Press.

—— (1992) *Mechanisms of Carcinogenesis in Risk Identification,* Lyons: IARC Press.

Jacquette, D. (1994) *Philosophy of Mind,* Englewood Cliffs, N.J.: Prentice-Hall.

Kant, I. (1963) "Duties to Animals and Spirits," in his *Lectures on Ethics,* New York: Harper and Row.

Kauffman, S. (1993) *Origins of Order,* Oxford: Oxford University Press.

King, M.C. and Wilson, A.C. (1975) "Evolution at Two Levels in Humans and Chimpanzees," *Science,* 188, 107–16.

Kitcher, P. (1994) "1953 and All That," in E. Sober (ed.) *Conceptual Issues in Evolutionary Biology,* Cambridge, Mass.: MIT Press, 379–99.

Klaassen, C. and Eaton, D.M. (1993) "Principles of Toxicology," in A. Amdur, J. Doull and C. Klaassen (eds) *Casarett and Doull's Toxicology* (4th edn), New York: McGraw-Hill, 12–49.

Koppanyi, T. and Avery, M. (1966) "Species Differences and the Clinical Trial of New Drugs: a Review," *Clinical Pharmacology and Therapeutics,* 7, 250–70.

Kornberg, A. (1995) "Science in the Stationary Phase" (editorial), *Science*, 269: 1799.

Kornetsky, C. (1977) "Animal Models: Promises and Problems," in I. Hanin and E. Usdin (eds) *Animal Models in Psychiatry and Neurology*, New York: Pergamon Press, 3–7.

Krebs, H. (1975) "For Many Problems there is an Animal on which it Can be Most Conveniently Studied," *Journal of Experimental Zoology*, 194, 221–6.

Kuhn, T. (1970) *The Structure of Scientific Revolutions* (2nd edn), Chicago: University of Chicago Press.

LaFollette, H. and Shanks, N. (1993a): "Animal Models in Biomedical Research: Some Epistemological Worries," *Public Affairs Quarterly*, 7, 113–30.

—— (1993b) "The Intact Systems Argument: Problems with the Standard Defense of Animal Experimentation," *Southern Journal of Philosophy*, 31, 323–33.

—— (1994a) "Animal Experimentation: The Legacy of Claude Bernard," *International Studies in the Philosophy of Science*, 8, 195–210.

—— (1994b) "Chaos Theory: Analogical Reasoning in the Biomedical Research," *Idealistic Studies*, 24, 241–54.

—— (1995a) "Two Models of Models in Biomedical Research," *Philosophical Quarterly*, 45, 141–60.

—— (1995b) "Utilizing Animals," *Journal of Applied Philosophy*, 12, 13–26.

—— (1996) "The Origin of Speciesism," *Philosophy*, 71, 46–61.

Lakatos, I. (1970) "Methodology of Scientific Research Programmes," in I. Lakatos and A. Musgrave (eds) *Criticism and the Growth of Knowledge*, Cambridge: Cambridge University Press.

Lancet (1978) Editorial (12 August), 356–7.

—— (1985) Editorial (19 October), 900–2.

Lasagna, L. (1984) "Regulatory Agencies, Drugs, and the Pregnant Patient," in L. Stern (ed.) *Drug Use in Pregnancy*, Boston: ADIS Health Science Press.

Lave, L.B., Ennever, F.K., Rosencrantz, H.S. and Omenn, G.S. (1988) "Information Value of the Rodent Bioassay," *Nature*, 336, 631–3.

Leader, R. and Stark, D. (1987) "The Importance of Animals in Biomedical Research," *Perspectives in Biology and Medicine*, 30, 470–85.

Lehninger, A., Nelson, D. and Cox, M. (1993) *Principles of Biochemistry*, New York: Worth.

Lewontin, R.C. (1991) *Biology as Ideology*, New York: HarperCollins.

Liggitt, H. and Reddington, G. (1992) "Transgenic Animals in the Evaluation of Compound Efficacy and Toxicity: Will They Be as Useful as They Are Novel?," *Xenobiotica*, 22, 1043–54.

Lin, T., Gold, L. and Freedman, D. (1996) "Bias in Qualitative Measures of

Concordance for Rodent Carcinogenity Tests," *Statistical Science* (in press).

Lubinski, D. and Thompson, T. (1993) "Species and Individual Differences in Communication Based on Private States," *Behavioral and Brain Sciences*, 16, 627–80.

McClain, M. (1992) "Thyroid Gland Neoplasia: Non-genotoxic Mechanisms," *Toxicology Letters*, 64/65, 397–408.

McKeown, T. (1976) *The Modern Rise of Population*, New York: Academic Press.

McKinlay, J.B. and McKinlay, S. (1977) "The Questionable Contribution of Medical Measures to the Decline of Mortality in the United States in the Twentieth Century," *Health and Society*, 55, 405–28.

Manson, J. and Wise, L.D. (1993) "Teratogens," in A. Amdur, J. Doull and C. Klaassen (eds) *Casarett and Doull's Toxicology* (4th edn), New York: McGraw-Hill, 226–81.

Marg, E. (1982) "Is the Animal Model for Stimulus Deprivation Amblyopia in Children Valid or Useful?," *American Journal of Optometry, Physiology, and Optics*, 59, 451–64.

Marshall, E. (1995) "The Trouble with Vectors," *Science* (25 August) 269, 1052–3.

Mason, S. (1970) *A History of the Sciences*, New York: Macmillan.

Maynard Smith, J. (1992) *Did Darwin Get it Right?*, New York: Chapman and Hall.

Mayr, E. (1982) "Is a New and General Theory of Evolution Emerging?," in J. Maynard Smith (ed.) *Evolution Now*, New York: Freeman.

—— (1986) "How Biology Differs from the Physical Sciences," in D. Depew and B. Weber (eds) *Evolution at a Crossroads: The New Biology and the New Philosophy of Biology*, Cambridge, Mass.: MIT Press.

—— (1988) *Toward a New Philosophy of Biology*, Cambridge, Mass.: Harvard University Press.

Medawar, P. (1984) *Pluto's Republic*, Oxford: Oxford University Press.

—— (1991a) "The Pissing Evile," in D. Pyke (ed.) *The Threat and the Glory*, Oxford: Oxford University Press.

—— (1991b) "Animal Experimentation in a Medical Research Institute," in D. Pyke (ed.) *The Threat and the Glory*, Oxford: Oxford University Press.

—— (1991c) "Is the Scientific Paper a Fraud?" in D. Pyke (ed.) *The Threat and the Glory*, Oxford: Oxford University Press.

Medical Research Modernization Committee (MRMC) (1990) *A Critical Look at Animal Research*, New York: Medical Research Modernization Committee.

Mill, J.S. (1961) *System of Logic* (vol. 3), London: Longmans Green.

Miller, J. and Loon, B. (1982) *Darwin for Beginners*, New York: Pantheon.

Mishler, B. and Donoghue, M. (1994) "Species Concepts: A Case for

Pluralism," in E. Sober (ed.) *Conceptual Issues in Evolutionary Biology*, Cambridge, Mass.: MIT Press, 217–30.

Mitruka, B.M., Rawnsley, H.M. and Vadehra, D.V. (1976) *Animals for Medical Research: Models for the Study of Human Disease*, New York: Wiley.

National Center for Health Statistics (NCHS) (1995) *Vital Statistics of the United States, 1991*, Washington, DC: Public Health Service.

Neese, R. and Williams, G. (1994) *Why We Get Sick: The New Science of Darwinian Medicine*, New York: Random House.

Neubert, D. (1990) "The Necessity of Animal Testing for Safety Evaluation and Medical Progress in Reproductive Biology and Toxicology," in S. Garattini and D.W. van Bekkum (eds) *The Importance of Animal Experimentation for Safety and Biomedical Research*, Dordrecht: Kluwer Academic Publishers, 191–218.

Newton, I. [1687] (1962) *Principia* (vol. 2), Motte (tran.), Berkeley: University of California Press.

Nicholson, K.G. *et al.* (1981) *Lancet*, vol. 915.

Nicolis, G. (1989) "Physics of far-from-equilibrium systems and self-organization," in P. Davies (ed.) *The New Physics*, Cambridge: Cambridge University Press, 316–47.

Nishimura, H. and Shiota, K. (1978) "Summary of Comparative Embryology and Teratology," in J. Wilson and F. Fraser (eds) *Handbook of Teratology* (vol. 3), New York: Plenum Press, 119–54.

Nomura, T., Katsuki, M., Yokoyama, M. and Tajima, Y. (1987) "Future Perspectives in the Development of New Animal Models," in *Animal Models: Assessing the Scope of Their Use in Biomedical Research*, New York: Alan R. Liss, Inc., 337–53.

Nonneman, A. and Woodruff, M. (1994) "Animal Models and the Implications of Their Use," in. A. Nonneman and M. Woodruff (eds) *Toxin-Induced Models of Neurological Disorders*, New York: Plenum Press, 1–15.

Northrup, E. (1957) "Men, Mice, and Smoking," in *Science Looks at Smoking*, New York: Coward McCann.

Nozick, R. (1974) *Anarchy, State, and Utopia*, New York: Basic Books.

Palmer, A. (1978) "Design of Subprimate Animal Studies," in J. Wilson and F.C Fraser (eds) *Handbook of Teratology* (vol. 4), New York: Plenum Press, 215–53.

Parascandola, J. (1995) "The History of Animal Use in the Life Sciences," in A. Goldberg and M. Principe (eds) *Alternative Methods in Toxicology and the Life Sciences* (vol. 2), New York: Mary Ann Liebert, Inc., 11–21.

Pardes, H., West, A. and Pincus, H. (1990) "Physicians and the Animal-Rights Movement," *New England Journal of Medicine*, 324, 1640–3.

Parrish, H.V. (1968) *Victory with Vaccines*, Edinburgh: Churchill Livingstone.

Patton, W. (1993) *Mouse and Man*, 2nd edn, Oxford: Oxford University Press.

Paul, J. (1971) *A History of Poliomyelitis*, New Haven: Yale University Press.

Paulos, J.A. (1995) *A Mathematician Reads the Newspaper*, New York: HarperCollins.

Post, S. (1993) "The Emergence of Species Impartiality: A Medical Critique of Biocentrism," *Perspectives in Biology and Medicine*, 36, 289–300.

Preston, R. (1994) *The Hot Zone*, New York: Random House.

Rachels, J. (1990) *Created From Animals*, Oxford: Oxford University Press.

Regan, T. (1987) *The Case for Animal Rights*, Berkeley, Calif.: University of California Press.

Reines, B. (1991) "On the Locus of Medical Discovery," *The Journal of Medicine and Philosophy*, 16, 183–209.

Reusch, H. (1978) *Slaughter of the Innocent*, New York: Bantam Books.

Ridley, Mark (1993) *Evolution*, Oxford: Blackwell.

Ridley, Matt (1993) *The Red Queen: Sex and the Evolution of Human Nature*, New York: Penguin Books.

Riordan, M. (1987) *The Hunting of the Quark*, New York: Simon and Schuster.

Rollin, B. (1989) *The Unheeded Cry: Animal Consciousness, Animal Pain, and Science*, Buffalo, N.Y.: Prometheus Books.

—— (1992) *Animal Rights and Human Morality* (2nd edn), Oxford: Oxford University Press.

Ross, M. (1989) "Relation of Implicit Theories to the Construction of Personal Histories," *Psychological Review*, 96, 341–57.

Rossini, M., Di Martino, E. and Bensi, G. (1990) "Transgenic Animals for Human Diseases and Gene Therapy," in S. Garattini and D. van Bekkum (eds) *The Importance of Animal Experimentation for Safety and Biomedical Research*, Dordrecht: Kluwer Academic Publishers, 213–22.

Rowan, A. (1984) *Mice, Models, and Men*, Albany, N.Y.: State University of New York Press.

Rowan, A., Loew, F. and Weer, J. (1995) *The Animal Research Controversy*, Tufts, Mass.: Tufts University School of Veterinary Medicine.

Rupke, N. (1990) "Introduction," *Vivisection in Historical Perspective*, New York: Routledge, 1–13.

Russell, S. and Nicholl, C. (1990) "Evolution of Growth Hormone and Prolactin Receptors and Effectors," in A. Epple, C. Scanes and M. Stetson (eds) *Progress in Comparative Endocrinology*, New York: Wiley-Liss, 168–73.

Russell, W. and Burch, R. (1959) *The Principles of Humane Experimental Technique*, London: Methuen.

Salmon, W. (1984) *Scientific Explanation and the Causal Structure of the World*, Princeton: Princeton University Press.

Salsburg, D. (1983) "The Lifetime Feeding Study in Mice and Rats – an Examination of Its Validity as a Bioassay for Human Carcinogenesis," *Fundamental and Applied Toxicology*, 3, 63–7.

Sassard, J. (1990) "Laboratory Animals and Cardiovascular Pathology: Means for Better Use," in S. Garattini and D.W. van Bekkum (eds) *The Importance of Animal Experimentation for Safety and Biomedical Research*, Dordrecht: Kluwer Academic Publishers, 81–8.

Sax, N. (1981) *Cancer-Causing Chemicals*, New York: Van Nostrand.

Schardein, J.L. (1976) *Drugs as Teratogens*, Cleveland, O.: CRC Press.

—— (1985) *Chemically Induced Birth Defects*, New York: Marcel Dekker.

Schiller, J. (1967) "Claude Bernard and Vivisection," *Journal of History and Medicine*, 22, 246–60.

Schmidt-Nielsen, K. (1975) "Scaling in Biology: The Consequences of Size," *Journal of Experimental Zoology*, 194, 287–308.

Shambaugh, G. (1986) "Thyroid Hormone Action," in S. Ingbar and L. Braverman (eds) *Werner's The Thyroid: A Fundamental and Clinical Text* (5th edn), Philadelphia: J.B. Lippincott Company.

Sharpe, R. (1988) *The Cruel Deception*, Wellingborough, UK: Thorsons.

Sigma Xi (1992) "Sigma Xi Statement of the Use of Animals in Research," *American Scientist*, 80, 73–6.

Silverstein, A. (1989) *A History of Immunology*, New York: Academic Press.

Singer, P. (1989) "All Animals Are Equal," in T. Regan and P. Singer (eds) *Animal Rights and Human Obligation* (2nd edn), Englewood Cliffs, N.J.: Prentice-Hall, 73–86.

—— (1990) *Animal Liberation* (2nd edn), New York: Avon Books.

—— (1993) *Practical Ethics* (2nd edn), Cambridge: Cambridge University Press.

Singleton, R., Ellis, G. and Burghardt, G. (1994) "Transgenic Organisms, Science, and Society," *The Brave New World of Animal Biotechnology*, Special Supplement, *Hastings Center Report*, Jan.–Feb., S4–S14.

Sipes, I.G. and Gandolfi, A.J. (1993) "Biotransformation of Toxicants," in A. Amdur, J. Doull and C. Klaassen (eds) *Casarett and Doull's Toxicology* (4th edn), New York: McGraw-Hill, 88–126.

Smith, E.L., Hill, R., Lehman, I., Lefkowitz, R., Handler, P. and White, A. (1983) *Principles of Biochemistry*, New York: McGraw-Hill.

Smith, H. (1961) *From Fish to Philosopher*, New York: Anchor Books.

Smith, J. and Boyd, K. (1991) *Lives in the Balance: The Ethics of Using Animals in Biomedical Research*, Oxford: Oxford University Press.

Sober, E. (1993) *Philosophy of Biology*, Boulder, Colo: Westview Press.

Stanford Committee on Ethics (1989) "Animal Research at Stanford University: Principles, Policies and Practices," *New England Journal of Medicine*, 318, 1630–2.

Stebbins, G.L. (1982) *Darwin to DNA, Molecules to Humanity*, San Francisco: W.H. Freeman.

Steinbock, O., Kettunen, P. and Showalter, K. (1995) "Anisotropy and Spiral Organizing Centers in Paterned Excitable Media," *Science*, 269, 1857–60.

Steinmetz, P. and Tilley, S. (1994) "Animal Models: Some Empirical Worries," *Public Affairs Quarterly*, 8, 287–98.

Tabony, J. (1994) "Morphological Bifurcations Involving Reaction–Diffusion Processes During Microtubule Formation," *Science*, 264, 245–8.

Taubes, G. (1995) "Epidemiology Faces its Limits," *Science*, 269, 164–9.

Taylor, P. (1986) *Respect for Nature: A Theory of Environmental Ethics*, Princeton: Princeton University Press.

Templeton, A.R. (1989) "The Meaning of Species and Speciation: a Genetic Perspective," in D. Otte and J. Endler (eds) *Speciation and its Consequences*, Sunderland, Mass.: Sinauer Associates, 3–27.

Thomas, R.K. (1986) "Vertebrate Intelligence: A Review of the Laboratory Research," in R. Hogge and L. Goldman (eds) *Animal Intelligence: Insights into the Animal Mind*, Washington, DC: Smithsonian Institute Press, 37–56.

Treit, D. (1985) "Animal Models for the Study of Anti-anxiety Agents: A Review," *Neuroscience and Behavioral Review*, 9, 203–22.

Trull, F. (1987) "Animal 'Rights' v. Animal Research: A Worldwide Movement Challenges Biomedical Research," in Charles River International Symposium on Laboratory Animals, *Animal Models: Assessing the Scope of Their Use in Biomedical Research*, Charles River, Mass.: Charles River, 327–36.

Vainio, H., Magee, P., McGregor, D. and McMichael, R. (1992) *Mechanisms of Carcinogenesis in Risk Assessment*, Lyons: IARC.

Wiebers, D., Adams, H. and Whisnant, J. (1990) "Animal Models of Stroke: Are They Relevant to Human Disease?," *Stroke*, 21, 1–3.

Willis, L. and Hulsey, M. (1994) "Worries about Animal Experimentation in Biomedical Research: A Reply," *Public Affairs Quarterly*, 8, 205–18.

Willner, P. (1991) "Animal Models as Simulations of Depression," *Trends in Pharmacological Science*, 12: 131–6.

Wilson, D. and Sober, E. (1994) "Re-introducing Group Selection to the Human Behavioral Sciences," *Behavioral and Brain Sciences*, 17, 585–654.

Wilson, J. (1977) "Current Status of Teratology," in J. Wilson and F. Fraser (eds) *Handbook of Teratology* (vol. 1), New York: Plenum Press, 47–74.

—— (1978) "Feasibility and Design of Subhuman Primate Studies," in J. Wilson and F. Fraser (eds) *Handbook of Teratology* (vol. 3), New York: Plenum Press, 255–73.

Withers, P. (1992) *Comparative Animal Physiology*, Fort Worth: Harcourt Brace Jovanovich.

Wolpert, L. (1991) *Triumph of the Embryo*, Oxford: Oxford University Press.

Woodruff, M. and Baisden, R. (1994) "Trimethyltin Neutrotoxicity in the Rat as an Analogous Model of Alzheimer's Disease," in A. Nonneman and M. Woodruff (eds) *Toxin-Induced Models of Neurological Disorders*, New York: Plenum Press, 319–35.

BIBLIOGRAPHY

Zbinden, G. (1963) "Experimental and Clinical Aspects of Drug Toxicity," in *Advances in Pharmacology* (vol. 2), New York: Academic Press, 2, 1–112.

INDEX

283

119, 126, 127, 129, 130, 133, 135, 139, 144, 150, 154, 158, 159, 163, 180, 195, 196, 204, 205, 231, 244, 255, 259, 265, 266, 273, 274, 276, 277, 281
toxicology 4, 15, 35, 41, 48, 60, 62, 66, 108, 119–121, 126, 143, 147, 162, 167, 187, 188, 243, 270, 271, 273, 275, 277–280
transgenic 2, 5, 180–192, 280

United States Department of Agriculture (USDA) 178, 249, 250, 268

utilitarian xii, 6, 160, 178, 219, 220, 225–227, 246–251, 254–256

vaccines 5, 6, 127, 260, 275, 278
virology 119, 126, 200, 273

weak models 2, 62, 107, 138, 139, 143, 144, 159, 165, 181
Wiebers *et al.* 24, 25, 128, 129, 281
Willis, L. 14, 57, 58, 167, 281
Woodruff and Baisden 164, 165

xenobiotics 15, 117, 120, 145, 147, 150, 153, 156, 158, 183, 187